T0165563

# After the Blackness of Midnight, A Glimmer of Sunrise

Wanda Hancock

Order this book online at www.trafford.com
or email orders@trafford.com

Most Trafford titles are also available at major online book retailers.

Printed in the United States of America.

ISBN: 978-1-4269-8257-6 (sc)
ISBN: 978-1-4269-8258-3 (hc)
ISBN: 978-1-4269-8260-6 (e)

Library of Congress Control Number: 2011914789

*Trafford rev. 08/18/2011*

 www.trafford.com

**North America & international**
toll-free: 1 888 232 4444 (USA & Canada)
phone: 250 383 6864 ♦ fax: 812 355 4082

# DEDICATION

To

The Men and Women who Serve In Defense of Our

Country; You Have Enabled Each of Us to Enjoy

The Freedoms we Have in the U.S.A.

Thank You and God Bless and Protect Each of You!

# Contents

# Lucas Comes Home From Afganistan

Lucas was driving his ATV on a mountain range to go to his family's old homestead. His great - grandmother was an Indian from the tribe of Cherokee and she had married a white man. They built their homestead in the mountains near the border of North Carolina and Tennessee. Once married, she no longer wanted to stay on the Reservation, but she maintained her Indian heritage both in culture and foodstuffs. Her husband worked on the trains in whatever capacity needed. Lucas had kept track of the homestead through his mother and grandmother. He knew very little about his grandfather except he worked in some coal mines. His own father worked on the farmland they had acquired and produced corn, tobacco, wheat, and some barley. They also had huge gardens with his mother canning quantities of vegetables needed for winter, as well as, canning or smoking meat, such as hogs, cows, and venison.

Lucas was going over these things in his mind while driving. He was going to take some much needed R&R from the last tour of duty in AFGANISTAN and had decided to participate in a program of some kind of "First-Responders" in the nearest town/city. He was a first-aid station helicopter pilot in which one picked up injured military and got them to a field hospital or wherever the injured marine needed to go. He enjoyed serving his country, but it was extremely stressful to see his fellow service personnel injured, often with life-threatening or mortal injuries. Near the last of his second tour, he was piloting the Apache and his partner stepped out of the helicopter to help get a severely injured man onto the chopper and his partner was shot from a hide out in the mountainous range. He kept the chopper grounded until he saw the AFGANS coming out of the hideout to capture/kill him and take the helicopter. He turned his chopper guns in their direction and fired. He already had his radio and listening equipment on and knew the ground crew knew something had happened. Thankfully this chopper was super fast-moving and he got out of ground range firing quickly.

Lucas kept thinking, God why not me instead of Randy. Why are so many young men and women dying for our country? No one in AFGANISTAN has asked for help nor do they want our help.

The mountains have so many trails and mountain caves that one doesn't see or hear an enemy. He kept wondering how devastated the parents and siblings would be when learning their loved one was killed or seriously injured in such a way their life was forever altered. Why were Americans here where they were fighting a war for which there seemed no reason?

Lucas began to wonder if he would ever make a difference for the better while on tours. He decided when this tour was over to go home and help First-Responders in what ever city he was needed. He said nothing to anyone about his decision; he had prayed and knew this was the right decision for him. He knew if he stayed for another tour, he himself, would never be able to help others, and possibly have a post-traumatic stress disorder that would hurt his sister and mother. His father was at end-stage Alzheimer's and didn't know anyone.

He picked up his cell phone before going off the paved road and called his sister. She told him their mother had fallen and broken her back and one hip. She was in the hospital near the military facilities. Lucas turned around and headed back to his sister's place and asked how his mom was today. They had known he was coming home, but he had told them he needed some time off and was going to the old homestead. When he got to his sister (Lucy), she told him mom was worse today; she was just readying herself to go to the hospital to see her. Lucas gave her a bear-hug and they went together to see their mother. He had not bothered to change out of fatigues and so was a bit rumbled, but he didn't really care. He needed to see his mother and she needed to see him.

They went into the hospital and went to the nursing station and asked what room she was in. The nurses told them their mother had to go to ICU; it looked like she had thrown a clot to the lung area. They went straight into ICU and their mother was weak and on oxygen, but she recognized both of them. Lucas and Lucy kissed her and asked how she felt. She responded in a low, tired voice and told them, "Not so good. Even with all this stuff, I can barely get my breath." She told Lucas how wonderful it was to see him. Lucy had been up yesterday, but she was in another room at that time. Lucas told his mom he was going to see one of her doctors, kissed her and said he'd be back soon. Lucy knew Lucas would find her doctor and get as much information as possible. He did. He found Dr. Corbin and asked what had happened to his mother and what could he and his sister do to help her, she wanted to go home. Dr. Corbin said that is very unlikely; the clot is very near the branch of the heart and lung vessel and was called a 'saddle clot'. "This is a clot we are unable to resolve with surgery, but we are giving her anti-clot medication even though she had a broken hip and back." They were keeping her comfortable as possible, but if that clot moved, she would die. The doctor assumed that since Lucas had his fatigues on, he had just been called home. Lucas told him no, that he had served two tours in AFGANISTAN, he would be working as a First Responder; he had flown choppers for his tours of duty to bring the wounded into a field hospital.

Dr. Corbin told him he was sorry about his mother, but the outcome did not look good for her. If she developed pneumonia from the inability to change her position very much, any strenuous cough would block her heart and lungs. Lucas thanked the doctor for his time and information. He thought his Indian blood was showing, because he did not think his mother would live through the night. When he got back to the room his mother was napping and Lucy looked straight at him. She said, "Let's go outside the room for a bit and tell me who the doctor is and what he said. I've been afraid that she will die, maybe tonight. I will stay here with her all night and you get some rest." Lucas said, "I don't take orders right now; we'll both stay and relieve one another. I don't want her to die alone."

They both went back into the room and a nurse was with their mother. She was checking the monitors and began to rub her forehead and hold her hand. She turned around when they came in, but did not turn loose of their mother's hand. "My name is Molly and I've been looking after her. She knows me and likes me, because as we were talking last night and she told me she had Indian blood in her; I told her that I too had Indian blood from the Santee tribe, and I would be with her as long as she needed. She told me she had a son and daughter, but her son was in AFGANISTAN and her daughter worked near here. She became very short of breath and

I told her I'd stay here with her, because my shift was over." She smiled and said, "I gave report a bit ago, I came in to stay with her tonight as well. She has been asleep or semiconscious since the two of you left. You can talk to her or hold her hand. If she's able she will respond. I will stand over in the corner, but I'll still be here."

Lucas and Lucy went over and rubbed her forehead and kissed her, but she barely responded. Lucas stood at the foot of the bed and motioned to Lucy and the nurse to sit down. In about fifteen minutes, Lucas began to notice her heart monitor had slowed down quite a bit. Lucy had her head down as though praying, but the nurse saw the same thing. She asked Lucas if he would like her to call Dr. Corbin. Lucas said, "Why, he's already told me about this, but she will feel no pain." Molly said, "Okay." Lucy was still praying silently, but she was aware of what was happening. In about ten minutes, the monitor flat-lined and all three knew she was gone. Their mother looked at such peace and Lucas and Lucy were at peace as well.

Molly told them she must make Dr. Corbin aware and left the room. In a few minutes, Dr. Corbin and Molly came back to the room and their mother was pronounced dead. He asked if there were particular services they wanted performed and they told them all that had been arranged. Molly asked them if they wanted her to contact the CHIEF and they both said no. She would have a memorial service at the funeral home and if any of the tribe was left, they were welcome. Molly asked if they would mind keeping her aware of the arrangements. They both agreed. Lucas and Lucy went to the Funeral Director and told him what they wanted done. He informed them he would indeed take care of the obituary and the arrangements they wanted. If the CHIEF was able, he could say a few words, but the service would be conducted by Lucas and Lucy's pastor. Their mother was also a member of that Church.

Lucas and Lucy went to a coffee shop and sat down with coffee and pie. They talked about their mother and how wonderful she was; how she had raised them Christian, but had not forgotten her tribal family either. Lucas reminded Lucy they needed to contact Molly to make her aware of the arrangements. Lucy had all the phone numbers needed and called Molly and told her where she and Lucas were. They invited her over for a cup of coffee; she said, "I'd love to come, but my brother has just came in, may I bring him with me." "Of course, you may."

In a few minutes Molly came in and introduced her brother Michael. They sat down and ordered coffee and pie. Michael seemed like such a nice guy, Lucy glanced at his left hand and he was not wearing a wedding band. They all began to chat and tell about their parents and the Indian side of their heritage. Lucas was so tired, but not so tired that he didn't check Molly out. She was a really pretty girl with long, chocolate brown hair that she had fixed in some kind of braid on the back of her head. She had large green eyes. She did not have a wedding band either, but although she had on scrubs, Lucas thought she was pregnant. As they were talking, Molly asked him where he was stationed. He told her that he had pulled two tours of duty in AFGANISTAN and decided to come out and work as a First Responder with any city or town where his skills might be needed. He told her he had been a chopper pilot to bring in the wounded or dead to the field hospital. He thought that as a First Responder for a city, those skills and well as others he had might be of assistance.

Molly didn't say much after he mentioned AFGANISTAN, but she seemed a bit uneasy. Michael spoke up and said that Molly's husband had been killed in AFGANISTAN; in some sort of ambush. She looked at her brother and said, "They probably aren't interested in all that. Their mother just died." Michael looked quickly at Lucy and said, "I'm so sorry for your loss. I knew Molly was a bit upset when she came home, but I had no idea we were coming to see you two. Molly loves her patients and often feels as if they are family when one dies." They chatted on for a while, but then it was time to go home. Lucas said, "Sis, can I bunk with you tonight?" "Of course, you silly goose, I love you and welcome home." They told Molly and Michael about the arrangements for their mother's funeral and invited both of them to come. Molly said, "We'll be there."

Lucas and Lucy went back to Lucy's house and prepared to get into bed. Lucy asked Lucas if he was hungry and he said, "No, the pie and coffee were enough." He went into his room and showered and went to bed. Lucy wondered a bit about Molly and Michael; they seemed as close as she and Lucas were. She wondered if Michael was married, since he and Lucy seemed to live together in the family home. She also began to go over how calmly that her mother had died. She did not seem in pain. She said her prayers, and then thanked God for His great goodness in taking her home without a drawn-out illness like their dad had. She planned to go to the nursing facility tomorrow and talk with her dad, although he didn't know her; she would try to tell him anyway.

The next morning she got up and got her shower and dressed in casual slacks, blouse, and jacket. She then began to prepare breakfast. Lucas came out of his room already dressed in casual slacks, shirt, and jacket. They gave thanks for their food and for their mother and the blessings God had given. They didn't talk a lot, but both of them seemed together on seeing their father. They went to the nursing facility and their dad seemed a bit clearer today; almost as if he knew them. They told him that mama had died last night from a blood clot; however she had died very peacefully and they both were with her. Their dad listened, but was unable to speak, but some instinct seemed to enable him to understand that his dear Lucia was gone. Almost immediately he was back in the same state as before; not knowing or speaking to anyone; not even acknowledging their presence.

Lucas and Lucy went to the funeral home to ensure their wishes were followed and to find out if the Chief of her tribe was interested in speaking a few words over Lucia. The Chief said, "Only a few of the tribe was left, but he would make those related aware that Lucia had gone home." They also insured that their pastor was ready to have the service the next afternoon. The funeral director told them yes. They were able to see their mother and she looked the same as last night when she died; at peace.

Lucas told Lucy he needed some time alone; he said he understood he wasn't the same man that she knew her brother to be, but he really was having some heavy thoughts that he must sort through, if possible. Lucy told him that was fine with her; she had to purchase a black or dark blue outfit for the funeral.

Lucas left and went to the back of their Church where there were a group of trees and a few stumps and he sat down to think. Should he go ahead and register with the military base and tell them he planned to stay home for a while and work as a First Responder with the city? He was still a Marine, but would only need to go to base for about three days every three months to practice his skills and check in with his Commander at the base. He had already prayed about what he could now do that would still be of service to his fellowman. Lucas decided to go on over to the base and make his Commander aware of his plans. The Commander gave him a good reference and told Lucas that his choice seemed ideal for him and the community.

Lucas knew he was slipping into a depression; he never felt like laughing or even talking much. He did not know what to do about the depression; he did not tell the Commander because he did not wish to be classified as 'post-traumatic stress disorder'. He would think and pray about seeing an off-base psychiatrist. He was aware of some flashbacks of battles and he felt a deep loss of his mother, but was unable to tell anyone about it. He knew that Lucy had noticed a change, but she didn't mention it to him; she simply loved her brother and assumed when he was ready, he would make her aware of what was bothering him.

Lucas left from behind the Church and went to the main hospital near the military base and put in an application as a First Responder and gave them a copy of the referral that his Commander gave him. The Chief of the Fire Department and Emergency Captain occupied the same office building and so he did the same with the Emergency Captain. He knew emergency crews worked closely with the Police Department and he might be used by each department when the need arose. All three of the departments were quite willing to take him on-board with salary quite adequate for him and a family should he desire a family. He told them he needed to leave; that his mother died night before last and the funeral would be later this afternoon. They all told him to take as much time as he needed before reporting to work. He thanked them and left to attend the Service for his mother.

# Their Mother's Funeral

Lucy was dressed and Lucas put on his suit and they headed for Church. They were surprised to see so many cars there. They went into the Church and sat together. Lucas looked over and saw Molly and her brother Michael in the next pew. They smiled and then sat quietly for the service to begin. The Tribal Chief was old, but spoke quietly some words of the tribal language and then sat down. Their pastor then completed the Service. The entire service was rather quiet and dignified. When it was over, they went to the gravesite and buried their mother. Lucas didn't shed a tear, but Lucy did cry for their loss.

Molly and Michael did follow them to the gravesite and sat with them. They felt like family, but of course, were not. Lucas looked at Molly quite closely and she really was a beautiful woman, and she was pregnant. Michael had his arm around his sister and Lucas understood that they two were very close as brother and sister. Lucas wondered how long ago her husband was killed, but he knew Michael would look after his sister. Lucas decided he would like to get to know them both better. So after the service was over, he invited all of them to dinner.

They all went to a nice restaurant and were seated very soon. Their table was located in a quiet section of the restaurant and they began to get to know one another. Michael was much more talkative than Molly and Lucy was more talkative than Lucas. They seemed like old friends who got together often, but Lucas and Molly seemed to focus more on one another. Lucas spoke up and asked Molly when her husband was killed and did he serve in the Marines. She said, "As a matter of fact, he did." She asked why he was interested and Lucas told her that he too was a Marine and dealt with repairing and flying helicopters. Molly said her husband was killed in the enemies strong-hold that no one knew was there. He got killed about three months ago and she wasn't sure he got her letter telling him about the pregnancy. "I hope he did, but one never knows for sure. Randy had always wanted a big family, so she really hoped he knew about their baby."

Lucas was in somewhat of a shock. He asked Molly if Randy ever went on flights with a 'fella' most folks called "CHIEF" because of his Indian background and his ability to sense strongly when something wasn't right. Molly said, "Yes, he did, in fact he was with 'chief' when he got out of the chopper and was mowed down."

"I was told by one of his buddies that the soldier he went to get was already dead, and the AFGANS riddled him with bullets. His buddy then said that 'chief' was never the same and chief didn't sign up for another tour of duty. When he left, none of us have heard where he was or what became of him."

Lucas became quiet for a while, he looked straight at Molly and said, "I'm 'chief', and his buddy was right. I kept the chopper hovering, planning to drag both bodies back, but the AFGANS came running to get the chopper and kill me; so I had to get out of ground fire. I was never buddies with any of the guys, although I really liked them all. Randy was a decent man and very friendly; I think I could have been friends with him. He was a professional in every sense of the word, but we rarely talked privately. I wish I could tell you differently, but what I've said is true."

Molly looked back at Lucas and saw a very depressed man who was a decent guy. He was a big man with dark hair and grey-green eyes. He and Lucy looked somewhat alike, but Lucy was very outgoing and talkative. Molly said, "I just noticed they haven't heard a word we've said; they have been carrying on a different conversation." Lucas said, "Well, that's fine with me. Would you consider going to dinner with me alone sometime when you have an evening off?" "Yes, I would," Molly replied. Lucas asked when she was usually off and she told him every other Friday, Saturday, and Sunday. Her other off days were Monday and Thursday, in rotation.

It seemed they all four realized it was really late and dinner had been eaten, but Lucas couldn't remember what he ate, but he really enjoyed talking with Molly. They all got up and said good-night and went home. Lucy began to tell him about Michael and how nice he was. "I'm planning to see him again soon." "That sounds great," Lucas replied. Lucas had given Molly his cell phone number in case she needed him for anything. He also told her about becoming a First-Responder and how he had that taken care of today. He told her that he would probably go up to the old homestead for a few days, to rest and try to get his head straight. Molly thanked him for the cell-phone number and gave him her own cell phone number.

The next morning Lucas told Lucy he was going up to the homestead for a few days. Lucy thought that was a good idea. "You need some mental and physical rest time." Lucas asked his sister if she knew a good mental therapist, he thought he was really depressed and couldn't seem to get himself back on an even keel. She said she would find the best one; Molly would know. Lucas said, "I have feelings for Molly, but I can't trust myself to tell her. I saw the way she cared for mom and the fact that she and Michael came to the funeral meant a lot to me."

Lucy said, "I know how you feel, because I have feelings for Michael. We talked a lot the other night and I believe he cares for me as well. At any rate, there is time to make sure of my feelings and I will ask Molly if she knows a good psychiatrist and therapist. I assume you want one off base." "You assumed right dear sister. I've already packed so I'll be leaving for the old homestead; I've got groceries and water and things I'll need. You keep in touch with me and I'll do the same with you." He left in the ATV and headed for the cabin.

The cabin was about two hours away and the scenery was pretty. When he got to the cabin, he unloaded his cooler and the things he wanted to eat, as well as some sheets. He and Lucy had kept it in good repair and there was a rather large cot to sleep on. They had also put in a bathroom and running water. There was still a porch on the front and back of the house. The smaller animals scampered about the yard and he knew there were several larger animals in the forest surrounding the cabin.

Lucas decided to go for a walk in the woods around the cabin. He took several paths and simply enjoyed the sights and sounds that were so different from AFGANISTAN. This was peaceful without fear of an ambush. It began to get chilly and so he decided to go back and sit on the porch for a while. When he got back he put a jacket on and sat on the porch and just thought about anything that popped in his head. When unpleasant thoughts came, he would analyze what he could and go to another place in his head. He went inside and decided to skip supper and the next day he planned to go to the Reservation to try and talk to the Chief.

He got up the next morning and went to the Reservation. He was able to see the Chief who was in his tent, outside his house. Lucas talked to him about his mother and thanked him for speaking at her funeral. The Chief asked, "What do you want Lucas?" Lucas told him that he would like to know more about his mother's people; what they did for a living, did any of them speak the language and how different it was today from when his mother was a little girl.

The Chief began to talk to Lucas and told him about the differences in the entire culture than when Lucia was a little girl. She was his aunt because she was the daughter of his grandfather, who was also the Chief. "As far as the livelihood, it was some different, but with the legal gambling, the young men did not learn about hunting, fishing and smoking food very much." Lucas and the Chief talked a long while and it was getting late, so Lucas thanked the Chief and got up to leave. The Chief brought him up short; "What is really troubling you Lucas?"

Lucas sat back down and answered the Chief the only way he could; "I really don't know for sure. It seems that often I go into my own head and feel an emptiness that I cannot explain." The Chief said, "I think I know part of what you are feeling. As an Indian, you only killed your enemies when they first began an attack; that was the accepted way of life. You were brought up with Christian values and believe it or not; those values are almost identical. We believe in the Great Father, you believe in God the Father, the Son, and Holy Spirit. We knew very little about the other part of the God-head until much later. You are dealing with a stress that comes from having to watch your fellow marines die a terrible death and are unable to do anything much to stop it, (at least in your head). But have you ever thought about the lives you did save? I've watched from a distance, your youth and growth into manhood. You are a good man, Lucas, but you are not God, nor can you ever be. Man does not understand the ways of God, but we see evil and wonder if He really sees it. Rest assured, He sees and will judge people on their deeds of evil, unless they repent. You see Lucas, I am a full-blooded Cherokee, but I am also a Christian who learned of God from

Missionaries who loved us without condemnation. Now, go home and rest well, very soon you will understand that your choice to stay out of war and work as a First-Responder is exactly what you can best do to help those in need."

# Back To The Cabin

Lucas headed back to the cabin with a much lighter feel inside. It seemed as though the Chief knew him better than he knew himself and could see inside him. Talking with him had definitely helped his mood and spirit. He made himself some supper and went down to the river bank behind the cabin and just observed the small river. It flowed so peacefully that he felt even more relaxed. It was time to go to bed. He said his prayers and thanked God for his talk with the Chief. He also realized he missed Molly. It had been only two days, but he missed her and wanted to see her. He decided to call her tomorrow. Lucas slept more peacefully than he had in a long time.

After making his breakfast and having coffee (from a percolator), he decided to walk some more and went into the forest and then down to the river bank. He thought about all the Chief had told him and how the Chief thought the First-Responder job would be good for him and the community. He wondered how the Chief knew about his interest in the First-Responders and then remembered; he was an Indian Chief who had ways of keeping track of most everything around him.

He got back to the cabin and called Molly. He told her what he had been doing and how he had enjoyed talking with the Chief. Molly seemed happy to hear from him and told him that she knew an excellent psychiatrist. He had helped her considerably after her husband died. They chatted as old friends and Lucas realized that he really wanted to see Molly. He told her he was thinking of coming home tomorrow and wondered if he could see her some time soon. She said, "Yes, as a matter of fact, I have tomorrow off." "Good, then if it's okay, I'll pick you up for dinner at about six o'clock." "That will be fine," Molly replied.

The next morning Lucas awoke and realized he felt much lighter in his spirit. He kept thinking about the Chief and the things he said. He also thought about his beautiful Molly – that thought stopped him short; Molly was not his, but he really thought he was beginning to love her. He, of course, would not mention that to anyone until he deemed it appropriate. Lucas also thought he would report for duty at the First-Responders on Monday. He would talk with Lucy about this particular decision when he could. He got home and Lucy had just come in from work. She worked as an admitting clerk in a hospital nearby. They hugged each other and Lucas told Lucy he was going out a while. She said, "Okay, I'm going out too."

Lucas showered and changed into slacks and jacket and went to pick up Molly for their dinner/date. He was rather excited inside about seeing her, but it did not show on his face. When he got to her house he rang the doorbell and Molly was ready to go. About that time Michael came in and asked Molly if she was okay and if she was going out with Lucas. She said, "Yes, we're going to dinner and you need to stop being 'big brother' with any decision I make. I love you and will see you in the morning." "Oh Lucas my little sister is gaining her spunk and bossiness back; okay, I'll leave the big brother in the closet." "Good," Molly retorted.

Lucas smiled inside and thought she was more self-reliant than he had assumed. He reminded himself not to act to brotherly or bossy.

They got to the restaurant where Lucas had made reservations and went inside. They were seated promptly, again in a rather quite area. The waiter brought the menu and a glass of water; he left them to look at the menu and decide what they wanted. He came back and Lucas asked Molly to order what she wanted; she ordered steak, green salad, and baked potato. Lucas ordered the venison roast, sweet potatoes (fried slices), a salad and kale mixed with turnip greens. They both took a drink of water and started talking about everything, mostly Molly's work and how long she had worked in ICU. Molly said she had always wanted to work in some area of critical care, because she felt her skills would be more utilized in those areas. She talked in general about some of her patients, but she did not mention Lucia for fear it would make Lucas more depressed.

Molly asked Lucas what his work had entailed in the Marines. He told her he was not only a pilot of helicopters, but also was a mechanic trained specifically for the flying birds. He smiled at her and said, "Basically, I guess I'm mostly just a grease monkey who happens to fly choppers." Molly smiled and laughed, a 'grease monkey", I don't think of you as any kind of monkey. You are a big Indian man with their morals and beliefs and work ethic." Lucas looked at her and had not realized that he did look more Indian than White. He was a big man, with reddish olive skin and his hair was dark, but had the texture of his fathers, soft and slightly curly.

Their dinner arrived and while they ate, Lucas told her that he had never felt a whole person; he had inside a quite spirit, but had never learned the Indian's ways of meditation, he was raised Christian and accepted Jesus into his heart as a young boy. However, even knowing Jesus, he still had a mixed feeling inside. What he definitely knew was that Jesus was his friend and Savior.

Molly told him about growing up with a white father whom she saw very irregularly and she and Michael were brought up by a beautiful woman who was not only their mother, but their teacher of both cultures. She died of pneumonia about three years ago. She assumed her father had died in a train accident; they had never seen him after their mother died, so she and Michael were very close. However, he sometimes tries to tell me what to do and 'baby' me, especially after my husband died. "We live in our mother's house and have since she died. I'm much stronger than he thinks but I am grateful for his being with me and loving me. He is the only man I ever really trusted. I cared deeply for Randy, but we never bonded as most husbands and wives do;" she wasn't quite sure why that was so.

Lucas told her about them growing up and his daddy farming and his mother gardening and preserving fruits and vegetables; as well as drying and smoking any meat that his dad brought home. He said his parents did have a bond, but it wasn't shown much to Lucy and me. "We knew he loved us, but he never taught me the farming aspect of living, but I learned from observation and helping him farm. He did teach me to hunt and fish and how to dry meat and hang it for my mother to smoke, so they had food all winter. After Lucy finished college, she noticed our dad had become very forgetful. He would ask mother when lunch would be ready when he had just had lunch. When I knew that Lucy was strong and able to care for their mother and dad if the need arose, I joined the Marines. The training and long runs and early mornings never bothered me, but some of the boys were not accustomed to that routine and it was pretty rough on them. That training and learning the skill to repair helicopters as well as piloting them was really great. It stopped being great when I lost my partner in an ambush that neither of us saw. We were to pick up our fellow marine and prepare him to be sent home. You know what happened to Randy. I asked God, why Randy and the other marine died and he lived. He told Molly he never felt he could mentally do another tour of duty. So he came home and had put in applications with the First-Responders in their city. His military Commander gave him an excellent report and all three branches of First-Responders wanted him on board. The Fire Department, the Emergency Squads, and Police Department, worked together." He planned to show up for work on Monday. He knew he needed to learn the routines of each branch in order to respond adequately.

They had talked so long neither of them realized how late it was. Lucas said that he would like coffee and maybe some pie. Molly said, "Well, I'd love coffee, but perhaps should forgo pie tonight. I might gain too much weight." Lucas asked her how far she was in the pregnancy and she told him four and one-half months. Molly was small in stature and he certainly couldn't see one ounce of fat on her. "He told her that a slice of pie with coffee would not put fat on her or the baby. I've noticed how small you are; was your mother a small lady?" "Yes, she was; about five feet and two inches and a small frame. I'm about five feet and three inches. The doctor says I am the proper weight and he also said that the baby was exactly the right weight." Lucas said, "Well, one small piece of pie isn't going to make you fat. Besides, I think you are beautiful." So she had a slice of chocolate pie. "Is chocolate your favorite flavor?" "Oh, yes, I could eat chocolate morning, noon, and night, but I don't."

They had their pie and coffee and Lucas noticed that Molly looked tired. He realized she must have been on her feet all day. Although he did not want to, he told Molly that since it was this late, he better take her home, lest her big brother think I've kidnapped you. "I would love to see you again soon, if that's agreeable with you." Molly smiled and said she had a wonderful time and would love to see him again. He asked her if she enjoyed the mountains and she said she sure did. Lucas said he did too and told her about the cabin on his old homestead. He and Lucy had kept it original except for electricity and running water that came from an old well on the property. "If you feel like a two hour drive, I'd love to show it to you." "That would be great," Molly replied. They stood up to go; Lucas had already taken care of the bill, and they headed back to Molly's house. They got out and Lucas noticed her brother was not home. He asked Molly where her brother had gone. She said, "I've no idea, but he will be home soon." When they got to the door, Lucas opened it for her and bent down and kissed her forehead. Thank you for a lovely evening and Molly responded in like fashion, only she couldn't reach Lucas' forehead, so she kissed his chin. "Good Night, Lucas." Lucas knew he was in love with Molly, but dared not mention it to her. He had to wait for a signal from Molly regarding her feelings.

# Lucas Reports for Duty

Lucas kept going over the conversation with Molly when they went to dinner. He felt his heart stir and realized he did not feel so dark inside.

When he got home, Lucy was not home. Where in the world could she be? Well he knew Lucy could take care of herself because he had taught her self-defense and offensive tactics. So he showered and went to bed. He laid thinking about Molly for a long while. He then began to think about going to work Monday. He was beginning to get some enthusiasm back for the simple fact of living. He prayed and thanked God for Molly and asked God to take care of her and make him aware if Molly had feelings for him. He went to sleep with a smile on his face. When Lucy came in, she silently checked on him. Her own heart was so relieved; whatever or whoever put that smile back on his face was wonderful.

The next morning Lucas awoke and began breakfast for the two of them. Lucy had to do some kind of paperwork today, so he chose to go to Church. After Service, he went back into the woods behind the Church and enjoyed the trees and quietness of the small forest. He then went home to make lunch and found Michael's car there. He went on inside and went to start lunch and found the two of them sitting at the kitchen table having coffee and talking. He asked them how they were doing and they both said fine. Lucas knew when to keep his mouth shut. Very soon Michael got up to go home. They said good-bye and he left. Lucy asked him if he enjoyed Church and he told her yes and that he had taken a walk in the woods behind the Church again. Sometimes Lucas needed peace and quiet and seemed to find it in the woods, alone. Lucas told Lucy he planned to go to the First-Responders headquarters and begin to learn their routine. He said he really believed he could help them. Lucy said, "I know you can and will."

Monday morning he showed up at the headquarters and told them he felt ready to go to work. He knew he had to learn the routines of each department and was glad to have this opportunity. They welcomed him and took him around to different stations to get to know the layout. Then each Captain would meet with him to tell him their expectations. They would also give him literature to study in the evenings. The Fire Chief asked if he knew how to cook. Lucas answered he could cook well enough to keep from starving. The Fire Chief laughed and said, "Well, you will have your turn in the kitchen and his boys liked good, well seasoned food." Lucas said, "I think I can manage that." With all the literature they had given him, he asked where they expected him to stay. They each said there was a small office with a desk and phone and special radios for any emergency. When any emergency came in, he was expected to go with that crew to serve anyway they needed. That was fine with him. They suggested he spend the afternoon in his office going over the literature and knowing enough about the various department rules to be a help and not a hindrance. So Lucas spent the afternoon in his office going over each piece of literature. He had practically memorized the material, when the Fire Chief came in and said, "I'm sorry Lucas, I forgot to take you to lunch." "That's fine," Lucas responded. "May I take the literature home with me and study some more this evening?" "Of course you may, however we need to fit you with a uniform that is unilateral for you. All the various groups know this uniform and know they could use you in any emergency. We also will give you a special phone/receiver to keep by your bed in the event we have an emergency at night." "That's fine," Lucas replied. "Now, I suggest you go home and get some dinner. I'll bring the phone/receiver to you to install in your home." "Thanks," Lucas replied.

Lucas took the phone/radio receiver home with him and installed it in his bedroom. He also received a phone to keep on his person at all times. The Fire Chief saw his ATV and was glad to see he had one, one never knew when an accident or problem arose that needed that vehicle. Lucas realized he was really hungry and so decided to wait and take Lucy for an informal dinner. He wanted to tell her about the work and how excited he was about it. Lucas called his sister and she told him she would be home in about fifteen minutes. Lucy came in and hugged her brother and asked how he was doing. Really well, he replied. "Let's grab a burger and I'll tell you about my day." "Okay," Lucy replied. They went to a small burger shack and ordered burgers and fries and Lucas ordered a hot dog too. "My goodness Lucas, you must have missed breakfast and lunch." "As a matter of fact, I did miss lunch."

While they ate their burgers Lucas began to tell Lucy about the first day at First-Responders. He told her about seeing the entire complex and meeting so many people and all the literature that he needed to study more tonight. He also told her about the phone/radio receiver that he had to keep in his house; "I've installed it in my room, it won't bother you." He said, "Lucy, I think this job is exactly what I need, I can be of service to so many people in various needs. For the first time in a very long time, I feel so much lighter inside."

Lucy told him she was so proud of him and that he actually seemed to be coming out of his "funk" and enjoying being home. She told him that she had been so concerned about him, but knew God would take care of him. She said, "Did you realize you were rather despondent when you first got home and then mother died and you seemed to withdraw further." "Well, I know the darkness inside me and it still shows up when I least expect it, but I believe I'm better too." Lucas asked Lucy how she was coping with mother being dead and him being a 'wet rag' around her neck? "How are you doing, inside I mean. You seem cheerful and comfortable even with dad in the shape he's in." I understand about Alzheimer's, however I didn't know how all the past weeks had affected her. Lucy answered and told him it had been pretty rough, but she had asked God to care for all of us, so she was in pretty good shape. Lucas said, "You are in great shape," and laughed. "Thank you, kind sir."

Lucy told Lucas that while they had a bit of time to talk, she wanted to ask him something. "All right, ask," Lucas replied. "How do you feel about Michael? I've seen him a few times and I'm beginning to think I might be falling in love with him. I'm afraid of that; you see I thought I loved a guy when I was in college, but he turned out to be abusive and mean, however, he was outgoing and kind like Michael seemed to be. With your fantastic instinct, could you maybe see him occasionally and let me know what you think?" Lucas replied, "I think, from what I've seen, that he is a pretty decent man. He looks after Molly well; at least at mom's funeral he kept his arm around her in a very protective manner." "Thanks," Lucy said. "Oh by the way, you have a special look in your eyes when I've seen you and Molly together, both at the funeral and when we went to dinner. Are you interested in her romantically?" Lucas looked straight at his sister and said, "Yes! I've asked her out one night for dinner and we talked a lot about many subjects. I know she is four and one-half months pregnant and she often wonders if her husband had received her letter to inform him of the pregnancy." I told her I didn't know; that while I liked all the guys, I was never close enough with any of them to become buddies. "I'm not sure I've ever had a buddy. I definitely have never felt for another woman like I do Molly. Now listen baby sister, do not go telling anyone what I just told you." Lucy said, "I won't, but the same holds true with you. Just keep an eye on Michael and see what you think about him after we get to know them a bit better."

The next morning Lucy was making breakfast for them both when Lucas came out in slacks and a jacket. She asked if he would have any particular uniform and he told her what the Fire Chief had said. They would fit him with a unilateral uniform that all fellows knew in all departments and when they saw him, they would know he would help in any way possible. "I'll be measured and fitted sometime today and when the uniforms are tailored, I begin wearing them; by that time I will have had time to learn each department. The Fire Chief said I was a big man and so the uniforms would need to be tailored to him. The other guys were already fitted and worked as needed. I didn't get to meet any of them, but I expect I will in the next few days."

Lucas and Lucy left almost at the same time for work. He decided to call Molly and see how she was doing. She told him she felt great. He told her about his first day at the First-Responders Headquarters and that he would be fitted today for his uniform. It is different from any of the other groups, but each department knew the uniform and therefore would not wonder what he was doing at any incident that needed First-Responders. He asked Molly when she had a day off; she told him Thursday. "Well, do you think we might have dinner this Thursday evening?" "Yes, that would be nice," and she would appreciate getting out some. So Lucas made a date for Thursday to pick her up about six o'clock.

The next morning Lucas was excited about going to work. He wanted to meet some of the other guys in the services and he was particularly interested the special group of First-Responders such as himself. He felt pretty competent in the various protocols that he had gotten from the literature and the various Captains.

# Lucas and Molly Go Out Again

Lucas finished the day and had been measured for his uniform. The uniforms would be ready in about two days, maybe three. That didn't matter to him; he was still learning about all the departments. He left for home and showered and dressed for his date with Molly. He did not remember ever feeling for a woman as he did her. She was not only beautiful on the outside; she had a pure heart. He could spot a 'phony' a mile away. He got to her house and rang the bell. Again, Molly was ready. Michael came out of the kitchen and told them to have a good time; he might not be back when they did, but he'd be back before Molly went to bed. He did not question her or act like a big brother quizzing a little sister; he had learned his lesson well.

Lucas and Molly went to a different restaurant than before; Lucas had already made reservations and he thought Molly might like this restaurant better. They were seated quite soon and the waiter brought out the menus and glasses of water with lemon slices. Molly sipped her water and looked at the menu. She had not felt well in a few days, but she wasn't going to break her date with Lucas. She ordered broiled salmon, a green salad and a congealed salad. Lucas ordered prime rib for one and potatoes and a salad. They sipped their water and began to talk again. Molly asked Lucas if he had ever been married? He said "No, I've really never met a woman that I could feel close too; until now."

Molly looked up at Lucas and said, "You do realize that I'm pregnant with another man's child." "Yes, I'm quite aware of that, but that certainly does not bother me; does it bother you?" "No, not at all, but I just wondered if you knew that Randy was a good man, he was not Indian and had very little knowledge of how this particular woman feels. I never tried to explain to him, but while we got along fine and I cared for him, there was no real bond present; although I don't think he ever knew that." Lucas asked her who would help rear her child like she wanted; she answered Michael would until he is married and he will even then make sure this child knows both cultures.

Molly did not eat with gusto; she only ate small bites and switched from salmon to congealed salad and then a small amount of her green salad. "Is the meal not to your liking, Molly?" "It's not that, I've felt a little under the weather for a few days. I see my doctor tomorrow and plan to mention not feeling well, I even missed a day of work which I never do." "Have you mentioned this to Michael?" "Of course not, he would think something terrible was happening and start his 'big brother' talks with me. I love Michael dearly but he feels so much responsibility for me and often picks me up and places me on the bed and dares me to get up."

Lucas asked Molly if she knew the sex of her baby and what she planned to name it. Molly replied, "No, I want to be surprised, it doesn't matter what sex as long as it is healthy. This baby means so much to me and not just because of Randy, but because I've always wanted children. I love this little one so much and I'm already telling him or her about how much I love him or her. Sometimes I play soft music to the baby and he/she will settle down. This is a very active baby even at this date. You reminded me of something, a name, so I'll ask the doctor tomorrow what the sex is and then I can plan colors for the nursery and begin to get some baby clothes. I'm becoming rather excited about knowing, especially since the pregnancy does not seem to bother you at all." "It certainly doesn't because it is part of you. Molly, perhaps I shouldn't say this, but I will, I love you and I know what I'm saying. Please don't ask any questions, because I know what I feel and I don't want to influence you in any way. Just know this, if you ever need me, just call."

They finished dinner and Lucas ordered some coffee, but skipped pie. Molly ordered coffee and water with lemon in it. "Molly, please don't think because I didn't order dessert that you can't. I know how much you enjoy chocolate, but I rarely eat dessert. I prefer plain food." Molly started laughing and said, "I still love chocolate, but I'm not sure that would be a good thing, since I've felt a bit under the weather for a few days." "Okay, will you please call me tomorrow after you see the doctor and tell me what he says about your health and the baby's?" "I sure will, but you will be at work." "That's okay; I still have my personal cell phone with me all the time, so please let me know." "All right I will," Molly responded.

They talked a while longer and Lucas noticed again that Molly looked tired so he said, "We'd better go home, since tomorrow will be a big day for both of us." "That's fine," Molly responded; "And I've really enjoyed being with you tonight."

Lucas took Molly home and walked her to the door and opened it. He put his arm around her and kissed her, she responded slightly. "Sleep well, Molly." "You too," she said.

Lucas went home and Lucy was in her room. He checked on her and saw she was asleep with a small smile on her face. He was glad she was having pleasant dreams. He went into his room and went to bed. He thought about Molly and their entire evening; he could hardly wait until tomorrow to hear how she was and to go to work.

He was really beginning to love this work and seemed accepted by everyone he met. He met the other two First-Responders; Carl and David. They had also left the service to join the First Responders unit. Carl was in the army and David had been in the navy. They both seemed like good guys, but neither of them talked much. He went to his office and realized Carl and David shared an office like his right next door. They decided to have lunch and go back to work. They ate in the multi-dinning room. All three departments had a section in which to eat with their comrades. They had lunch and went back to their offices. Lucas was double checking some information about each unit to ensure he would be ready when the time came.

Later that afternoon his personal phone rang and he answered to hear Molly say, "Well, I'm calling you like you asked." He knew she must be better because she seemed to be smiling when they spoke. "Okay, let me have it," he said, laughing. Molly told him her baby was a little boy and was in fine shape. She had picked up a virus, probably from the hospital and the doctor told her to take a couple more days off and take fluids and whatever she felt like eating. She said she had come home and sure enough Michael was waiting to hear how she was doing. She told him she had picked up a virus and it would be gone in about two days, but she needed to stay home for a couple of days. He asked how the baby was doing and she told him he would be an uncle of a little boy. He smiled from ear to ear and said he wandered how long she would hold out without finding out the sex of the baby. He gave her a big hug and said, "Now hit the sack dear mother of my nephew." So she was lying very quietly on her bed. She had already made the hospital aware that she was sick and probably couldn't come back to work for about three days. "That's fine; you take the time you need to get well." "Thanks," she told her supervisor. She told Michael she was going to take a nap and for him to have a good day. Molly also called Lucas to see how his day was going. "Fine," he said. "Do you think I might drop by a few minutes to see you this afternoon or evening?" "That will be fine," Molly responded.

Lucas continued his work and made some special notes on car accidents. He had put a good first aid kit in his ATV because he also knew first aide, he had also been a medic in the Marines. When it was time to leave, he decided to go to a baby store. He wanted to get Molly a tiny baby doll and a soft blue bear. He put them in a gift bag and went to Molly's house. When he rang the bell, Michael came to the door and motioned for Lucas to be quiet. The two men went into the kitchen and had coffee and Michael began telling him that Molly had slept a lot today, but the doctor thought she would be fine. "I've made chicken soup and a congealed salad that I know she likes and some lemon water with heavy lemon juice. She probably awake in a few minutes." Lucas said that she had called him after seeing the doctor. I had asked her to and she did.

"Michael, what kind of work do you do?" Michael told him that he taught school, primarily to guys who wanted to take shop to prepare to go to community college to complete a degree in car repair and upkeep, as well as some who wanted to learn farming skills and maybe open an open-air market. There were some students who were interested in cows and sheep for milk production and cheese-making. "They are good students and I enjoy teaching. It helps me to learn too."

Michael told Lucas he was interested in his sister Lucy, but although she talked well and they seemed to get along, he didn't know whether to make her aware of his feelings or not. "She doesn't seem to trust anyone but you." Lucas said, "Well, she is interested but is afraid she won't make a good decision. She was very close to a man while she was in college and he was outgoing and nice, but in reality, he became abusive and mean. If I had known that, he wouldn't treat another woman like that. I asked her if he hit her and she said only once when she refused to go to a movie. She had a big test coming up and needed to study. Needless to say, she refused to see him again. I had taught her self-defense and some offensive techniques, so I really never worried about her being able to defend herself. When she told me that he hit her; I was furious and ready to take him down." She said, "Oh, big brother, he's been taken down enough. I handled myself well and made him aware of the creep he was, and I also told the other girls in the dorm to watch out for him. He soon left college and I pity the poor girl he sets his eyes on again, but perhaps he will be a bit nicer now. As to whether or not to mention your feelings, I don't know what to tell you. She is interested in you very much, but does not trust herself to make a right decision. As a matter of fact, she asked me to get to know you because she trusted my opinion more than her own. You don't have to let her know I told you that.

"While we are talking you might as well know that I care deeply for Molly. I've told her," and she said, "You do know I'm pregnant with another man's child, don't you." I said, "Yes, but that did not affect my feelings for her one bit, because the baby would be part of her. I asked the sex of her baby and what she planned to name the child. She said that she wanted to be surprised, but now that she thought about it, knowing the sex would enable her to choose the right name and begin to fix a room for a nursery. I asked her to call me when she saw the doctor and let me know how she was and how the baby was. As a matter of fact, I brought her a baby doll and a blue bear for the baby. I hope she doesn't think I'm too pushy, but Michael, I've never felt for a woman what I feel for your sister. I know you don't know me well, but I'd like to get to know you better and not just because Lucy asked me too. I need to know if it would upset Molly in any way to keep asking her out for dinner or a movie. I also asked her if she liked the mountains and she said yes. When she is able I'd like to take her to see our old homestead. It's about two hours away and I wouldn't do anything that would tire her or be a determent to her. So think about what I've told you and make me aware. I'd rather you not tell her everything I've told you, because I still have very dark moments and must get away by myself to think things through. I talked with the chief when I was up at the cabin the other day and that conversation really helped a lot."

They were drinking a cup of coffee when Molly came into the kitchen. She got a glass of lemon water and asked the two of them how they were doing. Michael told her they were just chatting waiting for you to wake up. Lucas had asked you if he could drop by a few minutes this evening. "He came in a few minutes ago and since he is with you for a little while, I need to go pick up a few groceries." "That's fine," Molly said. He left and she and Lucas began talking. "Are you sure you feel up to being out of bed a few minutes?" "Of course, Lucas, I'm not helpless and I need to drink some water or juice rather frequently." Lucas reached down and got the gift bag he had beside of his chair and handed it to Molly. She pulled out a small baby doll and a little blue bear for the baby. "I wanted something that would make you smile when you saw it." "That is so precious Lucas, thank you." She kissed him on the cheek and assured him that she would treasure these gifts.

"We'd better go to the living room and you lie on the couch and I'll use a chair and we can talk a while." "That's nice," Molly replied. She brought her lemon water with her and lay down on the couch and Lucas asked if she needed a blanket. She said no, she was warm enough. She told him she had gone over so many male names and had gotten a book with names for newborns, but couldn't decide on a name yet. "Well, I don't think that must be done for about four months, do you?" "No," she laughed, "But Michael is already insisting that his nephew have part of his name. I told him I'd let him know if he behaved himself."

Lucas talked more to Molly about general things and about his work. He told her he felt so much lighter inside than he did for a long time. "I still sometimes need to be alone and walk in the woods; that helps me get my thoughts together more clearly. However, I've noticed since I met you and began a work with the first-responders, I rarely have flashbacks or that heavy darkness I had in the past. Thank you, dear Molly for your quiet spirit and loving heart. I am not trying to pressure you or make you feel anything except what you feel, but I do love you and would like to see you as often as I can." Molly said, "I don't feel pressured by you, I appreciate your love, because you would not say something that wasn't true. But to be honest, I care deeply for you, but I'm afraid to make a commitment to you, lest I make a wrong decision and hurt you or anyone else. However I do think of you very often and have a secure feeling when I remember you said you love me although I'm pregnant with another man's child. That is very special to me."

They talked on a while and Michael came back with the groceries. Lucas told him that since he was back, that he would go home. Michael went to put away the groceries and Lucas reached down and kissed Molly. He smiled at her and left to go home. Before Lucas got to the door, Michael asked him how he found the First-Responders job. Lucas told him that he really enjoyed what he knew so far. He had met the other two First-Responders and their office was next to his. He said that one was named David and the other Carl.

David had left the navy and Carl had left the army. We went to lunch but didn't talk about much of anything. My guess is that they both went through similar experiences like I did. They both occasionally had a far-away look in their eyes. When we finished lunch we went back to work.

The Chief told me my uniforms would probably be ready day after tomorrow and he expected me to wear them to work. Carl and David both had on uniforms and I like the way they look. My guess is that once my uniforms are ready, I'll be inspected and be ready to go to any calls that come in. That will be fine with me. I'm ready to get into the swing of things from each department. I know the job can and will be frustrating at times, but nothing can compare to hell of AFGANISTAN. Lucas said none of the men and women needed to be in that place, especially when no one wanted them there. Lucas stopped talking; he said, "Molly and Michael, I'm really sorry for talking like I just did. There is absolutely no excuse for my speaking negatively about our government. Please excuse me and try to forget what I said. There are still times I have flashbacks and I realize that is the time I need to be alone, preferably in the woods. That's the most peaceful place for me when I regress backwards. So please have a good night and excuse me for sounding off; it really isn't like me. Goodnight."

Lucas left and Michael said; "There goes a good and decent man who is afraid to show his true feelings, at least to me." Michael told Molly he had seen Lucy a few times and she told him that Lucas was pretty much a loner, but he would do anything for anyone. She has noticed that since he went to the cabin and talked with the Chief, he had been much less depressed. He is still not ready to see a therapist and Lucy thinks he may never be. His best therapy has been meeting you and talking with the Chief up near their old homestead.

"How are you feeling sis?" "I'm better after seeing Lucas, look what he brought me." She showed him the little doll and the blue bear. "That was so sweet of him. I'm feeling a bit depressed because I can't go back to work for two or three more days. I'm not used to this, as you well know, but I feel better after seeing Lucas. Now no more questions, I'm going to bed. I love you Michael and good night."

Lucas got into his ATV and headed home. He was disgusted with himself for sounding off like he did in front of Molly. She probably thought he was 'fruitcake' and may never want to see him again. He felt the darkness creeping back. I can't stand much more of this, dear God. What if I've ruined my chance to marry Molly and help her rear her son. He felt he must talk to Lucy and get her opinion. She would tell him the truth regardless of what he wanted to hear.

When he got home Lucy was still up and had a slight frown on her face. She asked Lucas what had happened to him today? "I know something happened because about an hour ago I began to sense that you were in trouble." "I am, Lucy. I will never understand why this happened. Michael had gotten groceries while I stayed with Molly and when he got back, I thought I'd come home because Molly looked tired."

Michael asked me about the work and I told him all I've told you and about meeting the other First-RESPONDERS today. I said I thought they had been some similar things that he had. While they were at lunch I'd notice a far-away look in their eyes. Neither of them talked much and I didn't either. We went back to our offices and finished up some work.

I had asked Molly to call me today after she saw the doctor and let me know about her and the baby. She did and I asked if I could come by a few minutes to see her.

"Lucy, everything went well and I had taken her a small doll and a little blue bear; hoping she would smile and like the thought. She did and kissed me on the cheek. Michael got back. We chatted and I enjoyed our quiet time."

"What I'm troubled about is that I told Michael and Molly that no one should have to go through the hell of AFGANISTAN. We aren't wanted there and our men and women, die daily for no apparent reason that he could understand." He told his sister that he apologized to both of them and said he didn't usually talk badly about our country. He asked them to forgive his rashness and please try to forget everything he said. "Lucy, only another soldier can possibly know the pure hell of war. The Chief told me when I was at the cabin that was because Indians did not kill without reason; the enemy started it first, but then they had no repulsiveness about killing an enemy and perhaps saving his family. I simply don't know what to do to find out if I damaged my standing with Molly."

Lucy spoke up and said, "Lucas, pick up the phone and ask her point blank. Molly is honest to the core and she will certainly tell you if she is upset." "Do you think it is too late?" "No, it's not even nine o'clock. Call her Lucas; I'll be in my room."

Lucas never knew his hand shook while he dialed the phone until he saw it. I must really be losing it, he said to himself. He rang her phone and she answered. "Molly, It's Lucas". "I want to know if I have damaged our relationship with you because of my rant about the government. That really is not like me; only another service man knows what really hard battles are and how it steals your soul to see them die." Molly stopped him right then; "You listen to me Lucas, the fact that you allowed yourself to show true emotion about something you see wrong is absolutely a good thing. You, in no way hurt me, or Michael, and I would tell you if you had. I feel very close to you and my feelings are stronger than I thought. I lay awake at night thinking about you, your integrity, your non-demanding way of talking with me and the fact that you said you loved me, even knowing I was carrying another man's child; you made me realize that my baby is mine to rear and love the best I know how. Michael had a somewhat reserved opinion about Randy, and he reminded me that Randy could never understand my strong sense of family. I know we had no real bond, as I've told you, so stop that worried brow. Just know I am beginning to feel that I've known you for a very long time and I do have feelings for you. Will you sleep peacefully tonight and know that I do love you, I'm sorry I've been unable to be sure enough of myself to tell you before. You see Lucas; we all go through dark nights, but the morning sun does rise. Do you think you can sleep and maybe come by to see me tomorrow after work?" "Oh, my dear Molly, you have helped me so much. Thank you and remember no matter what comes, (darkness of night or the morning sunrise) I do love you. I'll see you about six o'clock tomorrow. Is there anything you think you can eat or drink that I can bring you?" "No; not a thing but your sweet self."

Lucy came out of her bedroom and said, "Well, did she speak to you?" "Yes, she sure did and Lucy I told her I loved her and understood that my dark moods sometimes appear before I know they are coming. I don't ever want to hurt her or Michael. Lucy, we had a good while to talk the other night and he does definitely have strong feelings for you. He wanted me to know he would never do anything to hurt you. You don't have to tell him I told you that; you both will know when it's right. Now I'm going to bed and dream about Molly and thank God for her and the job, and of course, for you. I love ya sis, and goodnight."

The next day was Friday and Lucas awoke with a lighter spirit and could hardly wait to go to work. His uniforms would be ready this afternoon and the Chiefs would all inspect him and he would be ready to go out if needed. Meanwhile, he should review automobile accidents material. It seemed more traffic accidents happened on weekends or holidays and bad weather. Depending on the 'call' he would be given any cover-up gear needed and could keep it in his ATV.

His uniforms arrived about four o'clock and he changed and put one on for inspection. All the Chiefs seemed to like the fit and they already knew from watching how he carried himself; just like the other two guys who came of out the service to work with them. They had been with the First-Responders only about two months and mostly stayed with each other until a call came in.

When they all finished looking him over, they called the two other guys to come meet their comrade and inspect him. They saw Lucas and laughed, "He'll make two of us, but he looks good." Both Carl and David shook hands with him and welcomed him aboard. It seemed at that moment they became the 'three musketeers'.

Lucas went over to Molly's to check on how she felt and she said better, but still not up to working yet. "Lucas could this really be a virus and will it affect my baby?" Lucas reminded her that the doctor said she needed rest and it would soon be gone. "I suspect you are still weak because of the inability to eat much, but keep trying. I've learned enough to know the baby takes his nourishment from you, therefore you are going to eat (forgive the pun) for two. That little fella is still moving about, isn't he?" "Oh yes, he is very active and he kicks hard."

Lucas got up to go home and reached over and kissed Molly. She kissed him back and thanked him for reminding her that a baby does get his nutrients from his mother. Molly asked him if he was off this weekend and did he think they might ride up to his cabin. "My dear Molly, I don't know; absolutely I want to take you to the cabin, but I don't want to tire you anymore than you are and that's a two hour drive. Could we plan it another time as soon as you are well?" "Yes," Molly replied, "It is probably a good idea, because I had forgotten my feet are beginning to swell if I'm on them too much. Thanks for reminding me." Lucas kissed her again and hugged her. "I really can barely wait until you can ride and enjoy the cabin; by the way, there are two large cots there and I hope you trust me to treasure you without overwhelming you or smothering you. I love you Molly and I mean your soul, heart and body, but I would never do anything to injure any part of you. Do you understand me?" "Yes, I do Lucas and I promise not to attack you either." They both began laughing and the pressure eased considerably on Lucas; he had feared she might have felt that he was not really interested in her seeing his homestead. He kissed her again and left to go home.

When he got home Lucy asked where he had been; she had tried calling him at the office and they said you had left. Lucas told her he had dropped by to check on Molly and they talked awhile. "Lucy, what is wrong, has someone hurt you?" "No Lucas, not like you mean. You see daddy is very low and the nursing facility wanted us to come be with him. I didn't want to leave without you, so I was going to write you a note." Lucas said, "Absolutely, we'll leave right now. By the way Lucy, if you can't reach me by phone, I'll probably be with Molly or Michael. Now, come on and we'll get to the facility. How long has it been since they called you?" "About ten minutes, but I didn't want to wait. I have a bad feeling about this Lucas." Lucas didn't reply.

# To The Nursing Facility

Lucy and Lucas went straight to the nursing station and asked how their dad was doing. The nurse said, "Go on down to his room, he seems to be waiting on someone." They went in and kissed their dad. They told him that mama had died the other day from a blood clot. We were both with her when she died. He opened his eyes and for a moment or two seemed to recognize both of them. He could not speak, but they both told him they loved him. They held his hands and rubbed his cheek and forehead. They stayed with him for about twenty minutes and noticed his breathing slowing down. The nurse came in and stayed with them a while and pretty soon, their dad slipped away as peacefully as their mother. The nurse told them she had to get his chart; she did not remember which funeral home they had requested on his admission and she would have to make the doctor aware.

She left the room and Lucas went over and rubbed his father's hair, it was white now and as soft as silk. He had often wondered if his mother might have taught him a lot about their Indian culture. He was never a man to talk much, but he worked hard and provided for his family and had saved quite a bit over the years. Combined with Lucy's input, his own input and his father's social security they would take care of their father and still have funds left over.

Lucy was on his other side and softly rubbed his forehead and cheek. She cried softly, almost without a sound. Lucas knew she was grieving over their dad and mother. She too was sinking into her own dark place. Lucas prayed silently and asked God to comfort her and remind her that their parents were with Him now. He came around the bed and put his arm around Lucy. She turned into his shirt and began to sob, gut wrenching sobs. Lucas had never seen her cry like this and he was becoming afraid for her.

The nurse came back with the chart and a doctor followed closely behind. He examined their father and pronounced him dead. He asked if they had any questions and if there was any way he could help. He noticed Lucy's sobbing and told Lucas that she needed a shot to help her for a while. She would otherwise make herself sick; in mind and body. Lucas agreed and the nurse brought a shot and gave it to Lucy who seemed not to know or feel the needle. Lucas took care of the paperwork and made them aware of the funeral director and that all that had been pre-paid. Lucy was still sobbing and he kissed their father and took her home. He simply did not know what to do with Lucy, she had never broken like this; it was if her soul was torn. Lucas could tell she was about to fall, so he picked her up and put her to bed. She was still crying but wreaking sobs had let up, probably because the shot was taking affect.

He had left her room door open in order to hear any other sounds. He soon looked in her room and she seemed to be asleep, but not resting, she was twisting and turning and her legs would kick; this was so unlike Lucy, he was going into the pit with her. He decided to call Michael and ask if he could come over, that Lucy seemed in trouble. He told him that their father had died this evening and Lucy had to be medicated in order to stop the wreaking sobbing. She could barely breathe she was sobbing so violently.

Michael said, "Lucas, if you will let me off the phone I'll be there in a few minutes. I'm going to bring Molly because I don't want her alone either. She has had some more foot swelling and still doesn't feel well." Lucas said, "Fine."

Lucas went to check on Lucy again and she was still very restless, but asleep. In about ten minutes Michael and Molly came in. Michael insisted on Molly lying on the couch. "Lucas, I'm going to lay down with her and hold her. You might as well know I've asked her to marry me and I told her she could take the time she needed to be sure I am not like some other men." She told me that you were the only man she trusted. Lucas said, "That is fine, Michael."

Michael went into Lucy's room and lay on top of the covers and took her in his arms. He was whispering to her that he loved her and she was safe now. She almost immediately relaxed and Michael just lay and held her.

Lucas told Molly that when their dad died, he was shocked and scared at how hard Lucy took it. It seems she goes into her head and I was afraid she couldn't come out again. I took her in my arms and she turned into my arms on my chest and I could feel those deep, deep sobs. The doctor came in to pronounce dad and he told me that he would suggest a strong dose of medicine to keep her sobbing from making her physically and mentally ill. Molly told him that the doctor was right. She said that she wasn't sure, but with their mother dying rather quickly and the funeral, now came another shock and it was too much for her mental state at this time. She has been worried about you and she said; I'm a bit like that, and I need to be alone, but I'm afraid to tell Michael.

Molly told Lucas that she thought that Michael and Lucy had been attracted to one another since meeting. He talks a lot about how dear she is, but she doesn't trust many men. Michael himself told me about the man in college. "You may take my word, Lucas; Michael loves her and will wait until she can trust him. I think she already does trust him, more than I knew; she said she had feelings for Michael, but couldn't trust herself not to make a bad decision that would hurt him."

Lucas got up and checked on both of them, he told Molly, they are both asleep and Lucy is in his arms and much less restless, almost as if she does love him. "I could do nothing to stop her sobbing, so that's why I called Michael; I hope you don't mind Molly, I know you are having some difficulty with this pregnancy and you might have to reconcile yourself to bed rest for a while. I'm no doctor but I was in surgery when a pregnant Marine came in and the base doctor put her on bed rest because with so much stress on her body, she could not stay on her feet and keep the pregnancy. I flew her to the main hospital on base. I never heard anything else about her, but since she agreed to fly with me to the hospital, I thought she probably did what she was asked to do."

Molly said she had already thought of that, but kept hoping that wasn't so because she loved to nurse. "Well." Lucas said, "You can care for your precious self and listen to my rants. It did cause me great distress because I thought I had ruined any chance I might have had to build a relationship with you." Lucy said call her, she will tell you exactly how she feels. "Molly my hands were shaking as I tried to dial the phone. Molly, I almost hung up, I'm such a coward when it comes to causing you any distress."

"I will always appreciate your voice and words. I then hoped that maybe you would finally know, no matter my dark soul at times, I love you and would willingly die for you. That you must believe. I do love you and would love to marry you and help raise your little boy."

Molly said, "Lucas, I do love you, especially since you haven't seemed to mind that he has a different biological father. You are a kind and loving man and you make me feel safe. You have so many wonderful traits I love. Believe me I know the difference between lust and unselfish love. That is one thing with which I'm quite sure of the difference. Now I don't want to talk anymore about your dark episodes, we all have them sometimes; it does not change my love for you."

"When will the funeral for your father be?" "What is today?" Lucas asked Molly. "Today is Friday." "Well, I guess the funeral will be Sunday afternoon. I don't expect you to come because I still don't think you should stand up much, until you see your doctor. I might need Michael to help with Lucy. I've never known her to break before. She is not a superficial person, but her faith seems to stop darkness from creeping into her soul. But frankly, until I see for myself how she is doing, I won't be comfortable."

"Well if that is what's worrying you, rest assured I'll be fine or if you need me with you, you can push a wheelchair can't you? We'll put the legs of the chair up and I'll be perfectly fine. Now will you stop worrying about me and decide the time of the funeral, make the funeral director aware and he will take it from there. Your pastor also needs to know and the gravesite needs to be opened." Lucas looked at his watch and it wasn't as late as he thought. So he called his pastor and told him about their dad, and asked if he would be able to do the service about two o'clock Sunday afternoon. "Yes, that will be fine," his pastor replied. He then called the funeral director and told him the service would be at the funeral home Chapel and the pastor would do the service. But the gravesite would need to be opened. The funeral will be about two o'clock on Sunday afternoon.

Molly said, "Now was that hard?" "No, but I needed you to remind me of what needed to be done." Lucas asked Molly when she planned to see her doctor. Molly said that he told her if she didn't feel better two to three days, he needed to see me. He wants to check my blood and ensure that I'm not dehydrated, and ensure that I'm not beginning early labor. "Lucas, I didn't tell Michael, but I want you to know I will do WHATEVER IT TAKES TO SAVE MY BABY. Nursing so many years, although mostly in ICU or ER is what I know and I remember enough about prenatal care and postpartum care that I will listen to my doctors. My hope is that I simply need IV fluids and will be fit to work, but I can do what's best for me and the baby." Lucas asked if she would call him as soon as she knew. She said, "Yes, Lucas I will call you. Please don't forget that I love you too." Lucas said, "You do?" "Absolutely, I thought I had told you and made you understand why." "Thank you Molly, I'm sure you did, but I was so worried that I might have lost any chance with you, I don't think I remember. Please say it again." "Lucas, I love you now and forever. Now do you believe me?" "Oh yes, my wonderful Molly." He got on his knees beside her couch and hugged and kissed her. He got a bump to his lower chest. "What was that?" "I told you my son was very active and he kicks hard." Lucas started laughing; "Maybe he'll be a tough little tyke." He asked very quietly if he could touch her stomach. "Of course you may, most people never ask, they think when a woman is pregnant anyone can touch her stomach, man or woman."

Lucas laid his big hand on her stomach and pretty soon, he felt another kick. He couldn't help laughing out loud. "Oh Molly, you must get very little rest." "Believe it or not, when I go to bed and tell him goodnight and put on some soft music, he seems to know it is bedtime." "Well I'm glad for that."

They began to hear stirring in Lucy's room. He sat down and waited for her and Michael to come out of the room. She had a button mark on her cheek, probably from Michael's shirt. She yawned and said, "Lucas; did I give you any trouble when dad died? I seemed to go away somewhere and couldn't come back. I remember you holding me and I must have cried, because your shirt was wet. Then when I woke up it was Michael holding me; thank you Michael, I hope I didn't wet your shirt too."

"Well, I have to call the pastor and ask him about doing the service and call the funeral director to prepare the gravesite, and make everyone aware of what time we want the service." "Lucy, sweet, I've already done that with the help of Molly. It is all handled and dad will be buried beside Mother; everything is handled and I believe to your liking."

Lucas said, "Well you had a rough patch and so I called Michael who said he believed he could help you relax. He certainly did because both of you had a good nap. Now I'm going to order dinner brought out here for the four of us." He got his pad and started taking orders; "Molly, what do you want?" "Probably baked Salmon and a congealed salad." "Lucy what do you want?" "A small steak and some fried sweet potatoes and a salad." Michael said; grilled steak, potato and a salad. "I'm having venison steak, sweet potato and kale mixed with turnips. Do any of you want dessert?" Michael said he had ice cream, lemon sherbet and cookies in the kitchen and he would make coffee. Lucas called in dinner and told them to bring it as soon as it was ready.

Molly got up and Michael said, "Where are you going?" Molly said, "Michael, I'm going to the bathroom and I've been independent in that task for a number of years." "Sorry sis." "You keep forgetting to put the 'big brother' in the closet, but you are forgiven, I love you." Lucy said; "I'm next in line." "Okay," Molly said. Michael said, "There are two bathrooms in the house. I've been known to go wherever I was at night or in the woods." "Me too," Lucas said. "I guess men are not as concerned about that sort of thing as women might be."

Lucas told Michael he really appreciated him coming over and holding Lucy. He had never seen her in such a mental and emotional and physical state. The doctor said she needed a shot to protect her mind and spirit. She was sobbing so hard, "I was just plain scared. My baby sister in that state tore my heart out." Michael said, "Listen Lucas, I told you that I love Lucy and would wait until she felt comfortable telling me, if she does. Please let me know if she ever gets in a similar state again; I know you love her, but your arms are different and so is your scent. Just like babies know their mother's scent, grownups do too, it's not as obvious. I think she has been worried about you, your mother falling, and dying, and her dad in the state he was; she simply could not stand anymore. She went into herself and I believe I helped her come back."

The dinner arrived and the two girls came out of the bathroom and Lucas said, "Did you two wash your hands?" "Yes sir, did you?" quipped Lucy. Lucas hugged them both and said he would right now wash his hands and Michael would too.

They all enjoyed dinner, except Molly still only picked at her food. She sure did enjoy the lemon water and had two glasses of that. She also ate some of the salmon and congealed salad. She said everything was good, but she thought she might lay down a while. Lucy gave her a hug and Michael as well. Lucas helped Molly to bed and kissed her goodnight. Lucy would sleep in the other room and the guys would bunk on the couches.

Tomorrow would be Saturday and they would all get back to their original homes. Lucas heard slight snore from Lucy and knew she would sleep well. He listened at Molly's door and heard soft music. He assumed she would soon fall asleep. Michael looked over at Lucas; "You take care of your women, don't you?" "Yes, there is nothing lower than a man who would abuse a woman. I still get angry when I think about that guy that hit Lucy." Lucy said, don't worry big brother, you taught me to defend myself and I did very well and then I kicked his butt and told every girl on campus what a creep he was. He very soon left school. "Michael, you need to know Lucy is wonderful and very special to me and I believe you really care for her; however, she will never again let a man mistreat her in any way." I said just what would you do? She replied; "Beat the snot of them and then cause huge dental bills." I started laughing and knew my baby sister would be okay.

Michael started chuckling and said, "If she will ever marry me, I'll be sure to mind her. But Lucy is so sweet and honest and just plain fun. She could wake up a snow man, but I don't think there is a mean bone in her body. What I have noticed is that she takes up for the underdog when she sees one. I admire that quality." Lucas said, "Michael I wish you good luck with Lucy, you certainly have my permission if she ever asks me again." "And Lucas, you have my best wishes as you take care of Molly. I believe she loves you and I know you love her."

# Their Dad's Funeral

The next morning Lucas and Lucy got up and went home to ensure that everything was as it should be. Lucas kept a close eye on Lucy. She was quieter than she normally was, but didn't demonstrate any other emotion. Lucas fixed their breakfast and they ate after giving thanks. Lucas then asked Lucy how she was feeling inside. Lucy said, "You know Lucas; I am so surprised about yesterday. I knew dad would die soon after mother did and I don't know how I knew. When I watched him take his last breath, I felt like I was falling into a black hole and couldn't stop falling. You know daddy and mom were both Christians and had a bond between themselves that you and I weren't a part of. It seems we always knew we were loved, but outside of their circle. Sometimes I remember thinking I must have done something bad that daddy and mother couldn't reach inside me. Wonder why that was so?" Lucas said, "He didn't know but he remembered the same feelings; it felt to him that it was you and me. There was never any anger, but I would often go for a walk in the woods and then I felt better." Lucy said she usually went to a spot where only she knew and looked for "Indian money".

"Lucas, thank you for calling Michael last night; as soon as he put his arms around me and put my head on his shoulder, I felt myself beginning to relax. You had held me at dad's side, but it wasn't the same. I knew his scent and his arms immediately and I came out of that tunnel. He kept whispering to me that we would be fine. I don't remember us becoming a 'we', but he calmed my spirit and I'm so glad."

"Well," Lucas said, "Michael told me that he loves you and I told him you don't need my approval for anything; that you made your own decisions, but he does love you, and does not expect a little mouse. You are a very special woman and I adore you." Michael said he was quite aware of his Lucy and he would never try to tell her what to do, like he sometimes did with Molly. He said it seemed he was always trying to protect her. She would have none of that.

The day was fast becoming night, so Lucas and Lucy went to bed. He did ask that she keep her door open in the event she needed him. "I will worry-wart, but you leave yours cracked as well."

They made breakfast and thanked God for his help and love. They thanked HIM for Molly and Michael. They then tidied the kitchen and began to prepare to dress for the funeral. They called the funeral director and asked if they could see their father; "Of course you may," he replied. The two of them went over to funeral home and saw their dad. He too looked at peace. They saw a small piece of Indian jewelry on his suit; they had never seen that. They asked the funeral director to remove it and let them read the back. He did and the back of engraved: 'To Luke From Your Lucia Forever'. They told him to place it back on his suit. "We don't usually bury people with jewelry; we took your mother's wedding band and a tiny farm implement from her dress and I've stored them for the two of you. I'll do the same for this." "Thank you." Lucas looked back at his father with snowy hair and a smooth face that wrinkles seemed to have left. He glanced at Lucy, who was crying, but very gently. Nothing like she had sobbed before.

They both went to the Chapel and took a walk out into the woods behind the Chapel. They walked a while and said very little to one another; it wasn't necessary. Lucas looked at his watch and realized it was almost time to get seated for the funeral. They went in and the pastor talked with them a bit and went to his office.

Soon they heard something behind them and turned and looked. Michael had Molly in a wheelchair with the legs up and he positioned her at the end where Lucas was sitting and then he sat down beside Lucy. Lucas asked Molly if she was sure she should be out and she looked straight at him and said, yes! Lucas remembered that Molly did not wish to be questioned any more than Lucy would allow. He smiled and said, "I'm glad to see you and I love you." "Good," Molly retorted. Michael and Lucy were talking and that seemed to help Lucy remained centered.

In a short while people began coming in for the Service and there was no more talking. All sat quietly and waited on the Service. There was soft music playing over the speakers, but it was peaceful. The Pastor came out and held a short service. There were more people than Lucy or Lucas knew or recognized. The Chief had come down from the mountains and sat quietly. He paid particular attention to Lucy. When it was time to go to the gravesite, they walked down to the site and Chief walked on the other side of Lucy and spoke softly to her. Michael rolled the wheelchair to the gravesite and positioned her beside Lucas and sat beside Chief who was speaking softly to Lucy. Michael wondered how Chief knew of Lucy's breakdown; of course, he answered himself. This Chief knew everything around here.

They were finished at the gravesite and Lucy was still crying, but very softly. Chief touched her hand and smiled at her and said goodbye. When he left, Michael invited everyone to a quiet restaurant to have dinner and chat a while. They went to another restaurant and were seated soon. Michael had rolled Molly's wheelchair into the seat next to Lucas and he sat beside Lucy and held her hand until the waiter came with water and sliced lemon and then they looked at the menu. Michael still had Lucy's hand, under the table. They gave their orders; Molly ordered congealed salad, chicken breast grilled, and lemon water; Lucy ordered salmon with lemon sauce and a green salad. Lucas ordered a steak and sweet potatoes and turnips mixed with kale. Michael ordered a steak, baked potato, and turnips. The order was taken and they began to talk.

The funeral was very nice and respectful. Lucas said it certainly was, but he was surprised to see Chief come so far for their father's funeral. Then he realized the Chief had known about the deep darkness that Lucy had and was there to comfort them all. He had noticed Molly beside Lucas and smiled and left. They talked a while longer and Lucas noticed that Molly looked really tired. He said, "At the risk of a tongue lashing, I really think you need to go home." She smiled and said, "No tongue lashing today. That's probably best." She was going back to the doctor tomorrow and ask him why the fatigue and slight nausea? Lucas asked if she would please call him and she said she would. Michael had also noticed it was time to go. They all went home and Lucas asked how Lucy was feeling.

"Much better, but I think I too need a rest." "So go on to bed and I'll be around. Goodnight, sis."

Lucas went outside on the back porch and just marveled at the moon and stars. He could imagine his mother and dad having a grand time. Since he had found out just how close they really were, he realized he felt at peace about things he could barely remember. He went back in his house and also went to bed. He thought about Molly and prayed for her. He asked the Lord to ensure that she was all right and that the baby was. He drifted off to sleep thinking about her and tomorrow at work.

He got up the next morning and showered and dressed in his new uniform. He put on his "special" phone and then put his personal phone in his pocket. He came out to fix breakfast for Lucy and she was already awake and dressed for work too. They finished breakfast together and told each on they loved them and headed to work.

Several people came up to Lucy and gave her condolences, but few people knew about Lucas' dad's death and burial. When a couple of them said something to him, they assured him none of the chiefs would expect him to report today. Lucas said that he wanted to be here in case he was needed. There were a few road accidents, but no one was killed; two had to go the ER for fractured bone. He observed how every crew came together at the accidents. That was a good thing. He, Carl, and David went back to their offices and filled out a report. Lucas went next door and asked David and Carl if they were to take a swab for DNA and they told him not usually. One of the Chiefs let them know when one was needed, especially a crime scene. "Thanks," Lucas said. "Hey Lucas, would you like to go get some coffee? "Sure, where do we go, in the dining room or outside?" They said, "We usually go in the dinning room and get an idea of what went on at the scene when the others get back. You will find most of the guys are friendly, but pretty well stay close to one another. It's been about two months since Carl and I decided to sign up here. I've enjoyed the entire work and knowledge each one has."

David began to talk a bit about the navy and stress of submarines, as well as working on a ship where our planes may land and no one is safe from a fire attack. Often when you cracked the hole to come on deck, you'd see your buddy get mowed down and there was nothing anyone could do but open fire on the enemy in the direction from which came the shot. We would all cut lose on that area and several of the enemy, knowing they were outnumbered and outgunned, would hold up their hands and two of our own guys just mowed them down. That made me physically sick. I dragged that buddy down in the hole and prepared him for sending home on the next plane and often I went on the angel flight. That was terrible, but the parents, girlfriends, or wives were so grateful, I'd do it again. But my last tour was my last tour; I began to have flashbacks and awaken soaked in sweat, so I decided to join the First-Responders. Both the other men knew when to be quiet and give their friend time to compose himself. Well, it's about time to go home, we'd better tidy those offices or we will be chastised tomorrow.

They all went into their office. Lucas felt an immediate bond with his mates and that was something he was didn't usually do. He called Molly and asked if she was feeling better. Molly said, "Not really; would you have time to come over a few minutes. Michael has already gone to be with Lucy."

"I'll be there as soon as possible." It took him about ten minutes to get there. Molly called out for him to come into her bedroom. She said, "Lucas did you lie to me about Randy?" "Absolutely not! I don't lie! Molly whatever gave you that idea?" She said that she had gotten a letter from one of Randy's buddies and Randy told him that he was not married. He checked in the directory or whatever that is called, and it revealed he had no wife. "Lucas, I don't understand, he wanted a lot of children he said, then the guy that I got the letter from today said that Randy had received a letter from someone who said she was his wife and she was pregnant. He said, that's impossible, I have no wife. His buddy didn't know what to think and now, I think I'm losing my mind. Why would he do such a thing?" Lucas said; "I think Michael might have been right about his inability to understand you and seemed ashamed when he got the letter you sent about the pregnancy. Honey, I don't know what would cause a man to do such a thing; he must have already decided to divorce you before he signed up." "Then he could have asked for a divorce and I would gladly have signed the papers," Molly said.

"Molly did you ever receive any money from the Marines for Randy while he was in the Marines?" "No, I didn't need money because I was working and making a good salary. I've talked to Michael and he started crying; I've never seen my big brother so angry and sad." He told me to call you and if you could you would get here shortly. He was going down to the Marine Base and find out as much as he could. They were especially nice and went through the records and Randy had said he was unmarried. Also I never got his flag and I have no idea where his parents are, but surely they would know their own son. "I expected he had made the Marines aware that should he disappear, he should be sent to his parents. I've never heard from them. Randy wasn't interested in me getting to know them or even where they lived except somewhere in Ohio."

"Lucas, this is so frightening and hurtful, my baby needs a name. I can hardly bear this," but Michael said, "Stop worrying, you are getting too upset and could lose the baby." "Lucas, "I trust you as much as I do Michael, but this hurts so bad! What is so horrible about me that he could not love or even like me? I always tried to make him happy, but he didn't want me too close and knew nothing about how Indians feel about families."

"Molly, did you go to the doctor today?" "Yes, and he made me mad. The baby is big and I was not going to carry him four more weeks, if I didn't stay off my feet. I must stay in bed except to go to the bathroom. "No shower unless someone was with me." "Lucas, please think about what I've told you and here is the letter I received today. I'm very tired and afraid if I don't sleep, I'll start screaming and never stop. Is it to much to ask you to stay until Michael gets back?" "I would love to stay with you, but you do need to rest and I'll be right out here and I won't leave." He reached over and hugged her and kissed her and said, "Please take a nap, I'll be right here."

Lucas read the letter and sure enough that is what Randy had made clear; he had no wife and should something happen, his body would be shipped to his parents in Ohio. Lucas became so angry at a dead man, he did not know what to say or do. He sat re-reading the letter and his heart was breaking for Molly. He already knew what he planned to do, but he could not put anymore stress on her. He loved her and would marry her as soon as he could, but she had to feel certain about his love. He checked on Molly and went back out onto the porch and called Michael. He told him what Molly told him and "Michael, I read the letter; that son-of-gun man is dead or he would get a beating of his life. Molly is worried that she had done something to cause him not to love her or want a bond with her. I assured her that was not true. She is one of the most beautiful women with a pure heart that I've known. I desperately want to marry her. Her baby needs to have a name and that will take a worry off her, but I can't mention that tonight; she is too close the edge."

"Have you told Lucy about this? Yes, I too was so angry and up set that I needed Lucy's plain common sense. You might as well know, I have asked Lucy to marry me, but not to put pressure on her either. She too had been in a dark hole. I know we are all Christians, but why so much at one time?" "I don't know Michael, but we will get through it." Lucas waited a while longer and checked on Molly. She seemed restless and crying softly, but asleep. He was a big man; he lay down beside her and put his arms around her and she turned over and put her arms around his neck. Not even aware of him, she seemed to settle down. He put his hand on her stomach and the little one was getting active again. He kicked hard. Molly woke up and realized she was about to squeeze Lucas' neck off. "I'm glad to see you Lucas, did you feel my boy kick you." Lucas laughed and said yes he did. He will be a big baby. "How many weeks till they can safely deliver him." Molly said, "According to his size, it will be about four more weeks." "Well, I'll stay with you as much as I can. Please remember, I truly do love you and want to marry you. I don't expect you to give me an answer, there is too much for you to digest, but I mean what I say and I'm definitely sure I want you for my wife."

Very soon Michael came in and came to check on Molly. He saw that Lucas had his arms around her and she seemed the most calm he had seen her all day. Thank You, Heavenly Father. Michael said; "How about some congealed salad sis, or some lemon juice water?" "How about both," she answered. "Okay!" Lucas got up to go home and asked Michael how Lucy was feeling this evening. He said he thought she was doing better. Lucas kissed Molly and told her he would see her tomorrow afternoon about six o'clock. That would be great, she replied. The same routine continued for about two weeks; Michael went to see Lucy after work and Lucas went to stay with Molly. They were becoming very close and so were Michael and Lucy.

# MICHAEL'S HOSPITAL STAY

Lucas and the team got a call that there was an accident at the local high school and a fire, as well as, a man trapped under a car. When they arrived, Lucas immediately went to Michael and checked him. Michael was conscious and said, I think it is only my legs. The team picked the car up and Lucas slipped Michael very gently from under the car. They put him in the ambulance, but before he would allow them to leave, he told Lucas to keep an eye on Eli.

The student who accidentally kicked the lift and trapped Michael was really distraught. He told Michael he did not have to ever teach such a klutz. Michael called Eli over to sit with him until the squads could lift the car off Michael's leg. The boy was almost sobbing and was so embarrassed. Lucas gave Eli his handkerchief and Eli said, "I'm so very sorry 'teach', I wish it could have been me instead of you." Michael told Eli that he knew it was an accident. "Now you boys get ready to clean this place up. I want it clean and every tool we've used cleaned and put into place." The other boys were almost as shaken as Eli was. Lucas said he would go with Michael and give them a report. But, you guys heard what Michael said: He wants this entire place spick and span and every tool cleaned and put where it is supposed to be. They all said they could do that.

Lucas went on the ambulance with Michael and asked him where else he hurt. Michael said, "My back hurts some and my ribs." Lucas said, "Well, we'll find out what is wrong and I'll let Lucy and Molly know." "Okay, but Lucas, take Lucy with you to stay with Molly. She can use my bed and closet for her work clothes. I can't bear to think either one of them being alone." "I'll take care of both of them. I'll also have one of the First Responders keep an eye on you and keep me posted."

They got Michael into the hospital ER and the doctors and nurses began to see what was wrong. They did x-rays and cat scans and the only thing broken was his leg. They would take him to surgery and put the screws into the bones that needed them, keep him a few days, and let him go back on crutches. "I'll also keep the boys notified, especially Eli. He was badly shaken." "Thanks," Michael said. The medicine they had given him was already taking effect and so Lucas waited until they took him to surgery and then he left to go get Lucy and tell her what had happened. Lucy almost immediately started to the hospital and Lucas said, "No, Lucy. Michael asked me to tell you to go to his house and sleep in his bed and put your clothes into his closet."

"I'm to stay and keep watch over both of you and I've told you the truth. He has two bones broken in his leg and he is already in surgery. One of the First-Responders will keep a watch on him and keep me informed and I will keep you girls informed. Michael is worried that this will really put you back in a dark place as well as perhaps Molly to lose her baby. I felt this is the best thing to do as well." "Lucas, help me get packed then and I'll do what Michael wants. Thank you for being there; I think I would die if Michael did." "Let's focus on the good part, it wasn't his chest or head, it was his leg and I'll need you to help care for Molly too. Do you think you are ready to go?" "Yep, got my clothes, underwear and bathroom supplies." "Well, lets go over and make Molly aware of his status and you will be a great help to me. If Molly does have a big problem, you can certainly call the First-Responders for me."

Lucas helped Lucy with her bag and they headed over to Molly's. Lucas went in and asked how she was feeling. "A bit better today, not so much nausea and my feet are less swollen." Lucy came in and sat down beside Molly and Lucas told Molly that Michael had been in an accident. "He is okay, except he has two bones broken and is in surgery for them to be repaired." Molly looked at both of them and asked, "How do you know?" Lucas could feel Molly drawing back from him; Lucy said, "Molly, you know Lucas works with the First-Responders and they got the call to go to the school. Lucas would never lie to you and you are aware that I'm going to marry Michael and stay with you until he comes home. Lucas will bunk on the couch and watch both of us. Michael will be home in about a week and I know quite a few home-care nurses who will stay and ensure you and he are fine. I've brought my work clothes and put them in Michael's closet and Lucas will bring back his uniforms to go to work. He will stay close to both of us." Molly was crying silently and Lucas simply picked her up and held her close. "You know Molly, that I love you and Michael, and he told me to make sure you were all right. He did ask me to come back to the hospital when he got out of surgery and I assured him that I would. Do you believe me now?" "Yes," Molly said, "It is like too much is happening to all of us so quickly. Lucas said, "Yes, 'the darkness of midnight' seems to have sucked all the sunshine away. However, Michael will be fine and on crutches a while, but I will certainly get the home care nurse when Lucy finds one to her liking."

Lucas kissed Molly and held her warmly and Lucy crawled up on the other side of Molly's bed. Molly had stopped crying and told Lucy she seemed like a sister sitting on her bed. Lucy said, "I feel like I am and I'll certainly keep any folk away that you don't want to see. You know Lucas taught me self-defense and offensive tactics and I can whip anyone."

Lucas said, "Since she is through boasting, may I go see Michael and talk with him regarding what I've told you?" "Yes, thank you Lucas, and before I forget again, I do love you." Lucas felt like his heart would burst, it certainly beat fast enough. He picked her up and thoroughly kissed her and reassured her of his undying love. Lucy said, "Would you get on with it; this smooching can wait until I know how Michael is." Lucas kissed Lucy on the cheek and said, "I'll be back after a while."

Lucy told Molly she knew that Lucas loved her and wanted to marry her, but was afraid you might not be ready. "I just wanted you to know." Molly replied, "It seems like Michael feels the same toward you. He talks about how sweet and self-reliant you are, but what a kind heart." Molly and Lucy talked a long while and Molly asked if Lucy minded bringing them some juice or soft drink? Lucy took a soft drink and brought Molly some lemon water. "Lucy, do you really know a health care nurse who would come out to check on Michael and me sometimes." "Not at this moment, but remember I work in the hospital and get information on the best." "Thank you, Lucy. Is it time for Lucas to be back yet?" "I don't think he's had time to track everyone down, but he will return to us as soon as he can." Molly told Lucy that she and Michael had always been close, except sometimes he bosses me, but I love him dearly. Lucy said, "I do too, Molly."

Michael asked how Molly was doing as well as his dear Lucy. They both had to cry some and when I left they were in the same bed talking like sisters. Michael responded; "I sure wish we could make that happen." "Lucy seems gun-shy and Molly is in no shape to decide on another marriage, but Michael I believe she will be sooner, rather than later. When she found how Randy had lied about her being his wife; any love seemed to die, only great disappointment."

"Michael have they given you anything for pain?" "No, not yet but when I get settled they said they would. The pain is not too bad to bear. Do you know how young Eli is doing?" "Well, when I left those boys started cleaning every square inch of the shop." They told me to tell 'teach' that they would not let him down. I told them they were doing fine and spoke briefly to Eli, who was still pretty upset. I told him that I know you well and you will be fine and the last thing you would want was him to feel so bad. He said he knew it was just an accident. Eli said, "It was, but I'm the one who tripped over the lift." "Well, my suggestion is to give thanks to God that you nor Michael weren't injured worse and then put it behind you. Michael would not want you being so upset. And when he is able to see anyone, you boys take him a basket of fruit or something and don't stay long, because he will get tired." "That's a great idea," Eli replied.

Lucas turned to go and Michael said, "Are you sure Lucy is okay." "I'm sure," Lucas told him; "She is much stronger now and will make sure to take care of herself and Molly. I'll get a home care nurse to come over during the day to check you and Molly. Lucy said she would find the best. I'm supposed to bunk on the couch. There are certainly worse places," he said laughing.

Lucas got to Molly's and she was asleep and Lucy was napping on the same bed. Lucy got up quietly and came into the living room to talk to Lucas. Lucas told her all he knew and that he had been with Michael a good while. "They have him in a room with a bar over the bed with a 'monkey bar' that will assist him in movement. There was no other injury except his leg." "Oh, I'm so glad," she said. "Do you have a clean uniform? I'll take that one to the cleaners tomorrow and pick it up tomorrow after work." "Thanks sis, now do you want me to order some dinner?" "I think something light would be nice and I think Molly might enjoy lemon sorbet. She loves lemon as much as chocolate, but she is afraid to eat chocolate, but the lemon sherbet/sorbet will be good for her." "Okay, I will go pick up something light for all of us."

Lucas went to a seafood place and got broiled salmon, salads and stopped and got some lemon sorbet. He brought everything back home and told Lucy and Molly what he had gotten. They both ate a little of everything, but Molly really enjoyed the sorbet. They had dinner in Molly's bedroom and they all talked and chatted about most anything they could think of. Molly told Lucas she sure did like the sorbet. It was so refreshing. I'm glad, Lucas told her.

It was bedtime and Lucas did indeed bunk on the couch and kept both the girls doors cracked open. At about two o'clock in the morning he heard Molly screaming and sobbing violently. Lucas with Lucy behind him ran into her room. She was semi- awake, just screaming. "Lucy, I'll turn my back, quickly check to make sure there's no bleeding." "None," said Lucy. Lucas sat down on Molly's bed and took her in his arms. She continued to sob and Lucas asked who her doctor was. She awoke and realized she was awake and crying. She said, "I'm not in labor, I would know, I don't know what's wrong, but maybe I should go to the ER and have them call Dr. Jones." Lucas picked her up and Lucy put a light blanket over her and they headed for the ER.

They put her on a stretcher and asked how far she was in her pregnancy; about six months she answered. "But I'm not in labor, I've had a terrible shock today and I guess Lucas and Lucy thought Dr. Jones should see me. I do too, because I'm so upset I might bring on labor. I've been put on bed rest for four weeks and I've stayed put."

Dr. Jones came in and Lucy went outside. Molly said, "Lucas please stay with me." He looked at Dr. Jones who shook his head yes. He asked if she had any bleeding or cramping and Molly said no. She said she got a letter today and although her husband was dead; the letter was sent by a buddy and Randy had denied being married. The admitting records were checked and he said he was unmarried. Should anything happen to him, send his remains to his parents I don't even know them, because he was rather reserved about his family life. I knew he lived in Ohio, but not where and I assumed we would soon visit one day. Randy did get my letter telling him about the pregnancy, but he told his buddy that couldn't be possible because he wasn't married. I know we were, but I'm unsure if the "Justice of the Peace" ever recorded it. Michael hasn't been able to find out because he was in an accident today and is in the hospital. He broke his leg and is now in a room. Will it be safe to use a wheelchair to go see him? Dr. Jones said yes, she could, but she needed a sedative to prevent anymore upsets. It will not hurt the baby, except make him sleepy, he said, smiling at her.

"Molly, you and Michael are so close, but you cannot do any research about your marriage being registered. Is it so important now?" "Yes! I want my baby to have a name and I cannot stand being lied to." "Well, you may go see Michael for a short while but then I'll give you a small sedative and you must go back to bed." He looked at Lucas and asked who he was; he had noticed the uniform. Lucas said, "My sister and I are their dear friends." "That's fine, Lucas, but I'll ask you to push her in a wheelchair upstairs to see Michael." "I will," Lucas replied. When the wheelchair got there Lucas picked Molly up and put her gently in the chair and lifted the legs and left the room. Lucy was waiting outside and all three of them went up to see Michael.

Michael was awake and so pleased to see Lucy and Molly. He asked Molly what she was doing out of bed and Lucas said, "She needed to be checked by Dr. Jones, because I became afraid when she woke up crying." "Oh," Michael said, "Are you all right?" "Yes big brother and I love you." Lucy went over and kissed Michael. She said she missed him and would check on him every afternoon after work. "Okay," he said, "But I'm sleepy now, they gave me a shot too. I'm glad you are all okay and no more worrying about me."

Lucas took Molly back down to the ER and Dr. Jones had a nurse standing ready to give her a sedative. "Now you go home and to bed and be sure to call if you experience any cramping or discomfort." "I will," Molly said. About that time Lucy came back and Lucas carried Molly to the car and Lucy followed behind. Lucas could hear Lucy silently crying, but not sobbing.

By the time they got home, it was almost six o'clock in the morning and he knew he had to go to work. Lucy called in and told them she couldn't work today, but she needed to check on home health nurses who could check a man with a broken leg and a pregnant lady who was on bed rest. "That will be fine," her supervisor said. Lucas put Molly to bed and kissed her and she was already nearly asleep. He told Lucy he appreciated her staying with Molly today and handing the home health nurse. "No problem, Lucas, I want to see the nurse for myself, anyway." The routine continued with Lucy going to see Michael; and Lucas staying with Molly for about two weeks.

# Michael Comes Home From the Hospital

In about a week and a half, Michael was discharged from the hospital, but still needed his bed fitted with a bar to aid   in lifting himself.  The leg was healing nicely, but he would begin therapy at home three days a week to learn to use his crutches and keep check on his leg.  Lucy had found a wonderful nurse, who seemed about retirement age, but she enjoyed working with folks at home.  She was bonded and her credentials were great.  She came the next day and met Michael and Molly, as well as Lucas and Lucy.  Her name was Lucinda and they all laughed at so many names in one house starting with the letter L.  She assessed Michael and Molly and kept notes on each one's vital signs and other observations.

Lucas left for work, although late, he had phoned the Captain and told him the circumstances.  Captain said, "No problem, Lucas.  Your buddies are asking about you, so go back and tell them what has happened."  Lucas knew he was sinking back into a hole and was really afraid, because of Molly.  Some way he had to get her to marry him.

Both Carl and David were in their office.  "You guys got a minute?"  "Yep, come in."  They both took one look at Lucas and said, have a cup of coffee Lucas – fresh made.  Lucas took a cup of coffee and sat for a few minutes just sipping and the other boys did as well.

Lucas began telling them about his last tour in AFGANISTAN and how he and his partner were going into enemy territory to bring out their fallen brother. My partner jumped out of the Apache and headed toward the Marine and the AFGANISTAN troops came out of the cave like ants. He had been almost, cut in half by their bullets. I turned my guns on them, sent a rocket into that hideout. The only thing left were body parts and blood on the flattened mountain hole.

I got out as quickly as I could, leaving both men behind. His radio and other equipment were on and the base knew something had happened. I reported to the Captain and no one had known that particular hideout was there. There are so many caves and mountainous regions you can't even smell them. The other guys just smiled, realizing that Lucas was mostly Indian.

Anyway, I decided that after this tour I was through. I have never been the same sense. My sister and I are very close, but both parents died within weeks of each other since I've been home. We met two people that we seem to be close to; as much as any military officer can; and then I learned that the woman I'm very interested in was the wife of the guy that stepped out of the Apache. She is now about six months pregnant and one of his buddies wrote her a letter and she got it yesterday. In the letter, the buddy told Molly he didn't know what to think. That her husband (Randy) told him he wasn't married. This woman must be mistaken. Randy's buddy then went to base and checked Randy's records and again he had registered unmarried.

Molly called me (you've probably guessed I love her), but she asked me why I lied to her. I had no idea what she was talking about, but I told her "I don't lie." She handed me the letter and said her brother Michael had come in from work and she showed the letter to him. He started to cry and was so angry that if her husband was not dead, he might be. Anyway, Michael is very interested in my sister, and he asked me to stay with Molly until he could find out if the marriage was recorded. By this time, the courthouse was closed and he couldn't do anything. Molly told me that a "Justice of the Peace" married them and she had no idea if he registered them or not.

At any rate, about two o'clock this morning (Lucy & I were staying with Molly) because Michael had been involved in an accident at school where he teaches and a car had fallen on his legs. Fortunately, he wasn't injured in his head or chest, but he had to have surgery and is still in hospital.

As I said, about two o'clock in the morning, Molly began screaming and crying so badly, I thought she might lose her baby. Lucy and I took her to hospital and her doctor said she was not in labor, but must stay off her feet for four more weeks. He also wanted to give her a sedative, but she wanted to see her brother first. So they brought a wheelchair and I lifted her legs on the footrest and took her up to see Michael. Michael is very interested in my sister and Lucy is in him.

Michael asked Molly if she was listening to her doctor and Lucas said she quipped, yes, big brother. She then told him she was okay, but the doctor had advised a sedative to help her rest. Well, I need to speak to Lucy before my pain medicine kicks in, so off you two go. The doctor did indeed give her an injection and when Lucy came down, we put her to bed and Lucy sat up in bed with Molly until Molly went to sleep.

By this time it was about eight o'clock and I had to insure that Lucy was all right, because with both parents dying so closely together, she had a rough go for a while. "I'm sorry for going on boys, but that's why I'm late." "No problem," they both said and refilled his coffee cup and suggested he see the Captain about taking the rest of the day off. "No, I cannot do that; it's against everything I believe in; to slough off my work onto someone else." Carl and David said, we understand, but if you get too tired, just let us know. You too, have been under a number of stresses, almost together. "Thanks, guys, I'll see you later." They let him go without another word. They had some idea of the anger, rage, and hurt he was experiencing.

Lucas looked over any paperwork from the evening and night before. Nothing much seemed to have happened. He sat at his desk with papers spread out in front of him. He knew he was close to the edge, but Molly must come first. He asked God to please give him strength and knowledge on the best approach to take.

He suddenly began to feel so much lighter in his spirit; he also decided he would get on - line and find out the Justices of Peace in this area. He would then visit each of them and find out whether they had married a couple by the name of Molly Deerborn and Randy Black. He would then check the courthouse as well for any register of such a marriage.

It was soon time to leave work and so he said goodnight to all the guys and left. He knew Molly and Michael had the nurse and Lucy would pick up his uniform, so he called Molly and asked what they would like for dinner.

"Well, Michael said he could eat a horse; I'd rather have linguini with clam sauce and a congealed salad and some more sorbet; if you please." Lucas started laughing; "Did Michael snitch your sorbet?" "Well maybe a bite or two, but it is so refreshing and I read the label and it has a lot of calcium in it." "No need to explain, my dearest; lemon sorbet you shall have." He pretty well knew that Lucy would have a burger and fries and he thought that sounded good too. However, since they did not serve horsemeat at his particular restaurant of favor; he would get him a big steak, baked potato, salad, and turnips.

Lucas went to his favorite restaurant and ordered their dinner and headed over to Molly's. The nurse was still there and was so very nice. Lucas said, "I didn't know you would still be here, I'm sorry I didn't bring you dinner." "Oh, that's fine; when Lucy gets here I will go home anyway." Lucas asked how Molly had done today. "She has a bit of a backache. I rubbed her back, but I think she might be starting into premature labor. I think she is afraid of the same thing. She even let me put a bedpan under her instead of going to the bathroom."

"Lucas, it doesn't take a genius to know you care deeply for her and she does for you. If I'm not butting in, why don't you find a way to marry her before, the baby gets here? That way he will have a name. That seems to be her greatest concern; except she does not want you to think she would marry you just for her baby." Lucas said, "I've already told her that. She seems now afraid she will hurt me or someone else. She seems to have gone in a deep hole and I well understand that. Do you think if I told her again how much I love her and the baby, and really want to marry her; that she would consent?" "Well, it sure won't hurt."

"My pastor would come here and do the ceremony. He is a good man and would ensure that you were properly married. Molly told me about what's happened. I'll give you my phone number and if she agrees, call me and I'll see that my pastor marries the two of you. You might want to tell Lucy and Michael after you two have a talk." "Thank you, Lucinda."

When Lucy came in, Lucinda went home and Lucy hung Lucas' uniform in her closet. He told her he was going to get them dinner and asked if a burger and fries were all right with her? She said, "Yes, but Molly needs some more lemon sorbet." "I know, she told me. Lucy, Lucinda is a trustworthy woman and she told me that the primary thing that was worrying Molly was that she may be going into premature labor and her baby did not have a name. I assured Lucinda that I had practically begged Molly to marry me, but she's afraid I might just be marrying to give her baby a name. You and I both know that's not so. However, Lucinda said if I asked her again, she thought she might accept and that Lucinda knew her pastor well enough to know he would come here to marry us. She said he was a good man and I know they are all Christians. She said run this by you and give me your thoughts." "I can tell you right now, Lucas, she will accept. Now, go get our supper and I'll stay with Michael and tell him about the purposed marriage. The marriage could occur as early as tomorrow. I know it is Saturday, but that shouldn't be a problem."

Lucas went to pick up dinner and prayed all the way there. He asked God to have His will done and make this go smoothly. He thanked the Lord for Molly and for the love he felt for her. Lord, you know my heart, help Molly see it too. I do praise Your Name and ask You to let her carry the baby to term and to help Michael to get well soon.

He picked up their dinner and stopped and bought a large box of lemon sorbet and some lemon pie. When he got back to the house, he went in to talk to Molly. "Molly, you know that I love you and I really want to marry you. Lucinda said her pastor would come out here and do it and it would be proper. Do you believe me?" "Absolutely I do and Lucas, if Lucinda knows a real minister who knows we are all Christians, I believe it will help me a lot." "I'm worried that you will deliver prematurely and Lucinda is too."

Michael said, "Please try to help her understand that she is the one you love as well as the baby." "Okay, I'll send Lucy in to eat with you." "Great," Michael replied. Lucas told Lucy to put the sherbet in the freezer and to feed/help Michael. He had some serious talking to do with Molly. She kissed his cheek and said, "You'll be pleasantly surprised."

Lucas went in with Molly's dinner and leaned over and kissed her. She began to eat and wrinkled her face at him. "Is the food that bad or am I that ugly?" She started laughing and said, "Neither; I think, Lucas that Luke has decided he wants out of the small area." Lucas laughed and said, Can you eat some dinner now?" "I'd rather have sorbet," Lucas said, "Sorbet it is then. Molly, I'll get the sorbet, but I must talk with you. I'm hurting inside and I can't talk much about it; would you listen with your heart and head." "Of course, you know I will." Lucas went to get the sorbet and a spoon. He got down beside her bed and looked her in the eye and said, "Molly I want to marry you now and be a dad to your son." "Well Lucas, I love you and that would be wonderful. However, you must swear this marriage will be registered and that you are not marrying me for the baby, but because you love me." "I can swear about the recording of our marriage, but, God knows my heart and I've prayed for wisdom and for His will to be done. I know this is His will for us to build a life that will help other people and be a blessing to those around us." "Then I accept!" Lucas almost cried; "My wonderful Molly, thank you!" He told her that Lucinda's pastor would come out here to marry us and ensure the marriage was recorded and I will too, and as soon as Michael gets able, he will too. Molly laughed and asked if Lucinda really said that; Lucas pulled her phone number out of his pocket and showed her. "Lucas, I do love just you and I do want to marry you."

Lucas got on the phone to Lucinda and asked if her pastor would marry them tonight? "I think so, but the courthouse is closed." "That doesn't matter, it can be recorded in the morning and I'll see it with my own eyes." Lucinda said, "All right, I'll give him a call and make him aware of the situation and your requests." "Thank you, Lucinda."

Lucas let out an Indian whoop and Lucy came running, "Lucas, have you lost your mind?" "Nope, just found it." Both the bedroom doors were opened and Lucas said, "Molly will marry me and knows I love her! Oh my goodness, I forgot to kiss her after she accepted." He went back into Molly's room and she was calmly eating her sorbet. "Michael did you hear my precious man let out an Indian whoop before he even kissed me?" Michael yelled back; "Sure did sis and that is wonderful. Now please tell me what my nephew will be named." "I haven't asked Lucas, but I plan to name him Michael Luke Stone if that preacher makes it here in time." Lucy reached over and hugged her; "Did you know Luke was our father's name?" "No Lucy, I didn't, but I couldn't call him Lucas, because neither of them would know who I was calling; same with Michael, so therefore his name is Michael Luke Stone." Lucas picked her up halfway in the bed and hugged and kissed her plenty well. Lucy said, "Oh well, if you two are going to smooch, I'm going back to help Michael." She kissed Michael and told him how proud she was of both of them. Michael was in tears. "Lucy, he is a good man and will never hurt her."

Meanwhile, in Molly's room, Lucas had called Lucinda and they would be here in about fifteen minutes. Lucas said, "Molly, I'm sorry I didn't get you a flower, but I got you some lemon pie." Molly said, "Let's eat it after the preacher gets here and does his job." "That's fine."

About that time the doorbell rang. Lucas went to answer it and it was Lucinda and the Pastor. Pastor Jackson Jones had the papers and they left the two bedroom doors open so Michael could hear. He did a beautiful reading of Scripture and then the usual marriage ceremony. He then pronounced them husband and wife. He reminded Lucas that he would have to wait until Monday to get the marriage recorded. "That's fine," Lucas said. He had already kissed his new wife and then asked Lucy if she would make some coffee to go with lemon pie for their wedding reception. Lucy started laughing and of course that was done pronto! Rev. Jones asked why Molly had to be in bed? He said he knew she was pregnant, that Lucinda had informed him and how her husband was killed. He told them he thought God had brought them together and would keep them together. She asked for prayer because the little one seemed to want to come too early and therefore she had to stay in bed.

They all had coffee and lemon pie and then after another prayer and Lucinda acting as a notary, they went back to their respective homes.

# Molly Has the Baby

Molly ate a small portion of pie and coffee and stopped. She seemed uncomfortable but said she wasn't, but her back did ache a bit. Lucas said, "If you can turn a little I'll rub your back." He had seen that particular thing done on a TV program he had watched. Molly said that felt good. Lucas had not undressed and didn't plan to, but he would lay beside her tonight. Lucy could take the couch.

Molly said, "Lucas, do you like the name of our son?" "I really do, that is perfect. Like Lucy said our dad's name was Luke." "Lucas, do you feel like you are really a part of him or will you grow to love him." "Molly, he is already loved and prayed for and I love and adore both of you. Rest your mind; I'll be right here rubbing your back as long as you need." "Well, you need some sleep too." "I'll sleep right here with my two loves."

Since they had been married on Friday night, Lucas planned to go get them both a wedding ring that was just alike. He asked Lucy if she could guess at Molly's size. Lucy told him she had a pretty good idea and if it was too big or small it could be sized. "I'm planning to go get us a band that is identical, will you call Lucinda if Molly needs her? I won't be gone long, I know just what I want and I think she will like it as well." He would have both engraved with: 'Molly and Lucas Forever'. So after being assured that Lucy would keep check on her, he left.

He went to the jewelry store and got the two rings he wanted and got the size that Lucy guessed Molly would wear. On the way back, his emergency phone rang. He needed to be at a certain address, some lady was in labor and the ambulance had already left. They didn't know if she had delivered, but the call sounded frantic. Lucas got back very quickly and the ambulance was pulling into the driveway. They had the ambulance ready and headed inside and he opened the door and went straight to Molly's room. Carl was there and he was checking Molly's vital signs, but blood and water was everywhere. Molly looked at Lucas and told him she couldn't have the baby, he was too big and she would need a section. "These guys have already made the ER aware and they have called her doctor and a surgical team in." She looked so pale and Lucas was really frightened. Carl said, "I think she'll be okay, the water and blood make things look worse than they are." "I know there is no room for me, but I'll follow you all to the hospital; by the way, she is my wife." Carl shook his head yes.

The ambulance arrived at the hospital and Molly's doctor was with her. They had temporarily stopped the bleeding, but they would be taking her to surgery for a section. Lucas said, "Just a minute please." He went over and put Molly's wedding ring on her finger and it fit perfectly. He already had his on. The ER nurse said she would have to remove it or have it taped on. "Tape it on," Molly replied.

Lucas reached over all the tubing and kissed Molly and told her he would be waiting. "Thank you, Lucas."

As soon as they got to the operating room doors, he had to go to the waiting room. Carl came in and told Lucas to forget about work for a while. He would handle everything with the Captains. Lucas looked up at Carl and said, "Thanks." Carl saw the eyes of a tormented man who was really frightened as well. In a few minutes Lucy came in to stay with Lucas. She had called Lucinda, who was staying with Michael, who was all right except scared about Molly. Well I got her wedding band on, but the nurse said she would have to take it off or tape it on. Molly said, "Tape it". They had already started IV's but no blood. They didn't at this point think she would need any. The doctor told me that it wouldn't take more than about an hour and he would be out to talk with me. That was fifteen minutes ago. "Wonder why so long, Lucy?" "I don't know Lucas, but Carl saw me and said that he would handle things with the Captains. He also said Molly's vital signs were good." They sat for another few minutes and Lucas started to pace. "Lucas, there are a few trees right outside, I don't know if you saw them." "I didn't, but I'll be back in a few minutes." Lucas found a stump and sat down and began to pray. He prayed until he felt a lifting of his spirit and felt like Molly would be all right.

He came back into the waiting room just as Molly's doctor was coming in. He smiled at Lucas and said, "You have a healthy son and wife. She is still very sleepy and will be for a while, but you can take a look at your son, if you'd like." Lucas was on his feet in a second and wanted to know where he was. The doctor smiled at Lucy and said, "Right this way." Lucas looked at the little fellow and he seemed pretty big to be premature. The doctor said, "He weighed five pounds and eight ounces, but he would stay in the incubator overnight just to ensure his lungs were functioning well."

Lucas asked if he could see Molly for a minute and the doctor told him where she was and that he could stay a short while. Lucas followed him and Lucy said, "I'm going to talk with Michael." "Good." Lucas went into the recovery room and saw Molly who was quite sleepy, but she recognized him. She asked, "Is the baby okay?" "He looks great, has a bit of hair like you have; but I couldn't see his eyes. He was yelling pretty loud for a little one though. He weighs five pounds and eight ounces and is about 20 inches long." Molly smiled and said, "He has Indian blood and he will be tall." She asked Lucas if they had really gotten married and he assured her they had. "See, "I've got my wedding ring on and you had them tape yours on." She looked at her hand and asked when he did that and he told her he had bought them this morning and that he had put hers on in the ER.

Lucas was so thankful for Molly and the baby. He knew the little one and his precious Molly would be fine. When he had to go out, he went outdoors to phone Michael and Lucy. Lucy said, "Michael was thrilled with his nephew and so thankful that Molly was okay." Lucas was so confused; he was deeply thankful and so fatigued he could hardly stand up. He asked Lucy what today is? "She told him Saturday and he needed to come home for a while and shower and eat." He said, "But Molly might need me."

Michael said, "Lucas, Molly is in the best hands and when she gets out of recovery room, check to see if they have a lounger in her room. Then if so, check to see that you can spend the night and come home and shower and eat something." "Okay, I will, but after she gets out of recovery." In about twenty minutes, the nurse told him he could see her now. "She is still sleepy, but she is awake." Lucas asked if he could spend the night with her and the nurse said, "Yes, that's fine and we have a large lounger in her room." Lucas told the nurse thanks and went to see Molly.

This time when he saw Molly, she looked much better. Her color was good and she only had an IV and catheter. He bent down and hugged her snugly and kissed her. "Thank you, dearest Molly for marrying me. I'm also grateful for that beautiful little boy in that nursery. I know he has my last name, could you see it in your heart to let me be his real dad?" "Oh, my dearest Lucas, of course you are his daddy. There was never any question in my mind." She asked again if he looked okay. "He is beautiful and the only reason he is in incubator tonight is to ensure his lungs are working well. Sometimes, a section baby has a little difficulty with lung development according to Dr. Jones. But he also said, Lucas, I think this baby was more than six and one half months. It could be that I miscalculated or Molly did because her husband had just gone into the Marines. At any rate, he is healthy. He also said they could bring the incubator in here and let you see him and hold him just a little while."

Molly started to cry; Lucas said, "I thought that would make you happy." "I'm the happiest I've ever been, to be able to hold our son, even just a few minutes. Thank you, Lucas."

The nurse rolled the incubator into her room and asked Molly if she wanted to hold him. "Oh yes, I certainly do." "Well, I'm afraid you and your husband will need to wear a mask, but otherwise, the pediatrician said you could both hold him after a good hand washing." Lucas was at the sink scrubbing his hands and forearms as though he was prepping for surgery. Molly and the nurse started laughing; "I didn't mean to scrub the skin off Mr. Stone, just wash your hands." By this time Molly was already holding Luke and snuggling him close to her breast. The little fellow started searching for his food; at least that's what the nurse said and Molly agreed. "You see, Lucas, God made each of us aware of where to get food, in this case a baby automatically hunts his mother's breast." The nurse said, "I'm not sure there is any milk yet, but the simple act of his sucking will certainly help him become stronger." "Thanks," Molly said. Lucas said, "May I stay or must I wait outside?" "Oh Lucas, relax! We are married and this is our son and of course you may watch him nurse." Luke took hold of her nipple and started sucking like any little baby or animal did.

Lucas could hardly believe how quickly Molly had accepted all of him, his heart, his trustworthiness and his love for both of them. He put his large hand on the baby's back and rubbed gently. The breast and warm hand on his back seemed to make him sleepy and so Molly called the nurse to put him back in the incubator. Molly snuggled him and put him into Lucas' arms for a few minutes. Lucas had never seen anything so beautiful in his life. He said a simple prayer, "Thank You Dear Father, for Molly and this little one and I'll do my best to be the daddy and husband You want me to be." Molly said, "That's so precious Lucas, thank you for so many things." Lucas could tell his precious Molly was close to exhaustion. When the nurse came to take Luke back to the nursery, he noticed that his name was on a card on the incubator; Luke Stone. He just about lost it then. He held Molly and thanked her for their son and asked her to please rest now. He was going to shower and have some breakfast, or lunch, or whatever it was time for; he started laughing and told Molly that he had to ask Michael what today was. Molly smiled and said, "Well, just natural instinct from a father. I love you, Lucas." He kissed her and left for home.

When he got home, Lucy met him at the door and hugged him and said, "Welcome home, daddy." Michael said, "Did you see my nephew?" Lucas went into Michael's room and said, "Yes and I even got to hold him a minute. Michael he has dark hair, like you and Molly. Molly breast fed the little tyke and I rubbed his back and he was almost asleep. So Molly called the nurse to come take him back to the nursery. She is really tired, but so beautiful. I told her I was coming home to shower and eat and I'd be back to spend the night."

Lucy of course had followed Lucas into Michael's room and heard the whole conversation. She also knew Lucas was about out on his feet, so she told him to hit the shower and his dinner would be ready as soon as he got out. Michael told Lucy, "That is a good man who really loves Molly and the baby. I'm so thankful to God for him and for Molly and the baby. I've also thanked him for you, Lucy. I've told you before that I love you, but I know it will take time to trust or understand. You were transported back to college when you heard what Molly said about Randy and I understand. If Randy was not already dead; I'm afraid between Lucas and me, he would be. You know Indians don't start wars without notice to the other tribe, but he wasn't an Indian or even a descendant."

Lucy said, "Michael, I do love you, but please be patient a while longer and get well. I'm going to make Lucas some dinner and you too. What would you like? Lucas will eat anything I make, but I want to please you too." "Whatever you make will be great, just food."

Lucy had already laid our pork chops and so she made some potatoes and put together a green salad. She also opened a can of turnips and seasoned them with a little fat from the pork chops. She then seasoned the chops and rolled them in egg and flour and put them into hot oil in a cast iron frying pan. She had used cast iron as long as she could remember; most of it came from her mother and even two pieces from her grandmother. She also made some biscuits and had them baking in the oven. The entire house smelled wonderful. In a few minutes Lucas came out and looked so much more relaxed. He was hungry. He helped Lucy fix the plates and they took everything into Michael's bedroom. They had put a small table there and they all ate. It was good.

Lucas got up and told Lucy how great dinner was and he would see them tomorrow. He asked Michael what the doctor had said about him beginning therapy and using his crutches. Michael said, "He would see the doctor with his therapist on Monday. They would x-ray and make a decision regarding therapy and walking with crutches." Lucas said, "Good, the boys might be coming over sometime next week." He asked Lucy if she and Lucinda might have time to make snacks for them. Boys love snacks of every kind; and they never get full. Lucy laughed and said, "I think I can manage making something after work."

"Lucinda comes every day now to check Michael's leg and make him wriggle his toes and whatever; I'm not familiar enough with nursing to know what she does, but I'll make refreshments for the boys. Just let me know when they are coming over."

Michael said, "Lucas, how do you know so much?" "I told Eli that they could visit you, but not to stay too long. They are anxious to tell you about the shop. It looks great, so don't be surprised if they brag a bit." "Thank you, Lucas, I've been worried about Eli. He is a special young man, but has a number of challenges at home; I think sometimes he thinks of me like he wishes his dad were. He is fifteen, but has the eyes of an old man." "I noticed that too," Lucas replied. "Well, we'll keep an eye on him and maybe when he finishes school, he might want to work for one of the departments." "That's a great idea. He is really bright and ahead of his classmates in brain power, but because he feels so worthless, he doesn't show that he is really smart."

Lucas thought about Eli quite a bit that evening on the way back to see his wife. He still found it hard to believe that she really loved him. He knew about lust and infatuation, but not genuine love from a pure heart like Molly. He had no idea he was speeding until the lights came on behind him. He looked down and sure enough he was speeding. The officer came to the window and asked for ID and his car insurance; the usual stuff. He then glanced in the back seat and saw Lucas' uniform that he hadn't taken out of the car yet. The officer said, "Sorry sir, I thought you were speeding; had no idea you are First-Responder." "Officer, stop talking, I was speeding to go see my wife in hospital. She just had our baby and I wasn't paying attention. Now, there is no reason for me to be speeding, so give me the ticket that I deserve." "I could let you off with a warning." "You could, but you and I both know I was speeding and deserve this ticket; now let's have it so I can see my wife." "Sir," the officer said, "What is your name again; I forgot just that quickly." Lucas told him and got his speeding ticket. Lucas did not know it, but that young officer was totally perplexed; he planned to tell his Captain about this fellow.

Lucas got to the hospital without speeding and went directly into see Molly. To his surprise the baby was in a bassinet beside of Molly. Molly said, "Yes, they checked him thoroughly this morning and we can have time to bond. That is now the protocol and I, for one, am glad to have this particular plan in place. The pediatrician told me that he thought I had miscalculated his conception and that's what Dr. Jones said as well. I don't care as long as he is okay." Lucas leaned over and kissed Molly and asked if he could rub the baby's leg. "Lucas, his name is Luke and you are his father, so you don't need my permission to touch your son." Lucas looked at her a long while and his heart melted inside, but it did not show on his face. "Thank you, honey for reminding me. Now, will it make him sore for me to hold him? I've heard that babies can get sore if held too much." "Nonsense," Molly retorted; "That's an old wives tale." Lucas was so big and Luke was so little, he was almost afraid to pick him up; but he did. He snuggled Luke like he had seen Molly do and Luke decided to open his eyes. Lucas smiled and said, "Molly, he has your green eyes." "Yep, that's a fact;" then grinning from ear to ear, she said, "And he is beautiful. You forgot to add that part." Lucas started laughing and relaxed. Immediately Luke relaxed and they sat down in the chair next to Molly.

Lucas asked Molly how she was feeling, I mean physically. "I'm doing well, according to Dr. Jones, but when I'm discharged, I'm still not allowed to lift things much over ten pounds. The stitches look good, but the interior muscles haven't had time to heal. They took my catheter out this morning, for which I'm glad. When I go home, probably tomorrow, I'm still to rest as much as Luke does." Dr. Jones said, "Molly; you are a nurse; you know I mean that." "Yes, and we do have a home health nurse who comes daily to check my brother; she can check me as well." Dr. Jones said that would be great.

"Lucas, when you see Lucinda, would you ask her if she could add me to her list?" "I sure will. I'll also be around a while, just to ensure Luke doesn't gain six pounds in two days." Molly started laughing, "In other words, you want to be with us both for a while." "Yes," Lucas answered, smiling. "I do need to check with the Captain and let him know what is going on and why I'm not at work. I think Carl told me that he would take care of that, but that is not his responsibility." Lucas bent down and kissed Molly and told her he loved her dearly and he put his finger to his own lips and touched Luke's hand. Lucas told Molly that he would be back this evening, however, now he needed to see Lucy and Michael. He would remind them to ask Lucinda if she could check both of you, in case I'm not there when she comes.

Lucas left and went to headquarters and saw his Fire Chief, who was the only one there at that time. He told him that his wife had the baby and she had to have a C-Section, so he would need a few days off if possible. The Chief said that Carl had already told him. Chief said, "Lucas, I know you are a responsible man; there is no need to come see me or the other Captains when you need time off. It won't be very often, I'm sure, and remember you might also be called upon to work twelve to twenty-four hours, so stop the worry about your job." Lucas stood up and thanked his Chief and left.

He then went home and asked Lucy to help him make Molly's bed with totally fresh linens and to tidy the room. "Molly is probably coming home tomorrow and I really want your touch. Of course, I can do anything heavy like vacuum or whatever needs doing." He went in to see Michael who was feeling better today. He told Lucinda about his sister who had a C-Section and asked if she could check them both in the same visit. She assured him she could.

Lucy informed Lucas that she had already prepared the bedroom and the only thing needed would be a small crib. "There will be plenty of time to decide where the two of you live; frankly I've forgotten where we are at present." "Well, I don't know about that, at this time I'm only interested in Molly getting well and has everything she needs." Michael said, "I agree Lucas. Now don't you think you had better get a crib or something besides a dresser drawer in which he can sleep?" Lucas laughed and told him he was on his way to the baby store now.

Lucas went into the baby store and was bewildered. Lucy said for now a small crib; how small and what went with that small crib? Luckily there was a saleslady who read his face and realized he didn't have a clue what he was doing. She asked him how old the baby was and he said, "About three days, but my wife had to have a C-Section and I'm supposed to get the necessary items needed. We had no idea she would need a section and she was not due, but his little boy decided differently."

Oh, the saleslady said, "Well, I think I can help." She took him to a section of smaller cribs and he picked one he liked and hoped Molly would. The saleslady told him that he would need sheets, bumper pads, and something to stimulate him with hearing and seeing and using his arms and legs. She put together several items and then asked if they had bought clothes. "No, like I said, he decided to come early and we hadn't had a chance to do anything." The lady said, "That's quite understandable. Let me see what I think you will need and if your wife doesn't like anything you bring it back and we'll find what she does like." For the first time, Lucas smiled. It lighted his entire face and seemed to relax him. "Well, lets see," the saleslady said, "You'll need a small chest of drawers to store his clothing, sheets and diapers, as well as a few water proof pads to protect the sheets."

Lucas then went to a florist and bought beautiful red, yellow and peach roses with blue baby breath inserted. He also got Molly a box of good chocolates and one blue rose from Luke. He got home and took everything inside. He glanced over and didn't see Michael or Lucy. They came from the kitchen with Michael using his crutches and Lucy and Lucinda with him. He said, "Michael, you look great." Lucy said, "I told him that, but he only believes Lucinda." Michael asked how Molly and Luke were doing and Lucas said great. He said he had bought what the saleslady at the baby store said he needed. He told them he would set up the crib; and Lucy, "You need to show me where to put the little chest. Also, where should I put the flowers so they would stay pretty for Molly tomorrow?" He showed them the blue rose from Luke to his mother. Lucy gave him a hug and said she would put the flowers in the refrigerator until in the morning. Michael just smiled and went back to sit down; he had quite a workout today.

Lucas put the little crib together and asked Lucy what these things called bumper pads were. She showed him where they went and explained it was a safety issue when he began to kick and move about more. He was going to put the sheet on, but Lucy said, "Let me run them through the dryer for a while; it makes them soft." Lucas then brought the chest in for Luke's clothes; then he brought in another bag of toys. Lucas had all kinds of stuffed animals and tools and cars for Luke; Lucy hid a smile. Luke would have to grow a lot to play with all these things. She suggested putting up a shelf on the wall to put most of the toys on. Michael came in for a look and said, "I think Lucy is right. I have some shelving out in the garage; you can paint it and it should dry by tonight and then put the toys on it." Lucas asked, if either of them could think of anything else Molly might want or need? They both said, "No, that looks great."

Lucas was a little tired. He had dozed in the lounger in Molly's room, but he was still tired. He told Lucy that he was going to shower and asked if she would make him a sandwich. "Of course, Michael and I had one before you came back." He showered, ate, and kissed Lucy on the cheek and told Michael he had better rest because he knew his nephew had loud lung power.

Lucas went back to the hospital and went in to see Molly. She seemed fine and she was fairly sure she was coming home tomorrow. Lucas could sense something about Molly's voice and manner and wondered what had happened. He kissed her hello and looked at Luke who was sound asleep. Finally, he said, "Molly what is wrong?" "Lucas, I really don't know, but I got to thinking about what a good mother I had and I am unsure that I can be as good a mother as she was." She also said, "Lucas, you seemed to take to Luke so easily and for that I'm deeply grateful, but are you sure I'll be a good mother?" Molly seemed so venerable at this moment; Lucas picked her up and held her very gently. "Molly, listen to my heart and words; you know I have the same in-born instinct that you do. But have you considered the trauma your body has gone through for Luke? You labored before I realized what was going on, and I'm deeply grateful for Lucy and Michael being there. You need not worry about being a good mother; I know you are. Your body or your mind, have not had much time to recuperate and that's why you are wondering such thoughts. Rest assured you are a good mother already, didn't you see how Luke went straight to his feeding place. When you snuggle him he just snuggles right back in perfect peace." Molly smiled for the first time since he got there.

"By the way, Lucas since Luke decided to come early, I've not taken any time to get any necessities; such as a crib or even diapers." Lucas said, "Molly, please don't be angry with me, but I went this morning and got him a crib, crib sheets, bumper pads, one piece clothes and diapers. Plus I got him a bunch of toys. The saleslady outfitted me with anything the baby might need for stimulation. I also asked Michael and Lucy what they thought and they suggested I put a shelf up on the wall, because he wasn't able to play with everything at his age. I did not want to miss anything you or he might need. I know you are breast feeding, but I got some bottles and sterile water in the event he needed that. I got everything I could think of and if you don't like it, I can return it for what you do like."

Molly really started laughing then and held her stomach, "Don't make me laugh so hard, it hurts; but dear Lucas nothing you could do would make me angry at you. I can rest easy because now I won't have to think and write a list for you to get. Thank you my love, and thank you for reminding me that I've had major surgery and cannot think too clearly yet. But I will soon." Lucas said, "Does it hurt if I pick you up for a hug?" "Absolutely not and I'd like to hug you as well." They hugged for a while and Lucas noticed how long Molly's hair was, like a chocolate waterfall. "Do you want me to brush your hair?" "I'd appreciate that, it feels like knots are in it and no one had had time to brush it. I do well to wash my face and upper parts." Lucas got her brush and began at the ends and said, "I think I need a comb for this." Molly said, "I've got a big toothed comb in that drawer and it hurts less than a brush, but I had forgotten it." Lucas took the comb and started at the ends of her hair and got every knot out. Her hair was soft with a slight wave in it, not like an Indian hair. She told him what she remembered about her dad's hair, it was soft and curly. Lucas told her how beautiful it was, but honey, "I don't know how to braid it. I never had a need to learn." "Well, don't worry about a braid, it feels good to have the knots out. Thank you."

Lucas could tell that Molly needed a nap, so he told her he was going to sit in his lounger and rest while she did. "I imagine Master Luke will awaken both of us when he gets hungry." "Of course and he's none to quiet about it, either." They both began to relax and Molly dozed off to sleep. Lucas couldn't help looking at her; she was not only beautiful to look at, but she seemed to sense how he felt at times. He eventually dozed a while too.

About two o'clock, Luke began to wiggle around and cry a bit. Molly awoke right away and asked Lucas to hand him to her and to get a diaper at the end of the crib. Molly dried him and cleaned his bottom with a bath cloth and by this time, Luke was really crying. "Oh, my sweet baby, here is your food, now come on, take your nipple." Luke seemed to sense where to get his food and he began to suck like a much older baby. He ate whatever was in the breast and still wasn't satisfied, so Molly changed breasts. He then proceeded to eat again. Then he was finished. Molly asked Lucas to bring her a clean bath cloth to wipe her breasts. Lucas said; "May I help with that?" "Yes, if you would like, I've put Luke beside me and he isn't fussy, but he seems awake and looking around." Lucas gently cleaned Molly's breasts and looked at Luke. He did seem awake and looking for something. Molly said, "He has just become aware that he is not in a tight spot and can look around and wave his arms." Lucas kept staring at Luke. He seems to be able to wiggle any part of his body. "Isn't that wonderful?" "Yes it is wonderful. I counted his toes, fingers and looked him over from head to foot and he is older gestation than I thought. He has minimal skin wrinkles, like premature babies have."

Lucas told her that was great; he would grow much better with all systems on go; at least that's what he thought. "You thought right," Molly retorted. "I'm ready to go home today, but I'll have to wait for the doctors to check us both and then they will discharge us. Would you mind putting Luke back in his crib and I believe I'll rest a while." "Of course," Lucas responded. He also made sure her gown was covering her and asked if she needed a light blanket. She said "No, but thank you. Are you going to nap in the lounger?" "Yes, I will when you two are resting. I do love you so much," and he kissed her goodnight, again.

About five-thirty in the morning, Luke was again ready for his mother. Lucas had watched Molly change him and so he tried to tidy the baby and put a clean diaper on him. Luke seemed fine and when he picked him up, Molly was smiling at him. "Thank you for changing him; how did you learn to do that?" "I watched closely when you did it and just did what you did. I've also got a clean warm bath cloth for you to wipe your breasts." This little tyke is beginning to get restless for his mama, well, probably some food. Molly and Lucas smiled at Luke and Molly put him on the breast and he sucked like he was hungry; Molly then had to change breast and he continued to eat. "He must be going to be a big man." Molly said, "Yes, you know Michael is rather tall and our uncle was very tall; he died about two years ago."

When the feeding and tidying was complete, the nurses popped in and asked if they would like breakfast. Molly said, "Yes, for Lucas and me." "Okay," the nurse responded and shortly they had their breakfast of scrambled eggs, hash browns, bacon and juice and coffee. Molly and Lucas ate beside each other and enjoyed their first breakfast as husband and wife together. Lucas put the finished dishes together on a tray and moved them to the over bed table that he had placed near the wall. Then they waited for the doctors to come and discharge them home.

About nine o'clock Molly's doctor came in and checked her. He asked if her milk had come in yet. She said, "I don't think so; at least Luke has to suck on bother breasts before he seems satisfied. He slept between feedings about four hours." Dr. Jones told Molly the stitches looked good and asked about difficulty urinating. She told him, nothing seemed to bother her except she thought she got tired too easily. "Molly, you know your mind and body have been through quite a shock and you still must rest as much as possible for another ten days; you may walk to the bathroom and take a shower, but have someone with you." "I will, and I'm to see you in about ten days?" "Yes, but I'll leave instructions with the nurse and she will go over it with you and you'll take the instructions home. I'm going to give you a mild pain killer, because I know when you are up for any extended length of time; example: taking a shower and shampoo, the abdominal muscles will really begin to ache. So take a pain pill when you begin to hurt." "All right, I will; what should I do about the stitches?" "They will come out on their own when the time comes; if not, I'll remove the rest when you come in for a check-up."

"You need to remember, no sex for six to eight weeks due to the risk of infection." Molly said, "Well okay." When Dr. Jones left, Molly looked at Lucas and said, "I'm really sorry about this." Lucas looked her straight into the eyes of Molly and said; "Hear this, my precious wife that is no problem for me. When we are both ready there will be time enough to make love. I love you dearly, but you know I sometimes have very dark times, but it is not due to you. You seem to know instinctively when I need to take a walk in the woods or be by myself for a short while. That is not my rejection of you; you are the best thing in my life and I would lay down my life for you or Luke. Walking in the woods has always been a way for me to get my head clear and on an even keel. What I'm most afraid of is that I might have a flashback and awaken you or the baby. Sometimes that still happens and I'm unsure where I am for few minutes." Molly said; "I know about the flashbacks because Lucy told me. I am not feeling uneasy about them except I want so badly to help." "It helps me if I can just hold you a few minutes. Your warm body calms me down and I again sleep peacefully."

The pediatrician came in to check Luke and he said he was fine, but might need some sterile water between feedings. He also ordered a specific formula in the event Molly decided not to breast feed him. "Thank you, but I will breast feed him." "Well, I'll see Luke in about four weeks. You still need to rest some each day, so he will get enough nourishment."

# Molly, Luke, and Lucas Come Home

The nurses helped move Molly and the baby to the car and Lucas was driving. He gently lifted Molly with Luke and got her in the car. They thanked the nurses and left for home. "Molly darling, are you hurting? This is not the smoothest vehicle in which to ride, but I had put a pillow in for your back and bottom." Molly said, "Lucas, thank you my darling, stop worrying about me. We are going home and I can barely wait. I think Luke likes the vehicle quite a lot; he's sound asleep."

Molly said, "Lucas did I remember to thank you for my wedding ring? It came off when I pulled the tape off and I read the inscription. That means so much to me." Lucas put his left hand over and asked her to remove his ring and to read the inscription. "Lucas, you had the same thing engraved on our rings. Thank you so much. I'm also thankful that you love me and Luke, but most of all I love you for the wonderful man you are. I just wanted you to know before we get home and Michael and Lucy decide to steal our Luke."

"You know how excited Michael was and Lucy told me the other night, that Michael had asked her to marry him, but she simply could make no decision until she knew how you and I are. We were sitting on the bed like sisters and talked a long time. Lucas, Lucy is so much like you in so many ways. You know I'm a good nurse, but I won't be able to work for a few weeks, but that does not mean I forgot my nursing skills; especially in critical care. I will take as much rest as I can, but I plan on making dinner for you and Lucy when you get home from work."

"Molly you are supposed to rest." "I know Lucas and I promise you I will, but I can plan a menu and ensure the items are in the freezer or refrigerator and rest and then make dinner. If I need anything, I'll keep a list and you can pick those things up the next day. We can all four sit at the table and act like a normal family. That's one thing I can do to care for all of us and of course, take care of our son. Michael is up walking and practicing with his crutches; so I can keep an eye on him. I still would like Lucinda to come check him." "That sounds wonderful and perhaps you and I can take a short walk while Luke is asleep. The fresh air would do us both good."

Lucas was listening and could tell Molly was really getting happy that they had married and that he loved the baby. She also trusted him enough to say what she would need. There was no guile in his beautiful wife. But he also knew she had such a shock finding out about Randy and the fact that Luke wouldn't have a name, that he must hold her a lot and remind her how wonderful she is.

It still seemed at times like the black of midnight, even at noontime. Molly had dark times and he could hold her and listen, he felt she would soon get over being deceived by Randy and she certainly knows the difference between us. He planned to call Lucinda as soon as possible and ask when the pastor was going to register the marriage. He would also pay the pastor a gratuity for coming out to the house to marry them. He would see with his own eyes the marriage register and get a copy for Molly to ensure she was comfortable. He also thought about a baby book for little Luke, so Molly could keep records of growth, length and pictures of Luke. He would get a camera that took the shot and then it could be sent into her computer and have a hard copy to keep for Luke.

"Molly, it is Sunday isn't it?" "Yes," she said, smiling. "I thought so, but I've been a bit confused the last few days. As soon as we get everyone settled, I'll ask you make a list of groceries and paper products that might be needed. I'll also get a garbage can for our room and I'll take the plastic bag out each morning and keep a fresh one in the room."

"Lucas, my word, you think of everything; please don't try to do everything at once. I still very much want to spend some time with just you. Is that all right?" "Yes, darling, it is very 'all right'." "Thank you."

They reached the drive way and Lucas pulled the ATM up to the door and Lucas lifted them both out of the car and went into Molly's room. He himself was surprised at how pretty everything was. Molly's flowers were on a beautiful mirror and Luke's rose was by itself on his dresser, turned toward Molly with the card that read: 'To Mother from Luke'. The other flowers were from Lucas to Molly. Lucy and Michael, with the help of Lucinda had arranged the room and put the toys on the shelf he had painted yesterday. They had put the chimes and bells on the overhead swing and the bed was ready, even with a small pad to protect the sheet. There was a little blue bear, a small bunny from Uncle Michael and Lucy, and some rattles he could shake.

Molly was in tears, "How in the world did you all get all this done? It is perfect!" Lucas said; "I have to confess that the saleslady picked most of the things a new baby and mother and father need. I got so many toys, Lucy and Michael told me to paint a shelf that could hold them and get a few at the time for him to play with; I guess that is the best thing." Molly put Luke in Michael's arms and Lucy was right beside him, and Molly hugged Lucas until he thought he would lose his breath. She kissed him and told him how much she loved everything. Everyone knew she was getting tired and Michael and Lucy wanted to care for Luke a few minutes. Molly said, "Okay, but you stay close to me. Lucas and I will take a nap for a while. Keep the door open so I can hear him if he needs me." "We will," Michael and Lucy said, almost together.

Molly got into the bed and Lucas lay down on top of the covers and they kissed and hugged a while and Lucas told Molly to turn over and he would still have his arms around her and they could sleep. "Okay," she said, and was almost asleep when her head hit the pillow. He lay and held her and must have dozed off. He woke up to the smell of hot coffee, pork roast or chops, some vegetables and Lucy's biscuits. He glanced over and Luke's crib was missing. He eased out of bed and asked where his baby was. "Oh, he got sleepy and I brought his own bed in here so Lucy and I could keep an eye on him. He's slept almost as long as you all have, but I think he'll wake up pretty soon. He has already started to move around and stretch his arms."

"Yes, I think you're right." Lucas went into the bathroom and took the diaper off and wiped his bottom and forgot about a diaper being placed on top. Luke gave his daddy a good spray. "Well Luke, you have good water works too." Michael could hardly stop laughing. Lucas got a clean diaper and sleeper outfit and put on Luke. He looked so cute. Lucas took Luke up in his arms and said, "Are you getting hungry?" It seemed to him and to Michael that the baby answered, well maybe not words, but they both knew he understood. Lucas went to check on Molly and she was ready to scream. "Lucas, where is Luke, has someone stolen him." "He is right here in my arms, all clean and dry and with clean clothes on. I'm afraid that I didn't come off as well, I forgot to put his diaper over his front and I got sprayed."

Lucas handed Molly Luke who immediately began hunting his food. Lucas gave Molly a clean, damp, warm cloth to wash her breast and Luke really hung on and ate. Molly said; "My milk has come down, so maybe one breast will be enough."

That was not to be; Luke sucked until he couldn't get anything and then started wiggling. His mother changed arms and he attacked the other breast with gusto. "You think he will ever get full?" Lucas asked. Molly answered, "Yes, he will just stop sucking." That's exactly what the little guy did. Molly tried to burp him, but he didn't need it. "Okay, Luke, you really ought to play a little while." Lucas had brought the crib in and put Luke into the crib and handed him a rattle and a soft animal. He ignored the animal and rattled his rattle, he would shake his whole arm and it would rattle.

Lucy came into the room and said; "It's time for dinner. We can all sit at the table in the kitchen and I'll serve plates." Molly told Lucy that she too was a pretty good cook, but it would take a little more time. She would plan their dinner, ensure the ingredients were present and lay back down to rest. Luke would probably be ready to eat by that time and she would feed him and then start supper, so they could all eat together. Lucas and Lucy said, "That will be fine in about a week, but no stress on your body. When you get tired, you must rest. Michael will be with you and he can do some things, but after his work-outs, he is pretty tired as well."

They ate the most wonderful dinner. Pork Roast with roasted potatoes, turnips and kale combined; a congealed salad and Lucy planned ice cream and angel food cake with strawberries on top for dessert. They all thanked the Lord for the wonderful meal, for Molly, Luke, and Michael getting stronger and for His general provision and protection. They all began to eat and it was delicious. Molly ate more than she had before delivery and Lucas was glad to see that. They had their coffee with angel food cake, ice cream and berries on top. Molly said, "None for me please, I'm pretty full; however, did I see a box of chocolates in the refrigerator?" Lucy said, "You did, I forgot to put them on your pillow, but have a few now. It certainly won't hurt your milk and it will definitely make you feel better."

Molly looked at the box of chocolates, it was difficult to pick just two, but she finally made her choice. She offered everyone some, but they preferred the dessert. She took a bite out of one of the chocolates and said, "Yes, that's the right one." She ate it and had some coffee and then the other, it too was delicious. She reached over and hugged Lucas and thanked him for the chocolates, flowers, crib, chest, and clothing for Luke. "You are the best husband a woman could have." She tried to hug him tighter and kiss him, but said, "Ouch!" Lucas said; "I'm sorry darling I didn't think about the doctor telling you not to stretch. Let's have the rest of the coffee in our room and I'll get you one of the pills that Dr. Jones said take." "Okay," she answered. She followed Lucas to her bedroom and got into bed and he had the water and pill on the bedside shelf. She took the pill and drank the rest of the coffee and they talked a few minutes. Lucas realized that Molly was waiting for him to lie beside her and give her a good night kiss. He did so and had her turn on her side to relieve the pressure on the tummy muscles. In a very few minutes Molly was sound asleep.

Lucas eased out of bed and went back to the kitchen and asked if there was another coffee. "Sure," Lucy said. Michael said, "What did you tell Molly that the doctor said, I couldn't hear." "She must not do too much stretching until he checks her again in ten days. The pills are to help stop pain and help her sleep. She is already sleeping peacefully. Lucy, when Lucinda comes to see Michael tomorrow, ask her to help Molly get a shower. I would, but although she had me wash her breast before feeding Luke, I think at this time she would be more comfortable with a nurse or another woman." "No problem," they both responded.

They all three talked a while and Lucas told Michael he was going with the pastor to insure the marriage was registered. He told them he had been on-line and could find nothing about a marriage between Molly and Randy Black. Michael said, "I'm not surprised; as you both know Molly is a beautiful woman and an excellent nurse, but she got fooled so badly. I don't think he ever intended to marry her, but made her think they were married. I have not found out anything on-line either. "To see my Molly hurt and fooled like that makes me feel like a heel; I should have made my feelings regarding him clearer to her. There was no real love-bond from Molly, but she thought that would grow. Molly is so smart and a genuine person, she thinks everyone she meets is the same. But to see her hurt so badly, Lucas, I think I would have killed him if he were not already dead. I hope God will help me get over this unforgiving spirit I hold toward him."

Lucas said, "I've thought the same thing, but Lucy told me to take a walk while we were at the hospital and I simply prayed in that little grove of trees until I felt the burden lifted". "I don't know where your 'safe place' is to get alone with yourself and God, but I will say, when you settle this issue between yourself and God you will feel better."

"You know I would die for Molly or Luke, don't you?" "Yes, I do," Michael said, "I do know that and I think the two of you are good for one another and Luke is icing on the cake." "I think so too," Lucy added. "Well it is getting late and I'm going to lie beside Molly so she can sleep peacefully before Master Luke decides to eat. Thanks, Lucy for the good dinner and please make a list of meats, vegetables that you and Michael like; you know I like about anything and Michael can tell you some of his favorites, as well. I'll get the list in the morning and take it with me to the court house. I'll check personally the marriage register and make a copy for Molly. Then I will get all the groceries I can think of besides your list. I'll probably go back to work on Tuesday."

"That sounds great, but Lucas, you haven't got a good night's sleep since before Molly delivered. You might spend the afternoon lying with her and dozing yourself."

"You look 100% better since you know Molly is all right and that Luke is healthy, but you haven't taken any time for you." "Lucy and Michael, I've found when I lie beside Molly and just hold her, we both sleep well. Is that amazing to you?" "A little bit for me," Lucy said, but, you don't seem in such a dark place inside since Molly married you." "I don't think I am, but occasionally I find myself going back in my head to AFGANISTAN and hear choppers everywhere. I soon realize, it is just a memory, not real for me anymore. I still think about the guys for whom it is still very real. Maybe our men and women can come home soon."

Lucas changed into a tee shirt and lay down beside Molly and held her snuggly. She seemed to totally relax and soon Lucas himself went to sleep.

They both slept about an hour and suddenly Lucy and Michael heard Lucas scream, "Incoming, incoming, get you asses out of the way." He was sitting up in bed, but he did not look awake, although his eyes were open and he was using his arms like he was firing weapons. His shirt was wet and sweat was running down his face. Of course, Molly had awakened; she gently put both arms around Lucas and spoke softly to him, "Lucas you are home with me. I love you." Very quickly Lucas became fully awake and still looked confused as to where he was and who he was. Molly continued to rub his back and kept her other arm around him and he seemed to relax. He saw Lucy and Michael and then realized where he was. He turned and held Molly close and whispered, "Thank you; did I hurt you in any way?" "Of course not, you had warned me about sometimes you have flashbacks." "That one was bad," he said. "Would you rather I sleep on the couch and let Lucy sleep with you?" "I absolutely won't think of it; no offense Lucy, I love you, but I want to be with Lucas as much as I can." Lucas looked at Molly and said; "How did God grant me such a wonder wife as you and Luke? I think God knew we need each other and loved us all enough to put us together."

Michael and Lucy said almost the same thing. They sat down on the edge of the bed and asked if Lucas or Molly were hungry yet? "No, I'm not, but Molly may need some sorbet." Molly smiled and said, "That will be nice." Lucas went to get her a big bowl and a spoon and sat beside her. To his surprise Molly got a spoonful and put it in Lucas' mouth. He looked so shocked, "Molly, I got the sorbet for you." "Oh I know, but you need to know how good it is too." Michael and Lucy laughed and said, "Molly is getting in good practice when Luke begins with solid food. He'll probably love sorbet too!" Lucas swallowed and leaned over and kissed Molly, "Thank you for your love and the sorbet. I'm awake now and I'd like to see you enjoy your refreshment." Lucy and Michael left and went to have pie and coffee.

Molly ate a few more bites and popped another bite into Lucas' mouth. "I'll feed you and me, now hold me and mind me today." "Yes, dearest Molly." They completed the sorbet and Lucas set the bowl over onto the bedside stand. He had dried his face with his tee shirt and hugged Molly and kissed her until he felt he might lose control of himself. He said, "Now lie down on your side and I'll rub your back until Luke decides to eat." She did and dozed a while longer.

Lucas held Molly, but wondered what brought this particular flashback? He hadn't that particular one in a very long time. Lord, will I ever get past these midnight black soul thoughts? Will morning in my soul ever return? I pray it does. Thank You for Molly, Luke, Lucy, and Michael, as well as, Lucinda.

Molly had to feed Luke only once during the night. Lucas got up and changed Luke and handed him to Molly. As Luke began to nurse, he thought he had never seen such a beautiful sight in his life. A true mother feeding her infant and they happened to be his. He also noticed how beautiful Molly's breasts were. He thanked God in his heart.

It was almost time for him to go to work, so he showered and shaved and dressed. When he came out of the bathroom in his underwear and tee shirt, Molly was awake and glanced up at him and actually whistled at him. He looked shocked. Molly says, "I can flirt a bit, but you are good looking. Your work uniforms are in that closet." He dressed and all the while wondered why she flirted with him. His sweet Molly was reminding him, he was a real man and not just a convenience. WOW! That's something he had tried to forget until Molly was really well emotionally and physically.

He reached over and kissed Molly a bit more deeply than usual and said, "Thank you, Molly. You make me feel like a human man instead of a robot." "Well, believe me, you are no robot. You are my husband and I'm hoping these weeks will fly by so maybe we can really make love and you will know you are indeed my husband. I'll miss you today, but I'll be here tonight when you get home. Luke went back to sleep, but he said good morning too!" Lucas actually laughed out loud, said he would see her tonight and left.

Lucy and Michael were in the kitchen and had fixed him breakfast and coffee. "What was that whistle? It sure didn't sound like your Indian whoop." Lucas grinned and said, "None of your business." They all three began to laugh. "I'm going to the court house and wait on the pastor to come register our marriage and make copies and give one to Molly and the other to my Captain for my records. I'm also going to get Molly a camera that she can take shots with and run through the computer and put in a baby book for Luke. I think she will like that." Michael spoke up and said, "She definitely will. However, are you spoiling my sister?" "Oh, I hope so," Lucas laughed.

Michael looked at Lucy and said: "That man is really in love with Molly. He sees her as a woman, mother and independent wife. Lucy, I'm so glad." Lucy said, "Michael, I think Molly is not only trusting Lucas, but actually is beginning to see them as soul mates. We both heard her whistle at him; he came out of the bathroom in his underwear and went to the closet to dress. My bet is he thought she had dozed off to sleep. That bit of flirting helped him so much and I think it did her as well." "It did," Michael replied.

Michael took Lucy's hand and said, "You know I love you dearly and would love for you to marry me. You know me as well as anyone and you know that's true." Lucy replied, "Yes, and Michael if you are really sure about marrying me, I'd like to accept. I do love you very much and yes, I trust you." Michael almost fell trying to get to Lucy to hold her. She just walked into his arms and hugged him tightly. Michael said, "What kind of ring do you want and when do you think we can get married?" Lucy said, "The ring matters little to me, except you give it with love; anything you pick will be wonderful."

"By the way, will you wear a wedding ring that I pick out?" "I certainly will and will love it; why the question, Lucy?" "Michael, I don't really know; the question just popped in my head that you might not want or wear a wedding ring." Michael said; "My dearest Lucy, don't ever confuse me with anyone else. I love all of you and I always will." "Thank you, Michael." She kissed him a long time and he lifted his head and said, "Dear Lucy, I'm losing my breath and balance. Thank you for the kiss and hugs. Now, back to the wedding, when should we plan it and where would you like it?" Lucy said, "I'd rather wait until you are well and I'd like a short honeymoon, but I want to be married at my Church and by the Pastor who did mom and dad's funeral. Would that be all right with you?" You betcha!"

"I have a few friends at work who can recommend a good florist and to decorate the Church. I'd like to keep it simple, but that is up to you." Michael said, "I don't know much about weddings, but I think we could check out some florists together and go together to ask your Pastor to marry us. Does he require an independent interview with each of us?"

Lucy responded, "I don't know, but we can ask. About how long will it be before you can walk on your own or just with crutches?" "Shouldn't be but about four to six more weeks; I'm doing well walking with the crutches now, but I do get tired rather quickly. You can bet I'll work harder to get well soon." Lucy laughed and said, "Well, I'm not going to back out, but let's look at the calendar for a possible date." "That sounds great," Michael said, "But could we go to my room for a bit. I've been up quite a while." "Oh, Michael, I'm so sorry, I forgot." "Stop even thinking about it, we'll check things when I get back to bed." Michael wasn't too tired to kiss Lucy and they went back and Lucy helped him into bed.

A good while had passed when Lucinda came in. She checked Michael's leg and had him wiggle his toes. "They look good," she said. "Now, I'll go check on Molly to see how her stitches are coming along, as well as her milk coming in and anything she wonders about." Lucy said, "Lucinda, would you have time to help her shower today? She told me she felt so yukky, that a shower would be really great." Lucinda said, "Yes, that's a good idea and I'll make her bed too." Lucy said, "No, I'll do that while she gets a shower." So Lucy went and removed all the sheets as soon as Lucinda got Molly in the bathroom. She took dirty gowns and sheets and put them in the washer. She put on fresh sheets and a pretty clean gown for Molly to wear. She also found a nursing bra if Molly wanted to dress one day, she could still feed Luke. "I wouldn't think she would want the bra today, because the shower will have worn her out and she might be in some pain. I'll check all vitals and give her something for pain; but I might ask her to feed Luke first."

"That way they can both sleep for a good while." "Fine," Lucy said, "I'm keeping an eye on both of them today."

Lucas came back at about four o'clock and asked Lucy if Molly was asleep, because the door is shut. Lucy said, "No, Lucinda is helping her get a shower as soon as she finishes feeding Luke." "Okay, you come into Michael's room with me, I've got something to show Molly that I know will set her mind at ease and hopefully please her." He took a copy of their marriage certificate from his jacket and showed both of them and then he took the camera and baby book out of a bag. "Do you think her mind will rest easy and do you think she will like the camera and baby book?" Michael almost let out an Indian whoop, but caught himself in time. He told Lucas that he was as much a brother to him as Molly was sister. "She will be thrilled and frankly, I am too." Lucy looked at the wedding register copy and smiled and hugged Lucas. "Molly will be so happy and she will love the camera and baby book. I do too."

Lucas smiled and turned to go and Michael stopped him. "You know that I love Lucy, but what you don't know is that she has agreed to marry me as soon as I'm stronger. We are going to ask your Pastor to do the service in your Church and I'd like to ask if you would be willing to give your sister to me in wedlock?" Lucas looked at Lucy and she was about to jump up and down. She said, "It is true, if he still wants me when he gets better." "In that case, I'd be honored to give my baby sister to you to love, care for and cherish until you die." Lucy hugged Lucas so hard and was really crying. He said, "Lucy, what is the matter? You never cry so easily." Lucy said, "I really am happy and I can finally trust a man again. You know I've been around him in good and bad times and he has never yelled at me or even raised his voice to me."

"He has shown real concern and love even when I've been unable to. He is working hard to get well and we both decided to ask our Pastor to do the wedding at our Church. I'm planning to ask some of the girls I work with about a good florist and if they know someone who happens to do receptions." "That sounds like you both are certain of this. Lucy, honey, I'll help you guys anyway I can, but you will need to tell me what you need. And I would appreciate you making a grocery list for meats and fresh fruits and vegetables as well as canned goods or dried foods." Lucy told him she had the list almost completed, but he would need to purchase the things tomorrow after work. "I'll have dinner prepared and in the refrigerator and warmer and you and Michael can put it out on the table. Molly is still not well enough to assume any work except Luke at this time. Lucinda will tell us different if something changes." "That's fine, now would you check and see if Molly is out of the shower?" "Oh sure," Lucy said.

She opened the door and checked and Molly had just gotten out of the shower and her hair was wrapped in a towel and she was putting a clean gown on. She had already fed Luke who was sound asleep. Lucinda was giving Molly a pill for pain, so she could relax and rest. Lucy told Lucas all that and Lucas went into the bedroom. He lifted Molly onto the bed and covered her with a light blanket. Lucinda told Lucas that she had given Molly a pain pill and that she and Luke would probably sleep for a good while. Lucas said, "Honey I didn't know you were hurting when

I left. How can I help?" Lucinda smiled at him and said, "She wasn't hurting until after feeding Luke and then getting a shower and insisting on washing her hair. So I wrapped her hair in a towel and insisted she go to bed. Thank you for lifting her. Now I need to check Michael and then I'll be going." Lucas said, "Molly let me dry your hair and comb it while you look at some information I just got." He found the hairdryer and her big toothed comb and gently pressed as much water as possible into the towel.

Molly said, "What have you got that needs my attention, I think that pain medicine is kicking in, I might not quite understand, but if you'll stay with me, I'll understand when I wake up." Lucas smiled and showed her the copy of their marriage certificate and registration. "Really, is this my copy?" "Yours to keep and I got something else," he could tell she was pretty sleepy now, but he was going to show her the camera and baby book. "Oh Lucas, thank you so much; I really appreciate all the effort it took for you to do this, but it means so much." "Molly, I love you and I'll let you lean on my legs and I'll comb your hair. It is beautiful, but you don't need knots in it." So Lucas positioned himself on her bed and put her across his legs. He combed her long hair until it was smooth and almost dry. She was sound asleep and resting very well on his legs. He picked her up gently and laid her on her side and sat beside her and put all her hair on his shoulder so she didn't have a damp gown on. He rubbed her neck and upper shoulders and then he lay beside her. He didn't realize how tired he was and pretty soon he was asleep too.

Every thing was so quite that Lucy looked in the room and told Michael how Lucas had combed Molly's hair and had dried it pretty well and left the hair on his chest, I guess after he positioned Molly on her side, he knew it would be all right to take a nap as well. Luke had a tiny baby snore.

She went back into Michael's room and got up on the bed with him and asked what Lucinda told him. "Well, it will be at least five weeks before I can walk on my on, but for only a few hours. It looks like it's healing well. So let's get the calendar and check about our wedding day." Lucy got the calendar and in about six weeks, Molly would also be able to get out some. "Let's set it for this day, okay?" "Absolutely okay! Could we go together for me to purchase our rings? Sure, but Michael it is you I love, you really don't have to get me a wedding ring." "Well, I feel like I must and I'll get a plain band for me." Lucy said, "Oh no, you won't. If you are going to pick out my ring, I'm going to pick out the ring I want you to have." They both started laughing and enjoying thinking about their wedding. "Michael, I really don't want a huge showy wedding. A simple wedding to honor one another and God will be beautiful. Also, the girls I work with help each other find a good person to do their receptions. Michael, you are really sure you want me, aren't you?" "My darling Lucy, come a bit closer to me," he took her in his arms, she was lying on top of him, and he said, "Please Lucy, don't confuse me with a creep who hurt you. I would rather die than hurt you in any way. Please don't ever doubt that I love you and you only. Now please kiss me and I'll try to express myself a bit better." Lucy kissed him quite well and he repeated the process. "Now please listen Lucy, put all that junk behind you. God brought us together the same as he brought Molly and Lucas together." Lucy said, "I believe that. Can I still kiss you some and maybe hug once in a while?" "I fully expect to do a lot of it," Michael replied.

"What kind of dress do you want? I'd planned a dark suit, but girls are harder to fit and their likes and dislikes are different from mine; at least Molly's were." "Michael, I'll start looking in catalogues to find one I think I can wear you will like. Molly will give her opinion. This probably sounds funny to you, but if I had had a sister, I'd want her to be like Molly. I think of her now as my sister and I take her advice very seriously."

"Well, with your beautiful olive skin and hair, I think beige or white either would look pretty. But I want you to get what you want. I'll like whatever you get." They had both gotten tired and so they both dozed on Michael's bed. Both bedroom doors were open so either one could hear the other. They all five slept about two hours and there came a sound from Luke that only Luke could make. He was awake, wet, and hungry. Lucy went to clean him up and prepare him for his mother to feed him, but Lucas was already prepping him for his clean diaper and gown. Molly was just waking up and asked Lucas for a damp cloth to clean her breasts. He got the damp, warm cloth and cleaned her breasts and lifted Luke up to his mother. He ate like he had never had food. Molly said, "He's not full yet," so she switched him over to the other breast. "When we see the doctor, I'm going to ask him about water between feedings or something. I don't want him hungry." Lucas told her that was fine. The baby ate a while longer and just quit. "Well, I guess he is full." She wiped her breasts and his mouth and tried to burp him, but he didn't seem to need to burp.

Lucy went to the kitchen to begin dinner. She made some hamburger patties with a slice of white onion and put them in a sack, after seasoning the meat well. She put all four of the packs in the oven and it soon began to smell wonderful in the house. She made some roasted rutabaga, turnips, spring onions and squash, with all kinds of seasonings and put olive oil on them and in the other oven. She made a good green salad and a congealed salad that she knew Molly liked. She then made some tea and coffee. They could eat left over dessert.

Molly and Lucas came out the room and said; "Something smells wonderful." They all went into the kitchen and Lucas helped Lucy set the table and get the plates out and flatware. Lucas was used to helping Lucy cook because they went to work about the same time and returned home about the same time. If one got home before the other one, that one started dinner. Lucy put the patty sacks on each plate and took the vegetables and placed them in a platter, as well as the green salad. She also set out the congealed salad and told them they had to eat left-over dessert. No one complained at all. They prayed over the food and thanked God for His many blessings.

They all began to eat and Michael said, "I have some news that might interest you two. My beautiful Lucy has actually agreed to marry me and we have set a tentative date, depending on how quickly I can recover. Lucy, honey, bring that calendar so they can see." Lucy showed them the date and also began to tell Molly and Lucas about having the wedding at their Church with the Pastor who buried mom and dad. "There are girls that I work with who know good florists and people to make the reception." "We want Lucas to give Lucy to me in wedlock and we'd like you to be Lucy's brides-maid." "Well, I guess we can do that. I'm thrilled that you are getting married. I believe God has brought all of us together." "We do too!"

They continued to eat their dinner and Lucy said, "You have left over dessert." "That's fine," the boys said. Molly wanted another two chocolates. She picked out two and ate them with her coffee. "They are delicious and each of you should try one." Lucy said, "I would like one," and Molly handed the box to her. "Dinner was wonderful, Lucy, and I will try very soon to make dinner for all of you. I'm somewhat concerned with why I'm still so tired almost all the time."

They all went back to the living room and sat and talked for quite a while. Lucy noticed Molly trying to hide a yawn behind her hand. She was about to have Molly go to bed and Luke woke up and let out a loud yell. Molly and Lucas got to him, that yell didn't sound like he was hungry. He seemed fine, but Lucas figured he had been awake a while and did not like to be ignored. Lucas picked him up and took him out to see his aunt and uncle. Luke just looked around and then began to squirm. "I guess he is a bit hungry." He took him back to his crib, got a warm damp cloth to clean his bottom and put a diaper in front. He was dried and Lucas put him in Molly's arms and Luke began to nurse rather vigorously.

Molly said, "Wonder how long he has been awake? He certainly doesn't seem sleepy, but definitely hungry." Lucas said, "You know Molly, Luke seems older than the doctors said and he acts older. He looks around and really seems to make eye contact and I think he is growing pretty fast. He feels a bit heavier than five and one-half pounds." Molly said, "I think so too. We see the doctor one day next week and I'm going to have them give him a checkup." Luke had finished one breast and Molly changed arms and he went to work on the next breast. Then he was finished. Molly snuggled him and kissed him and said, "You need to go to sleep for a long time now." Luke looked at his mother and then at Lucas. He seemed to understand so Lucas put him in bed. He decided he wanted the rattle and Lucas gave it to him. He would shake it a while and soon he was sleepy.

Lucas helped Molly get a clean gown on and a warm, damp cloth to sponge her breasts and under her arms. "Lucas, please hand me that clean gown now and lay beside me for a while. I've missed you today." "And I've missed you, but so glad so much has been done." He took his outer shirt off and left his jeans on and lay down beside Molly. They hugged and kissed a while and Lucas said, "We'd better stop before I make a complete fool of myself." Molly smiled at him and said, "You are not a fool no matter what you do. I'll turn on my side and you sleep close to me tonight." "That's my pleasure," Lucas answered. They really were both asleep soon.

Lucy glanced into their room and all three were asleep and seemed at ease. She went back and asked Michael if she could sleep on the side of his bed tonight. "Of course you can my darling, however, I would like a hug and kiss goodnight." "Coming right up," Lucy replied.

# Lucas, Carl, and David Get to Work

The next morning Lucas went to work; but it seemed like a quiet morning. At about eleven-thirty, David and Carl were next door and the radios came on indicating a car crash into a moving train and some gas was coming from the train. It seemed the car's brakes had completely lost the ability to stop the car. Whatever had happened, the car would not move forward or backward; it hit the moving train.

They all responded and Lucas went toward the train, David went toward the car and realized quickly, they needed the 'jaws of life'. Carl was already working with the paramedics, but seemed no way to get the car from under the train. They brought the 'jaws of life' and a helicopter to fly the victims to the nearest hospital. Lucas knew how to use the 'jaws of life' and Carl did too. There were two people trapped in the car and they could not tell if there were train passengers or not; it looked more like a container than passenger train. The fire was totally put out and when Carl climbed up to the 'jaws of life', he connected the hooks well and Lucas helped on the ground. There was a young woman and little girl in the car, but the child looked dead. He couldn't be sure. He checked the chopper and prepared to take them to the nearest hospital. The rescue squad and fireman got the people out of the car and blankets were covering them to prevent shock. The other chopper pilot got in the second chopper and they headed back to their base.

Carl followed Lucas to the hospital and David stayed back with the rest of the team. Carl went into the emergency room and of course the room was set up for heavy trauma. The ER staff started IVs on both of them and the little girl began to cry. "Uncle Carl, Uncle Carl, hold me." He went over and talked quietly to the child, because she was on a back brace and had a rather severe laceration on her head. The staff had packed the wound on her forehead and it had stopped bleeding so much. They came to take the child to x-ray for films of everything and an MRI for her head. "Come with me Uncle Carl, Mommies asleep." Carl went with the child to x-ray and comforted her and told her they were going to take pictures, but she must be very still. "Well, mommy tells me to smile." "But these x-rays have to be done with no movement of your face." "Well, okay, but if they come out bad, I'm going to tell mommy that Uncle Carl told me not to smile." "Okay," Carl said. They did the MRI first and it was negative for any internal bleed. The other films showed a fractured left femur, but no other fractures were seen. Carl walked back with Karla to the ER.

He glanced around for Lucas who noticed Carl looking for him. Carl told Karla, he had to go to the bathroom and the nurses would be real close to her. He got to Lucas and stepped out of sight of Karla and asked him how his sister was doing. Karla said she was sleeping.

Lucas looked at Carl and said, "Your sister has a skull fracture, but the MRI showed no sign of brain bleeding. She also has a broken left arm and seems a bit confused. She keeps calling Karla." Carl said, "That's my sister and Karla is my niece. My sister's name is Grace and she is a really good mother; her husband was killed in the army. It happened about a year and half ago. She is also a nurse, so she knows what is happening, but I need to tell her that Karla is all right except that horrible cut on her forehead and a broken left leg. No internal injuries at all." Carl went over to Grace and bent down and gave her a kiss. "Carl where is Karla and how badly is she hurt?" Carl told her about the left leg, but she would need a plastic surgeon to fix that forehead. He said; "I don't know if they will stitch it enough to night or go ahead and call the plastic team in. When she was having x-rays, she told me to tell her when to smile. I told her that with this x-ray she must be very still. Well, if this picture turns out bad, I'm going to tell mommy that you wouldn't let me smile."

Grace smiled and said, "I am not quite as lucky. My skull is fractured, but there is not a clot present per MRI. Carl, you know there could still be leaking inside my skull and could mean surgery. Karla will need so much care. I'll check with a pediatric nurse I know who can do private duty with her and work with the physical therapist, but you must check them every day or so. You know I'll worry and that can set me back." Carl assured her that he would keep her posted on both of them.

Carl said, "Grace, you are already worrying and planning. I will be sure Karla is cared for, as well as you. The other guys will cover and Lucas will inform the Captains." "You mean that big Indian man who came in with you. He's a lost soul, Carl." Carl said, "He was until he could get this beautiful wife to marry him. He knew she was pregnant by a man who died in AFGANISTAN; but he fell in love with her no matter."

"We don't talk a lot, but when his wife went into premature labor and they had to do a C-Section, he was absolutely beside himself. I was on response team and told him she would be all right. She is and so is the baby."

"Now when will they do other films on you?" "I'm not sure, but probably in a couple of hours. Please check on Karla and find out if she is really all right and if they plan to take her to surgery today." Carl went over and Karla was holding court with a couple nurses and an intern. He heard her say if my picture comes out bad, I told Uncle Carl that was because I couldn't smile. Carl walked up about that time and Karla began introducing her new friends. Carl smiled and introduced himself and tried to ask what they planned to do about the forehead laceration. Before anyone could answer, Karla spoke up and said, "My daddy got killed in the 'service of our country', but Uncle Carl will help us. We have pictures of him, but I don't remember him much except he would toss me in the air and catch me."

Carl knew how Karla could go on talking about everything and he said, "Karla, you may talk to your new friends, but you must let them do their job." "Oh, excuse me," she told the nurses and doctor; "My mommy is a nurse and she works real hard. You probably do too; so I'll be nice and quiet, but could I have a glass of water?" "No not yet, Karla," one of the nurses said, "But I've got magazines you would probably enjoy." "That would be very nice," she replied.

Carl asked the intern if they would do her surgery this afternoon and he said, "Yes, they plan to. Do you know of any allergies she has." "I'm not sure, but her mother is over there and she is lucid and will answer any of your questions." About that time Dr. Knowles came in to see the intern about the cute little girl over there who acts like a grown-up. Grace spoke up and said, "She is my daughter. What would you like to know and what can you tell me about her surgery being done this afternoon?" "I'll check her," and he smiled at Grace. Dr. Robert Knowles was checking Grace out. She was pretty and her daughter was darling.

Dr. Knowles went over and checked Karla's forehead; "We will plan to do this, at three o'clock. Call the OR team and I'll need help from Dr. Wells too." Karla spoke up and asked, "Are you talking about my head? It doesn't hurt too much, because they put some medicine in it." "What is your name?" "I'm Karla and my mommy is a nurse and works really hard. Her name is Grace. What is your name?" "I'm Dr. Knowles," he responded and smiled at her. "You have nice teeth," Karla said, "And I do too. Mommy and my dentist told me to brush every morning and night and they would stay beautiful. But I got a little afraid the other morning because one of them is loose. Can you glue it back?" "This afternoon we need to take you to surgery to repair your forehead and that leg you seemed to have cracked." "Yes, I understand about surgery and casting and stuff like that."

Dr. Robert Knowles went back to Grace and told her that he and Dr. Wells would perform the surgery on Karla's forehead and Dr. Wells would check her leg while under anesthesia. "She is a very knowledgeable little girl for five years of age. She is definitely a talker." He asked Grace who her neurosurgeon was and when they would take additional x-rays? "I assume in a couple of hours. When will you be taking Karla to surgery?"

"If you have time and any surgery is needed on me, please let my brother know. He is a First Responder and still has his uniform on." Dr. Knowles looked at her and she said her husband had been killed in the army, so she and Carl lived together and took care of Karla. Lucas and Carl walked back in to see Grace. She introduced them to Dr. Robert Knowles and told them he would be doing Karla's surgery at about three o'clock.

"Lucas, you better get back to the scene and call me if I'm needed again." "I will, but Carl, I think the accident looked worse than it turned out to be. The reason for the "jaws of life" was that the train car was rocking and they could not get the car from under it without risking your sister and niece. She is so cute." "That she is. Grace and Karla live with me since her husband was killed. I'll get a nurse to insure they are both all right, but Karla will probably come home before Grace and I'll need to care for her or bring her with me. She is very precocious and out-going."

Lucas said, 'I'll let the others know what has happened, you stay where you are needed. All the Captains know you work all the time." "Thanks, Lucas."

Lucas got back to the scene and there were still officers around, but most of the debris had been taken away. The Chief of Police came over to Lucas and asked him how Carl was. He said he noticed Carl turned pale when he saw the car. "The occupants were his sister and niece and they live with him since her husband was killed in the army."

"Carl needs some time off and I told him I would make sure you knew." The Captain kept looking at Lucas and Lucas just stood there. "Sir, did you want something?" The Chief of Police said, "Did you really take a speeding ticket for speeding, even when the officer saw your uniform and knew where you were going and wouldn't take a warning instead?" It was this time that Lucas looked strange; "Oh I was speeding and the young officer was doing his best not to give me a ticket." I said, "You and I both, know I was speeding, now give me my deserved ticket and let me see my wife." The Chief started smiling; "That young man was so impressed, he came to see me the next morning and showed me the ticket and told me he tried to give you a warning." Lucas said, "Well that would be a lie and I wouldn't risk making a young officer think it was alright to cheat." The Chief said, "Thank you for your honesty; we knew we had a keeper when we saw all three of you First Responders. Now go on and write up the report and be sure to tell David about Carl. The two of you can cover for him until he comes back." "Thank you, sir."

Lucas went and knocked on David's door. "May I come in a minute?" "Sure, where's Carl." "David, Carl's sister and niece were in that car and injured rather badly. They are both talking lucidly, but Carl looks a bit shaken. I told him to stay with them and I would inform the Chief. I just talked to him and he said to go tell you. The two of us can handle anything that comes up. I'm going to write up the report and when it's finished I might go back to the hospital for a few minutes." "Lucas, you go home to the wife and baby, I'll check on Carl. When I stayed behind with the police, I figured since Carl got in the chopper, that you might need me on the ground."

"Frankly, I didn't think of it because Carl was pulling the hooks back into place. He never said a word and neither did I. Do you think we all have some Indian in us?" "No," David replied; "We've all just been to hell and back so many times, we simply wait for the next trip." Lucas said, "I think you are right."

Lucas went to his desk and got started on the report of the accident. David popped his head in and said, "I know what has happened, Lucas. I was the first to the site, I'll fill it out." "This isn't a problem and it's almost complete anyway. Then I think I'll go see Carl. I'll let you know if you wish." "I sure would like to know how they all are."

He finished the report and put copies every place where he was to leave a copy, and tidied his office and went home. He could feel himself slipping back a little due to Carl's problems and a depression that never seemed to leave either of them for long periods. He got home and went in and heard laughter from Lucy and Michael and Molly. "What's up?" he asked. "Well it seems your son just had a whopper of a B.M. Molly was a little surprised at the color and amount and scent. This is definitely a full-term baby. I can tell from this stool. He had a good bath and diaper change and seems as happy as can be now. Michael put his rattle in his hand and he swung his arm to hear the sound." "Lucas, Hello, I love you, and could you please take this trash can out?" Lucy said; "No I've got this handled." They were all amazed at Luke.

"Oh Molly, I've missed you and Luke today." (Michael had helped some with Lucy's chore). "It seems when I can't see you, part of me is missing." "Well, it is; my dear one. Now, come give your wife a kiss." Lucas smiled and gave her a smacker. He hugged and kissed her again and reminded her that he loved her. "Lucas, what's wrong?" "Well, Molly, today we responded to a car accident that involved a train and we needed the 'jaws of life' to get the woman and child out and into the chopper. Carl went with me and began getting the large hooks in place. The lady is Carl's sister and the little girl is his niece. He has taken care of them since her husband was killed in the army. The little girl (Karla) is about five years old and has a severe laceration on her head. They took her to surgery at three o'clock and Dr. Wells will aid with her leg."

"Grace is Carl's sister and she has a fractured skull, but seems lucid at present. Dr. Knowles seems as interested in Grace as her little girl." "Oh, I know Dr. Knowles is a great doctor and is unmarried and I expect that is why he checked her out. She must be a 'dozzy'." "I didn't pay much attention except to Carl. He has blond hair and his sister has long blond hair and I assume her eyes are like his. His are deep grey with blue, but seems like he is an old man. Of course he isn't, but he has an old man's soul."

In about an hour, Carl phoned Lucas that Grace would need to stay in bed with fluids tonight and they will re-check her with another MRI tomorrow morning. "They fixed her arm and she is a bit groggy. They finished Karla's face and said it was not nearly as bad as they first thought. That is a relief to know they are both 'out of the woods', at least at this time. The ER doctors and nurses have asked me to leave and they will keep me posted through out the night." Lucas told him that was a good idea. He would see him in the morning.

Carl went home and showered and started to bed. He knew he could not rest. There were too many thoughts and visions in his head. He had never wanted to explain about the flashbacks, because if they ever put you on the post-traumatic disorder, your career and most of your salary just disappeared. He decided on this last tour, he would come home and take care of his small farm and his sister and Karla. He found the First Responders much less stressful than the army had been. There were few places to hide, you ate sand all day and it was hot as blue blazes in the daytime, but chilly during the night. What finally made him know with certainty was toward the end of his last tour, when a squad of the enemy slipped up above the sand dune. He had just left to go to the latrine and they simply killed everyone in the dugout. It was mass killing with over twelve men/boys just chopped to pieces with their guns. Dear God, I still don't understand. I ask for forgiveness for the hatred I feel toward them, but God you know that was innocent blood spilled. The boys had not had rest in several days. Father God, help me forgive, as You have forgiven me. Amen.

He finally slept a few hours and got up to shower and go see his sister and Karla. He was a bit surprised when he noticed Dr. Knowles paid more attention to Grace than to Karla. He wasn't too surprised. Grace was a beautiful blond haired girl with big blue eyes. She did most of her nursing in Intensive Care Unit or the Emergency Room. Most everyone knew her and would ensure both of them were okay. He knew that much about that hospital.

Carl walked over to his sister, nodded toward the doctor, and asked if they had done her MRI this morning? "They did it a few minutes ago, but I've heard no report." Carl still looked worried and asked his sister if she was hurting anywhere. "Yes, dear brother, my head is aching, but I see and hear well and as you can tell I'm lucid. Now stop that frowning and kiss me." Carl bent over and kissed Grace's cheek. Dr. Knowles introduced himself to Carl as Robert Knowles; you probably know we were busy with Karla and Grace. "I've done the work on Karla's face and I think you will be pleased. You will be too, Grace." He turned to go check on Grace's MRI report for her.

Carl went over to see Karla and she was her usual chipper self, except, she told Uncle Carl her face hurt a little bit, but, "Look at my cast. You can sign it, if you want to." "I sure do want to." He wrote: 'Love You Karla, Uncle Carl'. "That's neat," Karla said, "But you could draw something." Carl said, "Well maybe another time when we all feel better." "Oh, I see," Karla said; "You don't want everyone to know what an artist you are." Carl winked at her and said, "Yea, they might want me to draw a monkey and I've almost forgotten how."

Both Grace and Karla had been moved upstairs last night and were across the room from one another. They could talk to one another and Karla talked about everything until Grace told her to let's go to sleep. Mommies' head hurts. "Goodnight, mommy, I love you." "I love you too, darling."

Carl was headed over to see Grace, but noticed Dr. Knowles was with her. They did not seem to be discussing any deep subject, such as her health or Karla's. They were laughing and talking like friends. Carl brought himself up short; He remembered that Dr. Knowles seemed as interested in Grace as Karla. He turned to Karla and said, "See you sweetie," and walked across into Grace's room. Dr. Knowles got up off the side of Grace's bed. He looked at Carl and told him Karla looked great (of course, I might need to boast a bit) "I'm a Cosmetic and Facial Structure doctor what most folks call a 'plastic man'. However, Karla looks good at present. She might need a touch-up when all the swelling is down and she begins to notice her 'looks' more. Her vital signs are stable and the cast seems loose enough that there is no swelling of toes or foot."

Grace spoke up and said, "Hi, Carl, I heard you chatting with Karla. She is her wide-open self, right?" "Exactly," Carl replied. "Dr. Knowles checked my MRI this morning and there doesn't seem to be any bleeding inside. In fact, the fracture seems more superficial than we once thought. However, my head still aches, but all the vital and neuro signs are great." Carl smiled for the first time and said, "That's great honey, but I expect you to get all your strength back and stop hounding the doctors to go home. You remember, I know you!" He looked at Dr. Knowles and asked when he should hire a private duty nurse for Karla. "I'm not sure, a lot of that depends on how Grace continues to improve." (He did not seem to notice that he had called his sister by her first name). "Well, that's fine, just let me know. Grace, since you and Karla seem in good hands, I'm going to the office." Grace reminded him of the shock he had when he realized she and Karla were in that car. "I've had worse; forget that sis, my mouth runs away with me at times. You know where to find me."

Grace said to Robert, "You and I have known each other a good while and worked in the same hospital. I don't think you understand that our government sent (at least three men) that I know into war and all three came back as a shell of their former selves. Neither Carl nor David ever married, but Lucas just married a beautiful woman who loves him and seems to well understand his need for quiet time. She too, is part Indian and they married the night before her baby came. Lucas knew she was pregnant with another man's child, but it did not seem to bother him whatsoever. Her supposed husband was killed in service. The fact was, he and she went to a Justice of the Peace and he never registered their supposed marriage. Molly became so upset that her brother thought she would simply escape into her head and never come back."

"Lucas was there shortly after she got a letter from his buddy. Her brother, Michael, called Lucas and told him what happened. Michael and Molly were very close as are Lucas and Lucy. Molly's husband declared on entry he was unmarried and should he be wounded or killed send him back to Ohio to his parents. Lucas is a very quiet, big man who looks more Indian than Molly. He went to see Molly; he simply went into her room and reminded her of his love and the several times he had already asked her to marry him. Michael said he kissed her gently and simply held her until she dozed off. Michael had recently got out of the hospital because in class, one of the students accidentally kicked the lift that held the car Michael was showing the students how to fix, but the car pinned him."

"Our neighboring hospital pinned the bones together and he had to stay a few days in hospital to ensure he could begin therapy and safely transfer home with a home health nurse coming to check on him. Lucy, Lucas' sister, and Michael are very interested in one another."

"Robert, I just realized I've talked your ear off; you have rounds to make and I've taken your time from the patients."

"Actually, Grace, I'm off today and I came to see you and, of course, Karla. I've noticed you for a long while, but you did not seem interested in any man. Last night when I saw how well you managed Karla and what a dear she is; I wanted to get to know you a whole lot better. When you are discharged, I'd like for us to go to dinner and I mean Karla as well, if Carl agrees. He is terribly protective of you two and well he should be. However, Grace, I've had non-professional feelings for you a good while. I'd smile and you smiled back, but that was it."

"Please don't think I'm boasting, but I have known the 'come-ons' from several of the nurses, but I'm simply not interested. I've never married, because I never thought of trying to build a life with anyone who had no concept of what a doctor's life entails. While I have extremely rare times away from home; but when I'm, "on call", I have to go to the hospital, that could put strain on any marriage." "I can understand that," Grace said, "I agree and if it was not for Carl and a neighbor I could not do rotating rounds either."

"Well, while you are in the hospital, may I come by and just sit and talk to you?" "That would be very nice," Grace said. "I'm also glad you are not a "skirt-chaser". You see I've noticed you more than you knew." "You have?" Robert asked, clearly surprised. "I'm so glad to have seen you today and will plan on coming by before I go home, if that's all right with you." "That's more than all right," she smiled up at him. Robert bent down and ever so gently kissed her. "Your neuro-surgeon thinks you are the greatest thing since sliced bread." "Oh Robert, he thinks of every woman he meets the same way. I might be a bit quiet, but I notice a lot of interaction between my co-workers." "Well, I guess I'd better go; I have surgery in the morning, but I' see you before I go home." "Sleep well, Robert," Grace replied.

Lucas was helping Lucy prepare dinner, but she shooed him from the kitchen. "You need to spend time with your wife and son; besides she has been uncomfortable today and refused to take a pain pill until Lucinda assured her that the baby can eat first and then she needs a pill. So she has been fighting sleep until she could see you." "Then I shall go hold my wife until she goes to sleep. I'll take my boots off and my outer shirt and lie beside her. She seems to relax with my just holding her." "That's because she feels secure with you and knows your scent and arms. I noticed this morning she noticed even more of you." Lucas, said, "Oh hush you little busy-body." As he finished his sentence Michael and Lucinda came in and he had walked up and down two steps. He was so excited and told Lucy all about it.

Lucas took his shirt off and slipped his boots off and took Molly in his arms and kissed her. She did relax and drifted to sleep. Lucas hadn't realized how tired he was, but while he was holding Molly, he went to sleep as well.

In about an hour, Luke awoke demanding something; not a quiet cry, just yelling. Lucas got up to change him and get him ready to eat. He was dry and comfortable and still yelling. Molly said, "Lucas, the crying is good for him because it does strengthen his lungs. Please hand me a damp warm cloth to clean my breast and he'll soon be too busy eating to yell."

Lucas helped her get her breasts cleaned and still held Luke. Luke hushed as suddenly as he began. " Wonder what's caused the yelling and then the sudden hush?" "I don't know, probably a dream he was falling. Give him to me and he'll eat." He took the first breast and then looked at Lucas while Molly was changing him over. He began to eat again, but when he finished, he did not go back to sleep. "Do we have a rocking chair," Lucas asked? "Yes, it's in Michael's room." Lucas went to get the chair and Molly was cuddling Luke and talking to him like he understood everything she said. He just cooed.

Lucas said; "I'd like to rock him a bit, if you don't mind." "Of course, Lucas he remembers your scent too. Did you notice when you cleaned him up and held him for me to prepare to feed him, he continued to look at you?" "I didn't notice," Lucas said, but then a big smile broke out on his face. "Molly, I think he likes me." "Of course he does and I love you so much, I'm about to squeeze both of you pretty tightly." Lucas said, "You need not do that, we'll come lie with you." "That would be wonderful." They had Luke between them, but he did not like such close quarters, so

Lucas put him on his left side and hugged Molly with his right arm. "This feels wonderful," he said.

After a while Luke decided he wanted to kick and play. So Lucas put his hand out so Luke could kick it. He seemed to like that, but he was getting sleepy. Lucas put him in his crib and he was asleep very shortly. Lucas then lay back down with Molly and held her closely. They began smooching a bit and Lucas said, "Well I'd better stop this, it is too wonderful and I almost lose control." Molly said, "Lucas you are wonderful and I love you so much. After I'm well, I'm going to attack you each day and as often as I see you." Lucas started laughing and said, "I don't think that will be necessary." He was still laughing when Lucy called; "It's suppertime." Lucas asked Molly if she wanted him to carry her to the kitchen and she said, "I can walk some, but not too fast." "We will take a slow journey down to the kitchen for dinner." The food was good. Lucy was a good cook.

They thanked her and Michael kissed her and thanked her for the food as well. He could now take a few steps without his crutches, but would get tired quickly. Lucy said, "That is great. You took five steps on your own." Michael grinned and said, "Yep, and I'm improving each day." Lucas congratulated him and Molly did as well. "I've forgotten when I take Luke to the doctor and even when I'm supposed to see my doctor." Lucy looked on the calendar and said; "Luke has an appointment at ten-thirty in the morning. You are to see the doctor on Tuesday morning at eleven o'clock." Lucy said, "Before you start worrying Lucas, Lucinda said she would take them both for their check-ups."

Lucas asked Molly how much a nurse made for extra work like that? Molly said, "I'd pay another day's wage." Lucas said, "That doesn't seem like very much to take Luke to his doctor. He might need diaper changes and water or his milk before he gets back." "That's fine," Molly reassured him; "I'll pump my breast and put his feeding in the refrigerator for Lucinda to take." Lucas said, "I never heard of such a thing; how can you pump your own breasts?" Molly told him that Lucinda had already brought a breast pump from the hospital and I know how to use it. Lucas shook his head and said, "I've got a lot to learn."

They went back to Molly's room and he could tell she was a bit tired. He just held her in his arms and told her to sleep a while. "I love you, dear

Molly." Lucas rested beside her until Luke decided he needed food. He got up and put a fresh diaper on and got a warm, damp, cloth for Molly to wipe her breasts. Luke ate like he had not eaten just a few hours ago. Molly nuzzled him and talked to him and he looked like he understood. Lucas rocked him again and pretty soon Luke went to sleep.

Lucas asked Molly if she was hurting and she said, "Only a bit, but not severe." Lucas thought she should take a pill and she did. He lay down beside her and they went to sleep. Luke slept until about six o'clock and again needed changing and feeding. When they were both settled, Lucas took a shower and dressed for work.

Lucas got a cup of coffee and knocked on the other door. Both of them said, "Come in." He went in and spoke to David and Carl. He asked how Grace and Karla were doing and he said they seemed better this morning. "None of the doctor's could tell me when they could come home; so I'll have to wait to hire a private duty nurse for them."

David asked Lucas and Carl if they either one got the name of the little red-haired nurse, who mostly took care of Karla, but had several times checked on Grace. Neither one of them had noticed her, specifically. Carl said he was going back to the hospital at lunch and he'd ask Grace if she knew her. "Thanks," David said. There was no 'small talk' and each man went about his paper work and reviewed some drills on the 'jaws of life'.

They all went home or somewhere to have lunch; Lucas to see what the doctor said about Luke and how Molly was doing. Luke had been a full-term baby and he was seven and half pounds now and twenty-two and half inches long. His muscle development, his neurological checks revealed a perfectly healthy baby boy. He was four and half weeks old and seemed in perfect health. Lucinda told the doctor how much he was eating and the doctor said that was fine. He suspected Molly might have to give him some water between feedings, but he is just right in weight and height for his age. Lucas reached down and kissed Molly and told her how proud he was of her and Luke.

He then asked Michael how he was doing and he said, "Great." "The students want to come over Wednesday after school and I told them fine. Lucy will make some muffins or something for them to eat; I know boys were hungry after school." Lucas said, "Don't worry about that Lucy, I'll pick up a lot of muffins and cookies and juice drinks. They will be fine with that." Michael said, "Thanks, Lucas. It seems I've grown too dependent on Lucy and I shall refrain from that." Lucy said; "Don't you guys talk over me as though I wasn't present. Michael, you listen good; I'll do what I want and you are not imposing on me. And, Lucas, stop acting like a big brother and let me make my own decisions. I would appreciate you getting muffins, cookies, and juice for the boys, because I have a staff meeting after work on Wednesday." She marched her little butt out from their sight and went to tell Molly how aggravating big brothers and finances could be.

Molly started laughing, "I heard some of the tongue lashing you gave them and I expect Michael and Lucas will mind their own business for a while." They both started laughing at that time. "I wonder if Michael will change his mind about wanting to marry me." Molly said, "Lucy don't be silly, he adores you and is frustrated because he can't do more for you. Let it pass and take both of them a cup of coffee and tell them you love them." "Thanks, Molly."

In a few minutes Lucy took a cup of coffee to Michael and Lucas, with some cookies on the tray. "Both my loves, do not worry about me, I'll let you know when I've had enough." Lucas said, "I just told Michael that you had certainly set me straight a few times; I assured him you still loved him." "Well I do love you both and Lucas you need to see Molly a little while, before you have to go back to work."

Lucas went back to Molly's room and held her and kissed her a while. "I do love you, Molly, but I need to get back to work."

In Michael's room, he looked at Lucy and said, "I'm so sorry, I didn't realize that I was talking over you and making demands that are not necessary." Lucy crawled up on his bed and hugged and kissed him and said; "No problem, you are forgiven and I love you." Michael looked like he might cry, so Lucy kissed him until he drew his head back and said, "Darling, that's wonderful, but I might embarrass myself further if you don't just hug me now." So Lucy and Michael just lay on his bed and talked a while. Lucy was tired and Michael noticed that she had gone to sleep in his arms. He was so thankful that he had not hurt her feelings, but had made her mad. Mad, he could handle, hurting her he didn't think he could stand that. She was so dear to him. They both slept until their nephew woke them up for his midday feeding. Lucy got up and went to help Molly with a bath cloth and change Luke and put him into Molly's arms. He went to work on the breast and drained it dry and then Molly put him on the next. He almost drained that breast as well. Molly talked quietly to him and he seemed to want back in his crib. Lucy put him back to his bed and pretty soon, he was asleep.

Lucas got back to work and Carl was pretty close behind him. They both wondered, but did not voice the thought that David just might be at the hospital. Carl had observed how Grace was interested in Dr. Knowles and he definitely showed interest in her. Carl had not asked Grace about the red-haired nurse that worked in the ER, but he would as soon as he could. Both Grace and Karla seemed to be improving rather quickly. Karla was her usual talkative self and again, Grace had company; Dr. Robert Knowles. So he stuck his head in the door and said, "See you soon, sis. You behave yourself and do what the doctors say." Karla said she absolutely was doing everything she was supposed to do. She told her Uncle Carl that her doctor did not glue her bottom tooth in. She said she had told him to, but he was busy checking her vital signs and preparing her for surgery. She couldn't understand how he could forget her special request. "Well, Karla, there comes a time in everyone's life when they begin to lose what is known as 'baby teeth'. That is normal and you grow your grownup teeth back quite quickly." Karla said that she hadn't thought of that, but it sounded like that's probably normal. "Your teeth are much bigger than mine and mommies' are too." "Well I will still keep them clean in the morning and at night." "That's exactly what you need to do Karla. I need to go back to work; is there anything I can bring you tonight?" "Yes, I need some new magazines and books; the ones they have given me are for babies. I've already read them before I came here, but I didn't want to hurt the nurse's feelings, so I said, thank you."

Carl thought that Karla might have noticed a red-haired nurse in the ER, so he asked Karla if she remembered a nurse who was in the emergency room. "You were talking to several and I thought you might remember her." "Well, Uncle Carl, I only saw one red-haired nurse and her name is Sheila and she is really nice." "Thanks, sweetheart; now I really must get to work." Karla reminded him about the books and magazines as he walked out.

David came in a few minutes after Lucas and Carl got back, but said very little. None of the guys talked much. They all got to work. They had to prepare for a fire drill with all the equipment this afternoon. So they began reviewing the instructions for the drill. When they got up to go the fire drill, Carl told David that Karla told him the red-haired nurse was named Sheila. She is very nice, according to Karla. David said, very quietly, "Thanks."

They got out to the grounds for the firemen to begin the drill and realized they were supposed to watch and learn at this particular drill. The Fire Captain came up and asked them if they saw anything that the guys could improve upon.

David spoke up and said, "Captain, one of the guys started his hose at the top of the flames; while on board ships, we were taught to start at the bottom and around and then quickly work upwards. One of the navy men would have a belt tied to him with his partner jumping in the sea, with a suction hose that would help to quickly extinguish the flames." The Captain said, "David, you are exactly right. Neither of the guys had been taught that step, but he would see they all knew and practiced until it was second nature. While we face different blazes, it's much the same as you said, except our older team goes up the ladders to begin working downward. These guys are new recruits, so they have to learn; that's why the mandatory drills."

By the time they finished the drill and cleaned up, it was past time for all of them to go home. The second team would be on call for two days and then the teams were reversed so every body was on the 'same page'.

Carl went to the hospital to see Karla and Grace. He asked Grace if she knew a red-haired nurse in the ER. "Oh yes, her name is Sheila and she is a good nurse." "Is she married," Carl asked his sister. "No, as a matter of fact, her husband was killed in battle in Iraq. Why? Are you interested in her?" "No," Carl replied. Grace knew not to ask anything more, but she was curious. She would ask Robert if he knew anything about Sheila.

Carl went over to talk to Karla and she talked about everything that had happened today. She said she asked Dr. Knowles why he did not glue her tooth in place. "He told me the same thing you did Uncle Carl. He must have heard you tell me." "Karla, doctors learn that very quickly from their own experience and in medical school." "Oh," Karla said, "Well, he is nice, anyway. He comes to see mommy every evening, but she doesn't know that I know." Carl said; "Karla, perhaps you better let mommy attend to her own choice of friends, just like she does you." "Okay, but I did wonder why he always came to see her after he came to see my head. I thought about asking him why, but I figured he needed to report on my condition. I'm almost well." Carl said, "Well that is part of it, but just between you and me, I think he is interested in your mom more like a woman, than just your mommy. You are growing up and very smart, so think about what I said. Sometimes I know your mommy likes adults to talk to; she has you, but you are her precious baby, no matter that you are growing up. Now, we must keep this information between just you and me, okay?" "That is very okay, Uncle Carl. I love you and I know mommy loves me, but it makes sense that she would need an adult to talk with since my daddy died." Carl said; "I know you are smart and kind and a good person. I love you too."

As Carl left the hospital, he noticed David's car in the parking lot. Well, okay, David! Good job.

As Carl was headed home, he decided to stop at a small restaurant that he usually came to when he was tired of his own cooking. He went into the restaurant and noticed several of the lights were out. They usually stayed open until ten o'clock at night. He started back out and heard a moan. He went toward the sound and saw the (chef or whatever they are called), lying on the floor and it looked like she had been badly beaten. He checked her and she was semiconscious. He called 911 and shortly the entire team arrived. The Captain of the night crew saw Carl, who had not changed clothes, but was in uniform; he asked him what had happened. He told them he often stopped for supper here after seeing Grace and Karla.

The medic came over and checked the girl who was coming to. Her name tag said Sarah, Carl had already seen that and had checked her pulse and observed her leg position. The medics put her on a gurney and into the ambulance. Carl asked which hospital they were going, because they were located almost equally apart from the restaurant. They told him and left. The Police Chief asked if he knew what happened. Carl said no, but he suspected robbery. He noticed the cash register open and some chairs turned over, before he heard the lady moaning. The chief said, he was probably right, but if that young lady got well, he would ask her to identify some suspects they had. "Fine," Carl said. "If I'm not needed, I need to check some things."

The Chief had seen Carl's face before he got over to Carl. He noticed such rage and shock, Chief spoke from a distance and immediately Carl's face came back like the flat expression he always wore. David was very much the same way; Lucas, well Chief could never see any expression differ in any situation. Chief thought to himself, these men have been to hell and back; yet they chose to operate as First Responders. This group was needed in any city, and they were proficient in any setting. He was glad he had these men on his team.

Carl left when the Chief dismissed him and went directly to the ER. He saw Sarah on a stretcher and an IV and oxygen had been started on her. David had seen Carl come in and he excused himself from talking with Sheila; "I'll see you about six o'clock on Friday." David went to Carl and said; "I'm truly sorry, Carl, I did not hear my phone or beeper." Carl said, "That's okay; I had already called 911 and told them I was on the scene. Sometimes I stop off for some dinner after visiting Grace and Karla."

As was his usual custom, Carl had his 'mask' on and told David, "Thanks, but I'm okay here." David went back and asked Sheila if she would keep an eye on that lady and the guy dressed in the same uniform that he had on? Sheila said that she certainly would and wanted to know if he needed anything else. David said, "No, just remember our date for Friday." He immediately left the ER and Chief was coming into the ER. He asked the Chief if there was anything he needed him to do. Chief said the crime crew was already there and didn't need any of them. So David went home and thought about Sheila for a while. She was really pretty and very smart. She didn't speak to him until he spoke; then she said, "What can I do for you?" He said that he had been to the ER several times with patients and thought she was extremely efficient. She asked his name and he said, "My name is David and I work with the First Responders." They began a casual conversation and talked a little while and David asked if she was married. "No," she responded. "Well then, would you consider going out to dinner on one of your days off? We can meet at a restaurant and that way you won't feel like you are out with a man you don't know and maybe we could get to know each other a bit better." Sheila said that she appreciated his thoughtfulness and they arranged the restaurant and time to meet.

# Carl Questions His Own Sanity

Carl called Lucas at home and told him what happened. "Carl, I'm sorry I did not hear my phone or radio." Carl said that he knew because he was the first on the scene and saw no reason to call you and David out.

Lucas could tell by Carl's voice that something was wrong, but he sounded angry instead of worried. Lucas asked Carl how he could help him. Carl waited a minute or two and said; "Lucas I know you have Indian blood and that your wife also does." Lucas said, "Yes, that we do." Carl asked if they would pray for him, he thought he was 'losing' it. Lucas assured him that they would, but suggested he and Carl meet for coffee. Carl said, thanks and they arranged a place to meet.

Lucas told Molly what Carl said and asked her to pray too. "Of course," she said. "Molly, honey, I don't like leaving you, but I believe Carl is in serious trouble. Molly said, "You go attend to him now. I'll pray for both of you."

He and Carl pulled up to the coffee shop at the same time. They went into the coffee shop and ordered coffee. In a few minutes Carl began to tell Lucas why he had gotten out of the army. He told him that what almost killed him was one night about ten or twelve troops had dug a trench in which they could get some sleep. Carl told Lucas that he had just gotten to the latrine and heard the shots. They were close and he pulled his pistol out of the holster and looked through the crack and couldn't see anything that caused such close firing. When he got back to the dugout, the enemy had stood over the guys and literally cut them in to pieces. They never knew what hit them. "Lucas, these were young boys that joined up to help our country. I'm almost ashamed to tell you, but I cried until I was sick. Why not me, why these innocents? I developed a hatred that I have still been unable to shake. I have prayed for God to take away the hatred I feel, but thus far it isn't gone. I made up my mind to come home and work on my farm and take care of Grace and Karla. As soon as I could I came home. I never said anything to my colonel. Once you've been put on the list of PTS, your salary is cut and there is no help for such people."

Their coffee cups were refilled and Carl continued about what he saw tonight. He said he often stopped by this little food place for supper, since he had grown tired of his own cooking. "When I went in, some of the lights were off, some chairs turned over and I heard a moan. I went over and found the owner of the shop, beaten so badly, that I almost didn't recognize her. I had noticed her for a long time and she really was a nice person. She treated every customer as if they really mattered. I checked to see if I could tell if her arms or legs were broken, but I could not be sure. I had already called in and the ambulances and police and firemen were there shortly. I saw no reason to call you or David, because there was nothing any of us could do. I did go to the Emergency Room and looked at Sarah. She had her name tag on and I already knew I was interested. When I saw this beautiful woman almost unrecognizable I became so angry; almost like the desert. David was there talking to that red-haired nurse that he was interested in, and he came over and said; Carl, my phone, did not go off. I told him there was no need; I had already called the squads."

"The reason I called you is because you probably know as much as one can know about how I felt. The thought came to me --- just kill yourself. But I can't do that, because it is wrong and Grace and Karla would be hurt badly."

Lucas said, "You are exactly right, sometimes the devil throws these darts at us. We are left on this earth for a purpose and I think all three of us have found the place we can serve others, without the bullets, guns, and planes blocking our hearing and forever wondering why not me instead of the others."

Lucas said he had never stopped at that little shop, but had seen it several times. "I believe Sarah will improve and my suggestion is to talk to her, no matter what she looks like." When I asked Molly to go out with me; she said you do realize I'm pregnant with another man's child. Yes, I recognize that and it means nothing to me except to see to your well-being and the child. "Molly is praying for both of us and I believe God hears every prayer. We sometimes think an answer is too far off, but it will come. My mother and dad died within weeks of one another. Lucy was very interested in Michael and Michael had told me he wanted to marry Lucy, but she hadn't answered him."

I took a trip up to our grand parents' cabin that Lucy and I had kept maintained. After Chief told me about my mother's back ground, I turned to leave. The Chief stopped me short. What is really bothering you, Lucas. I told him everything I could remember. The Chief is a wise and dear man. He told me that he had watched from afar and knew I was taught both cultures. I said, while that is true I cannot find that serenity I see in you. The Chief told me that while they called God, the Great Spirit, he had no idea about the other members of the Godhead. He said a group of missionaries came to talk to some of them. Although I am a Chief of the tribe, I'm also a Christian. He told me to go back to cabin and think about what he said. I did and I slept better that night than I can remember.

Carl looked straight at Lucas and told him that he had helped him tonight. "There is a reason we are here and I think we are doing what we are supposed to do. But, I really hope I'm not around when they catch this guy or guys, because I would kill them on the spot." "In that case, Carl I think perhaps you might tell the Chief of Police that you cannot help with this case. He will believe you and release you from responsibility when the creeps are found." "Thanks, Lucas. I'm feeling better now and I think I will rest tonight." They got up and Lucas paid for their coffee and both of them went home.

Lucas got back home and went into Molly's room. She was sitting up in bed and had been praying.

"How's Carl?" she asked, and Lucas told her what had made Carl leave the army "He was interested in the chef or cook or whatever she is, and he has not made her aware." After we talked, I told him about how much Chief had helped me and that I had slept better after that visit than in a very long time. "Carl, If you are interested in her; go over and talk to her and make her aware of your feelings." Carl said, "That's difficult because I want to kill whoever did this to her. She always makes her customers feel welcome and appreciated. So I think I will go over and see her for a little while. Maybe my presence will make her feel safe." "I told him I was sure of that. So I assume he went to the hospital and is still with her. Once Carl can bring himself to speak, he really speaks well. He has a farm and decided to move back and ensure that Grace and Karla were cared for."

Carl did go to the hospital and saw Sarah with an IV and the oxygen. There did not appear to be much blood from anywhere. Carl went up to her and took her hand and she tried to open her eyes. Carl told her he was a First Responder and had stopped off for supper. "I get a little tired of my own cooking and your food is good." "Thank You, Carl. You always leave a more than generous tip and I appreciate that. I am very glad you got there tonight and found me; I figured they would come back and kill me. They stole all the money and some cooked food and left me. I'm unsure what to make of that robbery. If they had been hungry I would have given them food. They did not have to beat me up so badly. I wanted a mirror, but the nurses said not until the swelling went down some. I might go into shock. Well, they have called in a plastic surgeon to check that bones are not broken and get MRI scans. His name is Dr. Knowles."

Carl said, "He is very good; He fixed my nieces face and it looks great." "Thanks for coming to see me when I must look a fright." "You look pretty to me and I want to get to know you. I'm not pushing you, but I've noticed your charm and behavior with all the customers. That is a gift."

"Would you mind me coming to see you after my work shift is over and is there anything I can bring you from the restaurant?" "No, but I live in the back of the restaurant and I'm afraid to stay there any longer. I'll know more tomorrow. Thanks for coming to see me Carl, and yes I'd like to see you as often as you can."

Carl went home and actually slept better than he had in a very long time. He did ask God to forgive his hatred for the enemy who took innocent blood. Only YOU, GOD can open my stony heart to forgive, but part of me wants to forgive them, but I mostly want to kill them. I'm not going to lie to You, God, because You already know everything; Your Son gave His life for every sin we as people do. Thanks, Lord.

Lucas was talking with Molly and remembered she was to see the doctor tomorrow morning. "If Lucinda is going to take you, please call me as soon as you can and tell me what the doctor says about you. Please mention your fatigue. I know he will know what to do." "Lucas, my darling, I've already got that on my list of questions, but thank you for reminding me. I love you. Now come lie with me and get some sleep. Luke will wake us up when he gets hungry." About five-thirty, Luke did indeed decide he was hungry and not ready to wait. Lucas got a damp bath cloth and cleaned him well and put a clean diaper on and a one-piece outfit. Luke was not having any of this without a fight; he screamed until Luke picked him up and talked quietly to him and told him his mommy would have breakfast soon. Lucas took him into the bathroom to get Molly a warm, damp cloth for her breasts and Luke simply looked at the lights. No more screaming. Molly said, "Lucas, when you pick him up and hold him, he feels secure and begins to notice things around him. I'm ready," she said, and Lucas handed young Luke to his mother. He was hungry and began to suck like a puppy or little pig. He ate all in that breast and began on the second, and then was finally full.

Lucas asked Molly if her breasts were sore when Luke pulled on them like he did. She said, "Sometimes the nipples get a little sore, but I put the cream on them and they are then ready for the next feeding."

"Molly, I love you and I'm going to take a shower and prepare for work." Molly said, "Lucas please hold me a few minutes first." "That would be great," Lucas said as he wrapped his big arms around Molly. They kissed good morning and just hugged and kissed until Lucas said, "Honey I probably need a cold shower now." Molly laughed and Lucas joined her in the laughter.

Lucas took his shower and shaved and came into their room to get into his uniform. Again, Molly whistled low and said, "My-o-my, what a man you are. You are one good-looking husband; just remember you are my husband." Lucas could feel himself more like a man than machine on the inside. He turned around and took her in his arms and hugged her so tightly, before he remembered she was so small he might hurt her. "I love you too! I will never forget your love and help as long as I live." He kissed her goodbye and left for work.

Lucas stopped off at a breakfast fast food and grabbed three biscuits that he and the others could have with their coffee at work. He knocked on their door and went in with the biscuits. "You guys probably hadn't stopped for breakfast, so I got us some biscuits." David said, "Well the coffee is ready. They got their mug of coffee and ate their sandwiches and then Lucas got up to go to his desk. "Thanks," the guys called after him.

They were reviewing some procedures on motor vehicle crashes and some additional info about trains. The Chief came in about three-thirty and asked them if they could go through a drill for kidnapping and procedures to follow, as well as their shooting skills? He already knew they were expert shots from military records, but he wanted to see each man's reaction. As usual, he could tell nothing by their faces, but David said, "We can do that Chief. Where will the kidnapping occur and how many stories are the complexes?" Carl asked if they could use paint bullets instead of the real thing? Chief said, "Absolutely, these are our trainees." Lucas said nary a word, except asked where they were going? Chief told all of them and they got their various vehicles and went to the setting for the drill.

The drill was well in progress and seemed to go well. Then one of the medics called out, "There is a man on the roof and he seems to be pointing a weapon toward us. We aren't sure where the victim is, but this guy is serious." Carl pulled his gun and with one shot had the paint splattered all over the guy on the roof. No one even suspected Carl, could shoot like that, nor could anyone imagine why he would. The Chief shouted, "Finish your task, get that victim out of there and you medics begin the assessment skills."

The entire team got themselves in high gear and the drill was over in a few more minutes. Chief said, "Carl, you did a great job, but these trainees haven't shooting skills yet and had no idea what to do about the man with the gun who was aiming at them. Of course, it was a shock, but you proved by the paint bullets that real practice entailed much more than just assessment skills. They have to think on their feet and respond appropriately every time there is an incident such as this. Would you consider training these guys on shooting for a three-week course? David and Lucas will cover the real stuff for a while." "Well, if that's where I'm needed I'll do it, but I don't baby my men. Sorry sir, too much army left in me." Chief said, "They cannot be babied, they must learn these techniques in order to save lives." Carl asked when they were to start and where would they have a mock village set up? Chief told him and also mentioned the pop-ups that were enemies or their own men or innocent by-standers. Carl asked if there were plenty of paint cartridges and Chief assured him there were.

David asked Lucas very quietly if they could help him and Lucas said; "He will be fine." So they both turned to go and review the drill for the Captain. The Captain told them they could all go home and he'd see them Monday. If an emergency came in, the other crew would come in to help however and wherever they were needed. The Captain said; "David, I want you to review well the new trainees fire problems; different men, same time limit; okay?" Yes Sir," David said.

The Captain asked "Lucas, I want you to train a special ops team in tracking and observing the enemy, how to do sneak attacks and why that is necessary in an American city. You will also have three weeks with an entirely different group." "That's fine sir," Lucas said. "I suppose you have a site for us as well." "Yes it's set up in an urban development that is especially known for drug smuggling and trying to get good kids hooked." Captain asked if each man understood his job for the next three weeks and would be able to assess each student? They all three answered, "Yes, we do, Captain."

# Lucas Goes Back Into Depression

Lucas looked at his watch and noticed it was after six o'clock and Molly had not called him regarding the doctor's visit. Neither had Lucy or Michael called. What could be wrong; he knew something did not 'feel' right. He left base and went home. When he walked in, he heard Luke fussing and nothing else.

He went into the room and took care of Luke, but Molly was sound asleep. This was not at all like Molly. Something terrible must have happened. He gently shook Molly and she woke up and looked at him strangely. He asked, "Where are Lucy and Michael or Lucinda?" "They went to have Michael's cast changed and special shoes put on to enable him to walk better." "Who has looked after you and Luke?" "We thought you would be home soon. I've tried all day to reach you; the phone rings and rings, but you don't answer. I thought about bad things happening to you and I could not stand that, so I fed Luke and put him to bed and took a pill so I would go to sleep. Lucas, where were you and why couldn't you answer the phone?" Lucas said; 'Molly my darling, my phone has not rung all day."

"All three of us went to some drills with the new recruits and the drills lasted longer than we thought. Then I really began to worry. What in the world could have happened to you? Please ring the phone once more." Molly said, "Okay, but I think something is wrong with it." She dialed the phone and it rang and rang. Suddenly Lucas heard the phone and followed the sound. The phone was in the uniform he wore yesterday. He forgot something so vital to keep informed about Molly. He sat down on the bed and said; "Molly, there is no explanation except I forgot my phone. That has never happened before. I think I might be losing my mind. I've had a very strange feeling all day and cannot put my mind around it."

"Molly, can you ever find it in your heart to forgive me?" Molly knew Lucas was close to breaking. She said, "Lucas please stop condemning yourself. That hurts me. Don't you think had I needed anything at all I would have called 911?" Lucas looked at Molly and she saw her big Lucas in tears. She reached as far as she could and pulled him to the bed beside her and locked her arms around him and kissed so deeply; he had no doubt she was fine, emotionally. She continued to kiss him and rub his stomach and chest and face and told him there IS NOTHING TO FORGIVE! "Now I'm fairly well and if you can find it in your heart, will you at least hold me a few minutes. This was an accident, nothing more and as I said, had I needed help, I would have called 911 even if it scared you." Lucas lay down beside Molly and used his big hands to wipe his eyes. He had not cried since he was a very little boy. He asked; "May I really hold you?" "I insist on it my darling Lucas." "I need confirmation that you are here and love me." Lucas hugged and kissed her deeply. "Never doubt in you weakest moment that I don't love you. I truly do, but I don't like me much." "Lucas, please don't talk about you like that. You are the dearest man I've ever known and I will always love you." She could feel the muscles beginning to relax in his shoulders and back. She rubbed his back and shoulders and he really began to relax. She continued to rub his back and shoulders until he was fully relaxed. Lucas said, "Thank you Molly, I was as close on the edge as I've been since AFANGANSTAN. Now turn over and let me hold you close to my heart." They lay cuddled until they both realized this was getting too much. Lucas kissed her lightly on the lips and told her again how much she had helped him.

"Molly, what did the doctor say?" "He told me that I had lost more blood than he thought and that I need a unit, possibly two, but my blood type is rare and it might be difficult to find it right away. That's the reason for the fatigue and caring for Luke has been a strain, because I thought I could not get him enough to eat. He told me that was silly; anyone can look at that baby and know he is well fed. But if you are worried, we'll put him on formula between breast feedings. I hadn't thought of that Lucas."

Lucas said, "Honey, hand me that damn phone." He called Carl and asked him if he could find anyone with Type A- blood. "As a matter of fact; I have, Carl said. I'll call some of the guys and ask if they have that type of blood. Is Molly bleeding again?" "No, but she bled more than the doctors thought and that's the reason for her fatigue." "I'm going to call David and ask him about his blood type and if any of his boys have Type A negative." "As soon as I hear from you guys, I'm going to take Molly to the ER to get the two units. Carl, thank you." "Go ahead and call her doctor and tell him you have found at least one guy with her type blood. As soon as I hear from my guys; David will check with his guys and we will meet you at the hospital." Lucas said; "I really appreciate this Carl."

Lucas reached over and kissed Molly and got her a warm bath cloth to feed Luke or pump her breast for later. As soon as he was sure she was alright, he would go to the drug store and get the formula. "Lucy will help when she gets back." Lucy came in and said, "What's going on?" Lucas told her how stupid he had been to leave the phone in his uniform pocket. I began to think I might be losing what mind I have left. Lucy said; "Lucas, don't be silly; it was only an accident and besides, Molly knows very well to call 911."

The phone rang and David spoke up and has two of his guys who have Blood Type A neg. "Carl and I will meet you at the ER and you let that doctor know to get his butt over there and start the cross-match for her transfusion." Lucas actually smiled; it seems my buddies are not going to let my precious Molly worry her little head about anything.

Lucas called Dr. Jones (that's his name isn't it, Molly nodded) and told him he had three young men who had Type A neg. and "You need to get to the ER and get things rolling." Dr. Corbin works ER and helps Dr. Jones frequently. "We are all First Responders, out of the service."

Dr. Corbin said; "I'm really glad you found blood, there is not one unit here and we were going to have some shipped from two-hundred miles away. I'll meet you in fifteen minutes."

Molly was crying now. "Sweetheart, what is wrong; we've got the blood and you will definitely feel stronger." "Who will look after Luke? He might miss me." Lucy and Michael came into the room and said, "Well he might, but he is used to us playing with him too. He will be fine. Lucinda told me about the formula and I've already gotten it and it is in the refrigerator." Lucas looked at Michael and Lucy could tell her brother was about to break, so she said, "Besides we make a pallet on the floor and get down to let him play with various toys. He is getting strong, Molly. Your milk is best, but the formula will tide him over until you can manage again." "Thank you both."

Lucas picked Molly up and put her into the ATV, but he had a pillow and small blanket in the event she wanted them. She told Lucas she had sponge-bathed her bottom and feet and hoped she didn't smell. "Well you do smell like your wonderful self and thank you again for bringing me back from the edge of insanity. I know you are part Indian and understand my feelings, but I have difficulty letting anyone get that close. You have truly stolen my heart and I will forever love you. Thank you, my dearest love."

They got to the hospital and Lucas brought Molly into the ER. Carl, David, and two of the guys were there. Dr. Corbin checked Molly and started an IV. He called the guys with the right blood to the lab and cross-matched all of them with Molly. "Okay, which one wants on the gurney first?" Carl said, "I will," and promptly got up on the gurney with his shirt sleeve rolled up and had even tied the tourniquet correctly around his arm. "Stick away doc, that's a special little lady for whom we are doing this." They got a pint from Carl and he told the nurse to give him some orange juice. Carl took the juice and drank it and the nurse gave him another.

Dr. Corbin checked the numbers twice and had one of the nurses with him check too. "They are the same, but Dr. Corbin, the blood had not been out of your hand since you drew it." "I know, but the man called Carl said she was a special lady. I had the feeling that any one of the three could turn me every way but loose unless I got on the ball." Lucas laughed and said, "We are all pretty close. Is Carl all right?" "Oh Yes, he's had two glasses of juice, but he seemed in a hurry to get his blood drawn first. I did and after his juice, he went upstairs."

Carl went in to see Sarah. She had much less swelling than yesterday, and her eyes could open. They seemed green, but he could not tell for sure. He asked how she felt and she said a bit sore all over. "The plastic man said I should be up and around in five to seven days. Carl, I'm afraid to sleep in my restaurant again. I've been thinking of selling it and buying another. I'm a good cook, but I'd prefer fresh vegetables that the produce stand near the restaurant can't always provide. Would you have an idea of someone who might want a well equipped kitchen and small restaurant to operate? I charge good prices and I really like to have the restaurant, but where it is located, I'm a bit afraid to stay."

Carl said, "Sarah I don't wish to make you nervous or upset, but you can have a room at my house until you are totally well. My sister Grace is a nurse and one of the doctors is really interested in her. My niece Karla is a handful, she is very precocious and very smart and talks like a grown up. You can stay in my room and with a key; I could stay in the back of the restaurant. I work every day, but I'm usually around and I have a small farm on which I can grow almost anything you might want."

"Carl, that is really nice of you, but you don't know me. What if I was a thief, or a really bad person, how would you know?" "Believe me, I know differently. I served two tours in Iraq and I can sense evil at forty paces. You don't have to give me an answer at present, but please don't sell your restaurant if you like it."

Carl told her he had to go see his sister and niece who were involved in a car/train accident. We used the 'jaws of life' and got her and Karla out and to the ER. They are both doing pretty well, but I like to check everyday. He went into Karla's room and she was her usual talkative self. She said; "Uncle Carl, did you bring me some books? I did better than that. I got you an electronic thing with which you can scan and get any book you want and read it there on the screen." "Oh Uncle Carl, I've wanted one of these forever, but they are a bit costly, so mom said I might have to wait until Christmas. Thank you so very much. This also has games and learning tools too." "How do you know so much Karla?" "Well, while I talk a lot, I also observe a lot of things around me. A man at the restaurant that mommy and I stopped at had one and I asked him about it. He showed me his and even let me practice a little bit. Thank you, again, Uncle Carl."

Carl went over to see his sister, Grace. Dr. Knowles was there and they got to know one another a little bit. Carl told him that Karla looked great. "Dr. Wells will probably put on a soft cast tomorrow and have the therapist teach her how to use crutches. She will need them a while."

"Sis, how are you feeling?" "Much better, not such bad headaches and the MRI remain negative for blood seepage."

"How long do you think you will remain in hospital or Karla?" "Carl, I really don't know." Carl said, "Well we might have a house guest who would occupy my room. He would sleep in the back of her restaurant. She was robbed and badly beaten a few nights ago." He turned to Dr. Knowles and said, "I think you fixed her face. She looks better today."

Dr. Knowles said, "As a matter of fact I did. She has no broken facial bones except her nose and I've already straightened it and put packing in. She will have some whoppers of headaches, but a traumatic injury that is life threatening is negative. She is a nice young woman. She said she is a cook with ambitions to run her restaurant with as much organic food as possible. She also would like to become a certified chef."

Carl said, "How do you get so much information out of patients?" "I just ask," Robert replied. "While we are talking I want you to know that I am very interested in your sister. We've worked together for quite a while but nothing came together except a smile. When she is well enough I'd like us to know one another well. I already care about her and little Karla."

Grace spoke up and said; "At least he is not a 'skirt-chaser'. So many of the doctors think they are God's gift to women (all women) and seem to think all women feel the same. I certainly don't. They put their pants on just like everyone else." Robert started laughing, "You see what I mean; your dear sister does not mince words, and I for one am glad."

Carl really smiled for the first time and said; "She has put me in my place quite a few times. My army career didn't bother her except she was glad to have me home. Grace, are you sure about this man?" Grace said, "Yes." Carl also knew when to keep his mouth shut and soon kissed his sis on the cheek and started to leave the room. "Oh, sis, I got Karla an electronic book reader so she can pick what she wants. She said, Uncle Carl, I've wanted one of these forever, but mommy said we might have to wait until Christmas. So don't blame Karla, I saw it and thought she would like it and got it for her, and I am not spoiling her. She is very bright and knows her own mind, just like her mother. Now, all of you have a good night."

Carl went back to see Sarah a few minutes and told her his sister thought it would be nice to have a house guest. "You can stay in my room and rest easy. Just give me a key to your door, when you are ready to go home." "Thank You, Carl."

Back in the ER, Molly had almost received one unit of Carl's blood and would probably take one more from one of the guys. They want to keep his name on file in case of an emergency. That was fine, but Molly would come first.

"Lucas said you guys don't know what this means to me; they were going to have to ship a unit from two hundred miles away. Guess we all three are where we are supposed to be." Molly spoke up and said, "Yes you are; and all of you are very dear to me and I appreciate you giving your blood." They had put an oxygen tube on her nose too aid the circulation of the new blood. It would also strengthen her.

She told Lucas if he was needed with the guys, that she would be fine. "I know honey, but I won't be unless I see you get what you need." "Thanks to all of you." That was all he said and each of the guys went out, except David, who was over in another part of the ER talking with a red-haired nurse. Lucas said, "He's been interested in her for long time, but somewhat afraid of flashbacks that could frighten her, however, he will take a chance with her."

Molly told Lucas she was already feeling stronger. She said; "I was so worried about him not having a last name and how Randy lied to me; I thought I was losing my mind. Yet Lucas, you had known all along I was pregnant with another man's child and it didn't seem to bother you. I want to thank you again for loving the person I am and Luke. Please rest assured that I consider myself forever yours, no matter what! I love you, Lucas, as a man, a friend, and father. However, with everything else I've told you, I love and honor you because of your integrity."

Lucas felt his heart begin to mend a bit, he knew Molly didn't lie and she did know he was a man and not a machine. Sometimes, he felt like a machine inside, or had no feeling at all. He would simply function in any role needed. He simply did his job. Feelings were not allowed to show. He told Molly that he wanted her to meet one of his buddies. He went over to David and said hello to his companion and asked if he wanted to meet Molly?

David said, "I'd love to, but let me introduce you to Sheila. She mostly works in the ER, but I come over and bug her sometimes." Lucas reached over and shook Sheila's hand. David took her hand and they walked with Lucas over to see Molly. Lucas said, "David, I'd like you to meet my wife,

Molly. She had a C-Section about six weeks ago, but could not get her strength back so the doctor tested and realized she needed a couple units of blood." Sheila said, "Hi, Molly; I had no idea they had found your blood type; the last I heard they would ship it from the hospital about two hundred miles away. I am so glad; you will begin to feel better quite soon." The two nurses realized about the same time that Lucas and David were surprised and didn't know what to say. Molly said, "David, when nurses get together they may seem to be talking in a foreign language, and our sense of humor may be offensive to sensitive souls; however that's only to keep us sane."

Sheila said; "I know you guys are probably the same, although I don't think David talks much. We have started to know one another a little and I realized early on that the military and nurses may do similar duties, it is defiantly not the same. Lucas, I'm glad to, finally, meet you. I've seen you several times always looking after Molly and I thought; she got a good man. I'm glad to have met you," and Molly said, "David, it is good to meet you. I'm also glad you helped Carl find the blood. I hope your boys aren't angry with you." David said; "No they are all good guys and eager to please. You have a good rest now."

Dr. Corbin came back to the ER and again asked Molly if she had any itching or anything other ailment. She said "No." "Well, we'll start the second unit. I don't remember the young man's name that gave this unit, but the other stood on stand-by in the event his was needed. Carl gave his unit first, had two glasses of orange juice and went upstairs to see a patient he knows."

When everyone had gone about their duties; Lucas asked Molly if she really saw him as a human man? Molly said; "I absolutely know you are a warm-heart, very loving man who just happens to love me. I'll never be able to let you know just how much I care for you. You don't make mistakes, Lucas, although the least little thing that happens, whether accident or not, you seem to go inside yourself and shut me out. That hurts me, and yet I do understand it. I hope the day will come when you can tell me anything and know I put that information in a safe place in my heart and then you turn lose of that. Do you think we might both be able to do that? You know that I'm part Indian too and that I feel very deeply, but cannot always let it show."

Lucas reached down and gave Molly a deep kiss and said, "Yes, I will try. Thank you for reminding me, I'm no longer alone in this world. I know I'm more Indian than White, but I've never achieved the level of serenity of Chief. That is a goal worth pursuing." "Yes, it is, my dearest."

Molly had half-way completed the second unit and could really tell a difference in how much stronger she felt. She knew she would still need to rest some, but not be a burden to Lucas or anyone else. Lucas sat in a chair beside her stretcher that one of the nurses brought over. He simply held Molly's other hand and talked with her.

Molly said; "Lucas, have you thought about where we will live when I am well? We are in Michael and Lucy's house, but two families don't need to be in the same house." Lucas said, "Well, I'd rather move to my house, but I'll discuss it with Michael and Lucy, when we get back. I think you will like the house. It's not as modern as Michael's, but it is very well furnished and comfortable. There is also a large closet that we could open up into the next smaller room for Luke. He needs his own room as well. We'll still have plenty of closet space. My thinking is that Lucy will like it better here, because she is already used to the kitchen and everything about the place. Nevertheless, I'll speak to both of them tonight." "I would like to be included in the conversation, please."

Lucas couldn't help laughing; "You sounded just like Lucy when she gave Michael and me a tongue lashing for talking over her. I'm sorry, sweetheart, but that's funny." Molly started smiling and said, "Yes it is, but also true. I'm still a bit tired, but I think that's because I was so worried about you and not taking a rest except after I fed Luke. I went to sleep, but I don't know how long I slept." Lucas said; "Not long at all, because I was home before six thirty." "Well, No that's not long at all, about two hours," Molly said.

Soon Dr. Corbin came in and checked Molly's vital signs and asked if she had any itching or any other symptom of reaction. She said, "No, I feel better." So he discharged her to be seen in two weeks.

# Molly and Lucas Come Home

Molly and Lucas got home and found Lucy and Michael and Luke were on the floor on a pallet they had made. Luke was cooing and seemed happy. "Welcome home Lucas" and Lucy said. "Luke had been a darling while you all have been gone. I fed him the formula and at first he did not want it and I told him mommy would be back soon and he could have his real nipples."

Molly started laughing; "I'm glad to hear he prefers me over the bottle. Anyway, I had the two pints of blood and I can already tell a difference. I'd like to sit down and hold Luke if I can." "Oh, of course you can. You look better Molly," Michael said. Lucy put Luke in Molly's arms and he began his cooing at her and then he saw Lucas. It sounded like he wanted Lucas, so Lucas picked him up and held him a while.

Michael looked at Lucas and said; "What's up Lucas?" Lucas said, "Michael and Lucy you two are planning to marry; is that certain?" "Yes, if she will still have me." Lucy said, "You bet we are getting married and rather soon. Why?" "Well Molly and I were talking while she was taking blood and wanted to talk to you all about where you were going to live and we would like the other place. While I prefer our old place, Lucy, I cannot just move in without your honest response, as well as Michael's." Michael said; "I would prefer Lucy and me to live here. She already knows the layout of kitchen and every room, but Molly and Lucy; Is that what the two of you want?" Lucy said, "Molly, I know you grew up in this house and I want you to be happy, but I would really like to live here with Michael."

Molly smiled at Lucy and said, "Yes, I would love to live with Lucas in that house. Lucas said there was a large closet that we could make a door into a smaller room and that could be Luke's room. That settles that except for the legal stuff."

"By the way," Molly said, "When are the two of you getting married?" Michael said, "In about three weeks, I think. My cast should be soft and shoes fitted and I can go back to work for a while, just to see how work affects my leg." Lucas was still holding Luke and he finally said, "I'm so glad for both of you. Where will you be getting married?" Lucy said, "We've talked about the Church that you and I are members of and I'd like Molly to be my bridesmaid and Michael would like you as his best man." Molly and Lucas said, "It seems you've been planning this for some time." Michael said, "Well I've asked her so many times, I'm pretty convinced she meant it when she said yes, so I don't want to waste any time making it legal." Molly said, "I'd like to help with the reception and check with a florist you all would like." "That sounds fine, but right now your son is asleep and you need to take a rest for a while. I know the blood has helped, but I also know you have had a rough day." "Well, I think I might lie down a while." Lucas looked at his sister and asked who would give her away; Lucy said; "I'm giving myself away. The two of you will follow us down the aisle and hand the right ring to the right person. Does that sound all right with you?" "It sounds very all right," Lucas grinned.

Lucas said he would put Luke to bed and lie down a while with Molly. "Good," Michael said, "She still looks a little tired." "I guess it will take a few hours for her strength to come back. That's what Dr. Corbin said."

Michael and Lucy looked at one another and hugged snuggly. "I guess we didn't have to bring the subject up after all." "No," Lucy said; "I've always known that Lucas loved that old house and it is nice, but I'd rather live with you here. I'm glad Molly thinks enough about our wedding to offer to help with the flowers and reception. You and I can pick out my dress; remember I don't want a fancy wedding. Michael, I really don't want a big fancy wedding, just few friends." Michael said, "I remember, and I'm in full agreement. I love you, my dearest Lucy."

"Why don't we make a 'To Do List' and that will make things much more organized. You know, invitations, people we want, florist, dress, Church, Pastor, Photograph person, wedding cake, cake squares, nuts, punch etc."

Michael said, "Lucy you already know this stuff." "I know honey, but we need to talk to the Pastor and ensure that we can use the Church and that he will marry us. I can pick up the invitations and bring them home for you to see, as well as napkins, linens, punch bowl and such as that. If you don't like, I'll exchange it. You can stay with Luke when Molly is well enough to go with me." "Lucy that is a great idea and the little tyke will be fine with Lucinda and me. Molly hasn't really felt like doing much of anything since she had the C-Section. That must be very hard on a woman's body. I've heard it is, but I know she is small boned and the pelvis could not deliver him without damage to one or both of them. Anyway, I'm really glad God brought them through; and Luke is so precious."

# DAVID GETS READY TO SEE SHEILA

It was getting close to six o'clock and David changed his tie three times and decided to wear just a nice shirt with a sport jacket for his date with Sheila. He was so nervous; he had not been this keyed up in such a long time. What if she didn't like the restaurant, what if the food was lousy, -- Oh stop this David, she is a beautiful woman with whom you are having a first date and that's to get to know her. He triple checked his dressed person and insured he had his wallet and credit cards and left to meet her at the restaurant. She wasn't there. Why not he asked himself, it was five minutes until six o'clock. He waited about three more minutes, and saw her drive up and to begin to look for a parking spot. His heart stopped fluttering so fast. She found one in a well-lighted area and got out and then closed her door with her hand. Smart girl, David thought.

He got out of his car and went to the parking lot to meet her and realized she too seemed nervous. It seemed like his nervousness left at that moment. He gently took her arm and opened the door and they went in. She was so pretty. He hadn't seen her hair in that style, long with some kind of smooth roll on top of the bottom layer. Her dress was pretty; it was a deep grass green and she had plain heels on.

They were seated fairly quickly and the table was in a quiet corner of the restaurant. The music was soft, but pretty and every thing seemed perfect for her. He asked her if she had a hard day at work; she said, "Not too bad. Frankly, I'm nervous. I've wanted to see you, but afraid you wouldn't like me as a real person. Most people only see the 'nurse' part of me."

David asked; "Is that why you seemed a bit nervous when you saw me? Rest assured, Sheila, while I see you as a nurse, I also see a beautiful woman that I would like to know well."

The waiter came with menus and they looked at them and David asked what she would like. "I'd like a small steak, medium rare, baked potato and salad." The waiter asked David what he would have and he said; "A large rib-eye steak, medium rare, potato, turnips and a green salad. We'll order dessert later." Sheila said; "Where will we put a dessert?" "We'll have room," he said. "I usually eat what is at the cafeteria on base, but I enjoy this food much better. I hope you do as well." "I'm sure I will. We nurses grab what we can pick up between patients. So this is a great treat for me." "You nurses must be on your feet all the time. Do any of you have foot problems?"

Sheila said, "I don't because I wear very good shoes." My instructors said, "You girls (there were few men then) make sure (even if you don't eat) you wear the best shoes you can get. It will save a lot of problems when you age." "Most of us just said, yes, Sister, whoever." "But I can tell even at my ripe old age of twenty four that she was right. I also try to care for my hands as well. We were not allowed to wear false nails in school, so I guess that's why I don't get them now. I do have a good pedicure about every month."

"Well David, I've done all the talking and I know little about you." "Well, there really isn't much to tell about me. I was in the navy and I decided to come out and work in a special squad with the police or as a First Responder. My parents are dead and my only living sibling has Alzheimer's. I would not wish that terrible disease on any family. He doesn't recognize me at all, but I see him occasionally. I'm twenty seven years old and I've never been married. Not much else to tell you, except I have a house in a small community outside of town."

"Have you been married?" David asked. "Yes, not the best marriage, but he was killed in the army in Iraq. No children."

Sheila said, "David, I don't believe I ate all this dinner and you have too. Where did the time go?" "I don't know, just seemed a few minutes, but I've so enjoyed our time together. Now let's order dessert." "Okay, but I don't want to get fat." "Well, look at the menu and we'll see what they have." "David, I'm afraid I'm a fool for chocolate anything, so I'd like a piece of chocolate cake and coffee." David ordered the same. They ate their dessert and enjoyed it. The night was quickly passing and Sheila had to work the next day. David said, "Do you know me well enough to exchange phone numbers and addresses?" Sheila told him she did. They exchanged phone numbers and addresses. When David took care of the bill he walked Sheila to her car and bent down and kissed her on the cheek. "Thank you for a wonderful evening and the pleasure of your company. Would you consider seeing me again on your next day off?" "Yes," Sheila said, "But I might have to call you, because sometimes the shifts are changed. Sorry but that's how nursing goes." "Well will you consider going out with me on your next day off?" "Yes I would like that."

Sheila got in her car and left; but she thought about David a long time. He was a decent man, but seemed drawn inside himself. She had heard that people in the service often, got home as very different people.

David in the meantime was going over in his mind every nuance of their conversation and how she looked directly at him when she spoke. He wanted to go out with her again, as soon as possible. He really liked her. I wonder why her voice became so flat when I asked about her being married. Had that been an abusive situation? He suspected it had been, because he had seen that look before. Well he would never abuse her or allow anyone else too, if he could help it.

# Lucy and Michael Prepare for Their Wedding

The next morning before Lucy went to work she went in to check on Molly. She had heard Lucas leave. Molly told her she felt much better and would love to have a shower and shampoo. Lucy said, "I'll stay until Lucinda comes and so you can get that shampoo and shower. Your color looks better today, but you still look a little weak." "Well, I am a little bit; Luke was up twice last night to eat and I can't always get back to sleep. But I don't think a shower and shampoo and decent clothes will hurt. I've got a nursing bra and some pads so I don't leak on my blouse."

Lucy said, "Okay, hit the shower then and I'll play with Luke if he awakens." "He won't because I fed him an hour ago." Molly got her clothes out and took her first shower in six and a half weeks. She had had sponge baths, but it wasn't the same. She shampooed her hair and got out and dried herself and her long hair. She then dressed and felt like herself again; well almost. When she came out, Lucy helped her comb her hair and plat it in one long, loose braid. She looked great.

Michael knocked softly on the door and said, "Molly, you look terrific. You think it's too early to be doing all this?" "No dear brother, I think it is fine. Now let's go get a cup of coffee." Lucy said, "I made some bran muffins and I think they are pretty good." "They are," Michael said.

Lucy then got ready and went to work. She was so glad to be back and she knew Lucinda would take care of both of them. She told everyone about her up-coming wedding and how it was to be very simple. They both wanted it that way. One of the girls said, "I know a great cake-maker and she is not expensive." "Could you ask her to bake it for us?" "Sure, I'll let you know tomorrow." Another one of the girls told her about the best florist around and so that was one more thing she could mark off her list. She would go to the wedding shop down the street and get some invitations and napkins. She already had a beautiful linen tablecloth. She called her Pastor and asked if she could come over after work. He said. "Certainly." She went in and told him that she and Michael were getting married and asked if they could use the Church and Reception Hall. "Of course, Lucy, do you want me to marry you two?" "Yes we both do. We want it kept very simple with a few friends and some flowers, but nothing really fancy. "Michael is recuperating rather quickly and they are fitting him with a special shoe with some kind of brace so he can walk down the aisle with me. Lucas and Molly will be best man and bridesmaid." "Well that is wonderful, and when will the wedding be?" She told him in about three weeks. "That should be plenty of time to get things organized and avoid me getting so nervous." "I think you are right, Lucy." Lucy left and went home and Michael was lying down with Luke and they were playing.

Molly was making dinner and whatever it was, smelled good. Molly had found a beautiful pork roast in the freezer and had put some spices, salt and pepper on it and seared the outside of the roast. She then put several rosemary and thyme sprigs around the roast and put about a fourth cup of white vinegar on the thyme and rosemary. She put it in the oven and set the timer. She had already put sweet potatoes to roast in the second oven. Before she could prepare the broccoli and congealed salad, Luke decided he wanted to eat.

He cried and yelled and Michael brought him to Molly to feed him. He asked his sister what she needed and she told him to wash the broccoli and put it in the steamer, but not to turn it on yet. She had the preparations for the congealed salad ready and asked Michael if he would finish that and put it in the refrigerator. Michael didn't want everyone to know he was a great cook (sounded sissy to him), but he helped his sister with most meals.

Molly took Luke to change him and feed him and he seemed happy now. She put him in his crib to play a while and went back to finish dinner. She played a little bit with him and decided he needed to sleep a while.

Molly had wanted to surprise Lucas and Lucy with their dinner already prepared, but Michael said, "Sister, it's time for you to rest now, while Luke is napping." Molly didn't argue with him, she was tired, but very proud of what she had been able to prepare. She lay down for a bit and went fast asleep.

Michael finished dinner and set the table and went to rest his leg a while. He was on the couch so he could hear the timer when the roast was done. He almost dozed until Lucy came in and began to chatter about how wonderful everything smelled. She also told him about seeing the Pastor and got permission to use the Reception hall, as well as the invitations. She showed him the invitations and the florist book and asked him to pick out the florist "look" he liked. Before he could do any of the above, Lucy kissed him until he almost lost his breath. "Honey, you are terrific, but no more right now." "Okay," she said; "But take a look at the florist book and please tell me I 'didn't jump the gun', that we really are getting married." Michael realized at that moment that Lucy was nervous. He said, "Lucy, my dearest, we are definitely getting married and I love the idea that you did what I'm unable to do at this time. Now, relax and let me tell you what I've been able to do today. I've walked around the house most of the day without one of the crutches and walked some without either one of them."

Lucy said, "Michael, I guess I was nervous, but I didn't know it showed." "Well, my darling Lucy, I'm part Indian as well as you. My hair might be blond and curly, but I'm still with Indian blood, and even if I weren't, I can tell nervous when I see it." Lucy sat beside him and said, "Thank you, Michael. I was worried that I might have taken too much for granted. The girls at work reminded me about the florist and a great cake maker."

Michael hugged her and kissed her gently and told her how much he loved and appreciated what she had done. "You are part of my heart, no matter whether everything is perfect for the wedding or not. I just want it legal and assure you that I want to spend the rest of my life loving you."

Lucy smiled and asked, "Who made that delicious dinner I smell?" "Molly did most of everything done today and fed and played with Luke; however, I noticed her fatigue and sent her to bed after she fed Luke and then I set the table and decided to take a rest off my leg for a while." "That is great," she replied.

Lucas came in from work and looked fatigued as well. "What in the world happened, Lucas?" "Well, today we took our groups and gave them a workout in various procedures needed for each area of service. I must be getting old; I could hardly stay ahead of that bunch." Carl and David looked about like I felt. We all three laughed about hardly being able to stay ahead of the groups and really observe and teach them. However, they looked like they had been run through a 'chopper blade'; not literally, but one of them asked David, "Is this what you teachers expect every day?" David said, "Maybe not quite so hard tomorrow; we had to see what you guys are 'made of'." They all hit the showers rather quickly and went home.

"Where is Molly? Is she sick?" Michael said, "Absolutely not; she has worked making dinner and tidying up, and feeding and playing with Luke. I sent her to rest and set the table. She wanted to surprise you and I told her if she did not rest, it would not be the surprise she had planned. So she went to bed and I hope asleep with Luke."

Lucas went quietly into their room and sure enough Molly and Luke were sleeping peacefully. He came out and asked Michael why she thought she had to surprise Lucy and me? Michael said, "I declare, Lucas, sometimes you are as dense as Lucy said I am. It's her way of showing you how much better she feels since the blood she received and how much she loves you and us. Now, relax, she is not sick!" "Okay, but she didn't have to do that." "I know," Michael said, "And I reminded her of the same thing and she told me quiet firmly to 'mind my own business'. I did. I played with Luke."

"By the way, Lucy and I are getting married next Saturday at the Church she grew up in. She talked to the Pastor and got permission for the Reception Hall and he said he would marry us. She also went and bought invitations and napkins and brought home a florist book for me to see what I want. That is what she did at lunch break and after work; so see, Molly saved us all some much needed time to rest. Lucy also got the name of a great cake maker and reception planner and will contact her tomorrow. This is pretty fast, but we want our wedding kept simple. She will ask Molly to help write the invitations tonight and tomorrow and then mail them. I told her protocol was not so important to people who loved us. Try to make your wonderful sister know I mean that!" Lucy piped up and said; "There you both go again, talking over me. I'm going to the kitchen and put dinner out for Molly. I do declare; I don't understand men."

Lucas and Michael smiled at one another. "I guess we could say the same, Michael." "Yea, we can."

Molly came out of the bedroom and welcomed Lucas home. She said; "I'd better finish dinner." Michael said, "Tread lightly Molly, you're treading 'where angels fear to trod'." "What do you mean Michael? Lucy has worked her butt off today or she would be home. What have you said to her?"

"Nothing, Molly, Lucas and I were just talking and she was sitting right here beside me, she said, loudly, I'm going to the kitchen and help Molly finish dinner. I guess I made her mad." Lucas spoke up and said, "Honey, he was just trying to tell me about their wedding and I know my sister; she has a short fuse and something we said set her off." "Well, I can just imagine!" "Now what?" The men just sat there and shook their head. "Never in a million years will I understand."

Molly went in the kitchen to help Lucy finish dinner. Lucy said, "I love my Michael and brother, but sometimes I could pinch their heads off." "What did they say?" "Nothing so much, Michael was telling Lucas all about our wedding next Saturday and I wanted to tell you and what I've done today." Molly gave Lucy a hug and said, "Sit down Lucy and I'll make us some tea. They are just men – what can I say?" Lucy started smiling and then she and Molly were both laughing out loud. "Molly, I think I'm more nervous than I should be about getting married. You know I love Michael and I know he loves me, but the closer it gets, the more frightened I become. I saw our Pastor today and asked him about marrying us and about the use of the Fellowship Hall for the reception. He said that would be fine. I then went and bought the invitations and some napkins. I talked to the girls at the office and they told me about a great florist and cake maker. I have a very old, quite beautiful table covering for the cake and snacks. I didn't get a chance to tell you or Lucas and it made me mad."

"Molly, I'm so sorry I let my temper show, but Michael needs to understand, I'm a person with feelings and beliefs too!" Molly said, "Lucy, stop worrying about it, we have a great dinner and we can call them in to eat and they will have forgotten or will say I'm sorry, with no understanding of what they are sorry for, except you got upset."

Lucy went into the living room and told the boys that dinner was ready. Lucas says, that smells wonderful and went on to the kitchen. Michael tried to stand without his crutches and finally made it and asked Lucy to come close to him. She did and he said, "I'm so sorry, my dear Lucy, I would never hurt your feelings if I knew it. I love you with everything in me and I'm grateful for all you accomplished today. Will you forgive me?" "Yes, my dear Michael, I was simply trying to take a load off of you and I wanted to tell Molly and Lucas myself about our wedding. I know that might be selfish, but you understand; I am still a little nervous about the wedding." Michael held her and kissed her and reminded her again and again that he absolutely thought she was the greatest. Lucy said, "Let's go to the kitchen, dinner is ready, and I love you too!"

They found Molly and Lucas hugging and Lucy began to laugh, well, "I guess we can all eat now." "It smells wonderful," Lucas said, "And I am hungry." He already told Molly how much he appreciated all she did, but he did not want her to stress her body or emotions. She reminded him that she would not.

They sat down to eat the most delicious meal that Lucas could remember in a long time. The pork roast was perfectly done, as were all the side dishes. As they were eating, he looked at Lucy and said, "I'm sorry, sis." "All is well," Lucy said.

Lucy began to tell everyone about the marriage ceremony, the cake maker, the florist, the invitations, and her grandmother's hand-crafted tablecloth that she wanted to use, if it was okay with Lucas. Lucas said, "I think that's a great idea. How can I help?" "I don't know if we need anything else or not, I'm planning to talk with Molly after dinner and maybe get her ideas of anything I might have forgotten." Michael said, "Well, sweetheart, we were going to buy our wedding rings and your dress. Is that still what you want?" Lucy said, "Absolutely!"

Molly said, "Michael, I want you to take Lucy somewhere special for your honeymoon. That is something I doubt you have thought about, but it is necessary. You two can get to know each other's moods and feelings, likes, and dislikes." Michael said, "I want that too, but I haven't had a chance to ask Lucy where she would like to go." Lucy said, "I'd like to go to a quiet mountain retreat somewhere that you and I both can enjoy." "Done," Michael said, "I know just the place. I'll also be stronger on this leg next week and we can purchase our rings and your dress." "That is a great idea, and I can prepare the office that I need a few days off for my honeymoon."

# Lucy and Michael Get Married

All the conversations and preparations continued.  The cake maker was going to make a chocolate cake with dark chocolate mousse between the layers and cover it with white cream cheese frosting.  It would be decorated with some pine trees on the bottom layer (for their Indian heritage) and flowers of different kinds on the second layer and then the top layer would be decorated with roses.

The florist would decorate the Church and Reception Hall on Thursday.  The floral decorations consisted of pine boughs with pine cones and cream candles in the center (for the window seals).  The front of the Church would have larger pine trees interspersed with real cedar that would indeed give a beautiful fragrance to the Church.  They would also put some larger cream candles at the ends and center of the arrangement.  It looked and smelled wonderfully like the forest.  The Reception Hall was arranged beautifully with Lucy's grandmother's hand-crafted tablecloth, the same type of forest type greenery, the beautiful cake and small cake squares, nuts, mints, etc. on the table.  The large punch bowl contained a mint and mango punch that looked gorgeous.

Michael and Lucy went by the Church to see the Pastor and get a look at the floral designs.  Michael told Lucy, he thought the whole thing looked like them.  Lucy agreed.

On Wednesday, (before the Thursday decorating) Michael and Lucy went to pick up their wedding rings.  Lucy had chosen a plain wide gold band for Michael and he had chosen a wide gold band with etching of roses around the band. He had her ring engraved with: 'Lucy and Michael Forever in Love'. When Lucy saw that, she almost cried and said, "I want the same on your band;" of course it was done.

They then went to a bridal shop and looked for Lucy the dress she wanted. Michael asked if he could see it on her and of course she said he could. She had chosen a beautiful cream beige dress with tiny roses down the front from a sweetheart neckline. With her coloring, it was perfect. Michael said, "Lucy, you are beautiful in that dress. Do you like it?" "Yes, I do," she said. "I just wanted your reaction before I said anything." "Well it is perfect for you."

The florist had prepared a bouquet for Lucy that consisted of cedar boughs and cream roses down the center. It was exactly what Lucy wanted. They had prepared all the members of the wedding with proper flowers.

When the time came to go to the Church, Molly fed Luke and asked Lucinda to please look after him until after the wedding. Lucinda had been checking Michael and Molly frequently, so Luke knew her.

When they got to the Church, they were surprised at the number of cars that were there. There were about twenty invitations sent out, so they didn't know who else would come. Michael and Lucy looked at each other and someone behind them said, "Hey." The photographer snapped several pictures of them. Lucas and Molly had stepped aside when they saw him. Then he motioned for all four to get together so a picture could be taken of the four of them.

As they entered the Church, Lucas noticed the beautiful scent first of all. Michael and Lucy looked at one another and smiled and walked down the aisle together. Molly and Lucas followed with their rings. The Pastor did a beautiful ceremony and the only music was quite without words or voices. It was just what Lucy had wanted. When the Pastor pronounced them husband and wife, Michael kissed his bride and they started out. When they got to the vestibule, there were ladies there that showed all of them to the Reception Hall. There were quite a number already in the Reception Hall sitting in chairs that folded, but looked comfortable. Michael and Lucy saw the boys Michael taught, smiling and showing thumbs up. Lucy saw all the girls with whom she worked, plus a few others from the hospital. They also saw the First Responders that Lucas worked with and they were smiling at Lucas. That was a surprise.

Then it was time to cut the cake. Michael cut a small bite for Lucy that he easily got in her mouth; however, Lucy had a bit more difficulty reaching Michael's mouth. She had never noticed how much taller Michael was than she. She noticed that the ladies who attended the buffet were from their Church and she must remember to thank them. By this time they had stood in the reception line for a good bit and she knew Michael's leg was hurting. She looked at one of the boys (Eli) who brought Michael his crutches.

Lucas spoke up and said; "You all know there was an accident where Michael works and he has progressed, but still needs the crutches at times." They all clapped and wished them well, ate cake squares, nuts and had cups of punch. They all said how beautiful the wedding was and how good the food was. Slowly most of the people left and the ladies from the Church told Lucy not to worry one bit about the gifts they got; they would take them to the house. "Thank you so much," Lucy said. "You all have been wonderful; as you know, mother and dad died so close together and I've been unable to really focus for a while. Fortunately my beautiful Michael has helped immensely." They thanked them again and hugged Lucas and Molly and left for their honeymoon. Molly had made sure everything they needed was packed and Lucas put it in their car.

They had neither one changed clothes and after they had driven a few miles; Michael asked Lucy if she felt like driving. "Of course, Michael, are you in a lot of pain?" "Well yes, but I took a pain pill before we left and I don't think it would be safe to drive after that. I need to stretch this leg out." He put the seat back as far as it would go and let out a sigh. "I love you Lucy and thank you for marrying me. I love you with all my self until death parts us." Lucy said, "I do too, now put your head back and let the pill take effect, but first you better tell me where we are going." Michael laughed and said, "I drew a map and the reservations are made and all the info you need is over the sun visor." "Thanks," Lucy said.

Lucy drove about two hours and found the turn-off to their destination. Michael had been sleeping and when she got to the location, he awoke. "I'm sorry sweetheart; I didn't realize I was that tired. I'm also embarrassed that you had to drive on our honeymoon." Lucy looked at him and reached over and kissed him. "You are so precious looking asleep, the only reason I didn't kiss you while driving is that it wouldn't be safe, but I was tempted." Michael relaxed and realized that his dear Lucy was in no way upset with him. He was feeling so much better; but had made arrangements for their bags to be taken to the rooms. He took the reservations while on his crutches and with Lucy went to the desk. Michael told them he had made accommodations for the car to be parked and for their bags to be brought to their room. He also planned for their dinner to be served in their room. "That is arranged, sir."

They followed the bellman to their room and he unlocked the door and gave the key to Michael. It was the honeymoon suite with a fireplace and king sized bed. There were roses on every table and in their bedroom. The bellman asked Michael if he would like assistance with unpacking and he said, "No, they would be fine, however, we need a pitcher of ice water with lemon and lime in it." "I'll bring it right away, sir." The water was there within minutes and a large menu for to look at and when they got hungry. There was a refrigerator and coffeepot in the suite.

Michael noticed that Lucy was really nervous. He said, Lets sit by the fireplace and rest a while and I'll get us some water." "No, I'll get the water," Lucy said. She got up and got them both a large glass of the water. It was good after the drive and Lucy was getting bit tired now. Michael lay down on the couch and said, "Sweetheart, let's just lay here and relax a while. I know we are both tired and I am a bit nervous. I'm not as innocent as you are, but believe me we both need a good rest before we have dinner." Lucy said, "Can I get out of my wedding dress; I'd like to save it. I'll put my robe on." "That's fine, darling. I'm not going to ravish you, so relax and do what feels comfortable for you; although I would like you to lie on the couch with me." Lucy grinned her special grin and said, Okay then." She slipped her dress off and her bra, leaving her slip and covering herself with her robe. She then came back and lay beside Michael. "Did you put the soft music on?" "Yes, it's soothing to me." Michael put his arm around her and kissed her gently and then said put your head right here. "Now let's take a little nap." "That sounds good to me."

Michael woke up in about an hour and Lucy was curled up as though she trusted him. He had thought, so often, she was afraid to trust anyone. But she looked like an angel lying there in his arms. He realized again, he had totally lost his heart to this wonderful, fiery woman. He loved her with every fiber of his being. He had failed to remove his shirt but his jacket was completely wrinkled and Lucy had drooled every so slightly on his shirt. He tried to put his coat over the spot and she woke up and stretched and looked at him, "Are we really married Michael?" "Yes, my love, we are. Look on my finger and yours." She said, "I thought I dreamed it. I guess I was more tired than I realized. Did you sleep?" "Yes, darling, I did. I too was exhausted."

"Well, at the risk of being called sassy, I'm hungry? Are you, Michael?" "And I'm not sissy either; although because of my curly hair, some of the guys used to call me that. It did not take but one of them getting his butt kicked until that nickname went away permanently. Blond, curly hair makes a boy sissy, I guess. I don't know why I told you that, I've never told anyone, not even Molly. You, Molly and Lucas seemed to have gotten the Indian coloring; guess mine came from my dad." Lucy said, "Just for the record, you are not sissy in any sense of the word." "Thank you, sweetheart."

"Let's look at the menu and find what we want to eat." They looked and Lucy ordered a small steak medium rare, a baked potato and a green salad. A slice of German Chocolate Cake and coffee, Michael ordered a larger steak, medium rare and French fries, salad and broccoli and for dessert he wanted lemon pie with lemon sherbet. "Also, bring a large pot of coffee, please."

Michael got up to take his jacket off and hung it in the closet; he had forgotten the drool spot on his shirt. Lucy said; "Oh, my word, I've drooled on your shirt just like Luke does." "No worry my darling." "I'm not worried as much as embarrassed; I must have slept soundly"

There was a quiet knock on the door and the food was brought in and set up on the table in front of fireplace on the other side. It was a two-sided fireplace and for that Lucy was glad. The waiter said, "Just put the stuff on the rolling cart and outside in the hallway when you are finished. We will pick it up later." "Thanks," Michael said.

They ate their dinner and chatted about the wedding and everything. Michael put his fork down and asked Lucy if she was on birth control. She said, "Yes, for a number of years; Why?" "I didn't bring any protection and should we decide to make love I don't want you pregnant for a while. I saw what Molly went through and I'm not ready to see you in any way uncomfortable." He seemed to relax and Lucy finished her cake and coffee and asked him the time. "It is about eleven o'clock. Are you planning to catch a train?" "Don't be silly, I just don't know where I left my watch."

"Have you eaten all you want, Lucy?" "Yes and it was very good. I'm still sipping my water. I drink a lot of water." Michael put the dishes on the rolling cart and put them outside in the hallway. He came back and lowered the fireplace and said, "We have one in our bedroom and I would like to lie down with you." Lucy said, "Let me put my gown on." "No," Michael said, "You really don't need a gown; I want to see your beauty and I'll keep you warm." "Well Michael, since you are giving orders, I'll go first! Now lie on the bed and keep quite and still." "May I kiss you?" Lucy sighed and said, "If you must." Michael realized he had been had; his sweet Lucy was teasing him in the sweetest way. She removed his shoes and socks and sang, "This little piggy went to market," but before she could finish they were both laughing and the atmosphere had lightened considerably. She removed his trousers, and attempted to remove his tie and shirt. But the tie would not do right. "Lucy, my love, it's removed like this." He loosened the tie and she took it off over his head and then took his shirt lose and rubbed his chest. He asked if he could move now? "No, I'm not finished." "Okay." She removed his shirt and lay on top of his chest. He said; "If I said please, may I hold you now." "Yes," she replied and started laughing. "Michael I love you and I've been trying to tease you into lighting up." "I'm much better and I love you." He hugged so tightly and looked astonished. "You little minx, you had already taken that bra off and I hadn't noticed. How could I miss such a thing?"

"I'm not dead and I certainly should have noticed how soft your breasts are. What's this?" "A slip, that prevents seeing through my dress." "Okay, the tables are now turned. You stay where you are and I'll finish the undressing." "May I hug you? If you must; I must." Lucy reached around his neck after he had removed her slip and robe and hugged him tightly. She also kissed him until he felt senseless. "Honey, wait a minute, the underwear has to go and so does yours." "Oh, I forgot." She slipped his underwear off and put it on the foot of the bed. Before she could grab him again, he pulled her panties off. "Those are pretty, but you won't be cold." Lucy laughed and they kissed and hugged and nuzzled one another a good while. Michael's voice was husky and he said, "Are you ready my darling?" "Yes," Lucy replied. "Sweetheart, I think I'll have to lift you up on to me; my leg does not want to cooperate in this matter." Lucy said, "I have two good legs." "That you do, and beautiful." "Well, what next?" Michael looked at her and said, "Just sit down on my erection." Lucy did as she was told, but that hurt. She must have made a face, because Michael said, "Lucy, I did not know you were a virgin." "You didn't ask," she said and kissed him hard. He moved her gently and she trembled, "What was that?" "Your orgasm." "It felt good but it hurts too; is that normal?" "You are very normal and I love you. I'll go easy and try not to hurt anymore." They kissed and Michael rubbed her buttocks and back and suddenly he was moving her rather vigorously. He kissed her gently. "Lucy, you are wonderful." "I think so too," she retorted. Michael started to laugh and said; "Now honey, I can't carry you to the bathroom, but you go and I'll follow." "Okay," she said. They went into the bathroom and Michael got her a warm, wet bath cloth and told her to wipe herself gently.

He also got a damp cloth and realized he had blood all over himself. He really must have hurt her. He went to his suitcase and got some cream and told her to put some on herself. They went back to the bedroom, they had never turned the lights out, and the bed was a bloody mess. "Oh Michael, what will the staff think?" "Stop worrying, they will think you were a virgin; however, I'll change the sheets so we can sleep on dry ones tonight." Michael said, "I've had sex before, Lucy, but have never made love and the sex was not with a virgin. My darling Lucy, if I had known you were a virgin, I'd have put some deadening cream on you. I'm sorry for the pain." Lucy said, "That's okay, but will it hurt like that each time we make love?" Michael held her close and said "No, but until we know you are over the hymen split, we will use this cream and making love will feel good." Lucy hugged him and said, "Thank you. I didn't know you didn't know I was a virgin. I've never been married; that one man tried to rape me, but that didn't succeed." Michael held her close and said, "Let's lie down and get my weight off my leg." He held her for a long time and Lucy was very quiet. "Michael did I make you mad at me? I didn't know what to expect and I assumed you knew everything." "My darling Lucy, you have not made me mad in any way; it is such a surprise in today's world for women to remain virgins until marriage; well I was just very surprised. You are so beautiful and it is still hard to believe that you haven't had sex before." "Michael, that is something my mother taught me; to stay pure for the man I knew I loved and that he loved me. So I have." "That is the most wonderful gift you could ever give me," he said. Then he asked why she was on birth control? "Oh that, to help regulate my periods and make them less painful."

Michael held her in his arms like the finest piece of crystal ever made. He repeated how much he loved her and would until the day he died. He could feel her body relax and he simply held her until she was totally asleep. He pulled the covers over them and he dozed off as well.

Lucy woke up in a little while and looked at Michael. "I'm going to get a glass of water, would you like one." "Yes," he said. She brought them some water and snacks left in the refrigerator of cheese, grapes and crackers. They ate a little snack and Lucy said; "Michael, could we try making love again, but this time with the cream and with a towel under me." "Oh yes, I'll get the cream and put it on you and then I'll be on top this time. That way I can control my movements and see all of your wonderful self. I love you Lucy, don't ever doubt that." "I won't." They began to hug and kiss and massage one another and Michael said, "I'm going to enter now; let me know if it hurts at all." He entered her so gently and she said, You feel good and I like your stomach on mine and your chest on mine." "Me too," he said. He began to move slightly and then a bit more vigorously and she trembled and said, "That didn't hurt, but what was it?" "Your orgasm sweetie." "Oh, that's nice." Michael continued his gentle movements and then much more vigorously and Lucy felt his release. "Oh my goodness darling, you feel wonderful. Did you feel any pain?" "No, just you and I might become addicted to you; but I'm kind of tired and sleepy now. That's as it should be my wonderful Lucy." He eased out of bed and to the bathroom and there was still some blood on him, but nothing like before. He sponged her down and put the cream on her and lay down beside her, pulled up the covers and they both slept until late in the morning.

They woke up and ordered breakfast and it too was delicious. Michael asked what Lucy would like to do today. "I'm really not sure, Michael. I too have been fairly rung down and worried about Lucas and Molly. I'm glad that Lucas wants the house we grew up in; I knew he did, but he was giving me first choice. Back to your question; I would like to rest today and get my mental qualities together. Did you have something special you wanted us to do?" "No, in fact, I need the rest as well, since so much has happened and my leg has ached a good bit." "Then we relax, watch some TV and love one another." Michael said, "Lucy, please let me tell you again that I love you, and I would never have hurt you so badly had I known you were a virgin." "Michael; I know that; now stop with the bad feelings and focus on our wonderful life we will have together." He smiled and said, "Thank you, my dear Lucy."

Back at home, Lucas and Molly were enjoying time with just themselves and Luke. Lucas had asked for a few days off to move and the Captains all said; good, your recruits are almost worn out. "They said their teachers were good, but they did not know how strong and steady all three of you were and that you all three did not talk much, but worked in such an organized way, they thought you all were in the same unit in service."

I told the recruits that we would take a week off from the official training due to First Responders who had some personal business they needed to attend to. They said, "Good, we will take this week to work out and be ready when they come back." The Captains said, "Fine, but you may be needed when an incident occurs."

Lucas and Molly were packing their things and decided to take some boxes over and let Luke see his new home. "Molly, I insist on lifting the boxes, but I'd appreciate you packing the things that are yours or mine and we can have Michael and Lucy's place back in order when they get home."

# David Pursues the Woman of His Interest

The Captain had given Carl, David, and Lucas a week off. David decided he was going to make the best use of this time. He had seen Sheila several times and they had dinner one time. He was getting anxious to see her for a longer period of time; so he went to the hospital where she worked and saw her in the ER. They were not really busy tonight and so he went over to talk with her a while. She was sitting at a desk and so he walked up behind her and said, "Hello there." Sheila was deep in thought and looking at some forms and when he spoke, she jumped.

Sheila turned around and for just a second, there was fear in her eyes; then she smiled and said; "Well, hello yourself." David said; "I didn't realize you were working, you are usually on your feet." "There are occasions when we have to catch up on the paper work." David smiled and asked when she would be off again, that he would love to take her to dinner. Sheila replied; "I have a three day stretch off, starting tomorrow. I've worked overtime and covered for one of the other nurses who was sick and I told the supervisor if I didn't have a rest soon, I would simply crawl up on a stretcher and sleep right here." Her supervisor said; "Well, we can't have that, I know you are tired, so take the next three days off and do nothing but what you want to do, but no working."

David said; "That sounds great. Would you like to take a day trip up to mountains and look at the scenery and any crafts or things we might see?"

"I would so enjoy that, I always relax when I can see the scenery without driving and I enjoy seeing the Native American's crafts. They now have some history of the tribes in this area. A friend of mine and I had time off and decided we would do that, but it has been months ago. They had little shops in the village and we ate candy and junk and complained about getting fat, but that's just girl talk. She works upstairs in the O.R. Well, David, I've talked your ear off; did you need something tonight?" "Yes, I do; I want to take you to the mountains and maybe visit the historic sites, but I don't know where you would rather go." "Oh, they are very close together and we could see both."

David asked her how late she slept after working the evening shift. "If you are planning to take me up there, I'll get up as early as you need. That break will be wonderful. As you just heard, I get rather excited with time off to do anything I want." "Well, why don't I pick you up about eight o'clock and we can have breakfast and enjoy the entire day. I like time away and sometimes need it."

"The Captain gave all three of us First Responders a week off. We are each teaching a group of recruits certain skills and this week is certainly needed, those guys worked hard and Carl and Lucas said they had a bit of trouble just staying ahead of them; I did too."

Sheila said, "Eight o'clock would be fine; we are going in casual clothes aren't we?" "Absolutely, it is time for R&R. I'll see you at eight in the morning. Sleep well."

David left the ER and felt like he had won a lottery. Sheila was so pretty and smart and he really liked her. He thought of her so often, he had to call himself up short. He knew her husband had been killed in Iraq, but something in her voice when she told him about it, made him wonder if it had been a satisfactory marriage. That moment of fear in her eyes made him wonder why she was fearful. Well maybe he could find out tomorrow; he certainly did not want to frighten her again.

The next morning at eight o'clock straight up, Sheila's doorbell rang. She had been up quite a while, showering and shampooing and dressing in slacks and a light weight sweater. She had also had a cup of coffee. She opened the door after checking her peep hole and said; "You are very prompt. It is just now eight o'clock." David stood where he was until she invited him in. He stepped inside and just smiled at her. She was really pretty and he had never seen her in anything but scrubs, and she had a terrific figure. He handed her a box of chocolates and said; "Just in case you get the 'munches' before we get breakfast." She reached up and gave him a brief hug and said, "Thank you. I like chocolates."

David said, "Are you ready to go on our adventure?" "Yes, I am," she replied and reached over and got her purse. They got in the car and headed for the mountains. After about an hour, David saw a road sign that showed a restaurant that served breakfast all day. He pulled onto the exit and they went to the restaurant. They had been talking a lot and Sheila said, "I didn't realize I've been talking so long and you've hardly said anything, and then you saw the sign for breakfast before I did." "That's great," David replied. "I like the sound of your voice and laughter." They went into the restaurant and ordered breakfast. It was fantastic; eggs, French toast, bacon, sausage, and hash browns. Sheila said, "David, this is delicious, but I don't think I can eat all this." "That's fine, the coffee is really good; I like the added spice they have added to it." "I do too," Sheila responded. They ate most of the terrific breakfast and while David paid the bill, Sheila went to the bathroom. She came out and he was waiting on her.

They returned to the car and started off again. The scenery was beautiful. You could smell the different trees even with the windows closed. There was a lull in the conversation; David asked Sheila if he had asked if she was married or did he just assume she was unmarried because she had no wedding band. Sheila said, "Yes, you asked and I told you my husband had been killed in Iraq." He said, "I was so busy looking at you, I guess I forged ahead without any manners at all." Sheila said, "No problem, it was not the best marriage, nor even a mediocre one. I'm sorry he was killed, but I would have left him when he came home. I had already planned to leave before he announced that he was going to Iraq."

"I'm a very strong woman, but after a time of constant emotional and even physical abuse, I had enough. I was raised to take my marriage vows seriously and I did; but he did not. I was never good enough, or pretty enough nor could I do anything worthwhile. One time he said, At least you can nurse and make some money. That really hurt me, but I grew to not care. David, please don't think that I'm a cold, uncaring woman because of what I've just told you. I've dated very little since he died and did not plan to; but this guy named David came to the ER and he had such a genuine smile and looked me directly in the eye when he spoke, well, I decided to take a chance."

David said, "Thank you for telling me and believe me, I believe every word you've said. When I came into the ER, I had asked one of my buddies if he knew you and asked if you were married. He didn't know, but asked his little niece if she knew your name. She said, 'Oh, yes, her name is Sheila and she is very nice.' Carl's sister (Grace) and Karla had been in a car/train accident and Carl was there to check on them both. He had been with Lucas when they brought his sister and niece out of the car and he simply got on the helicopter and came with Lucas. Carl never said a word about the passengers being his loved ones; he just did his job. He is a fine man and I'm glad we work together. He came out of the Army, I came out of the Navy and Lucas came out of the Marines. None of us talk much, but we all know something about what the other went through in Service."

"Sheila, am I going the right way?" "You sure are. "Why?" David said; "I have not dated anyone since I left the Navy, which was not too long ago and I've been listening and talking and am unsure where we are. There are things only another Service person would understand about war. I simply don't want to do anything to cause you discomfort or embarrassment, but I'm not very adept at dating a beautiful woman. Usually the women I saw only saw a uniform and (forgive the boasting) a fairly nice looking man who was quiet and they thought they could manipulate me. I've had sex many times, but I have never made love to a woman, because I've never allowed myself to get that close to a woman before. I'm just going to tell you; I have very deep, caring feelings for you and I want you to be able to trust what I say and do. If I make a blunder, please tell me so I won't do it again."

Sheila realized at that moment that David was not at all like the men she had known. He was really a caring person who felt deeply, but was unable to express it. Sheila said; "David, you can believe me as well. I have trouble letting my guard down and frequently push people (men or women) away. You mentioned Grace a while ago. She is one of the finest women I know and honest to the core. She had a good marriage and a beautiful little girl. When her husband was killed, she went home to live with her brother, Carl. She and I are pretty good friends and I've told you the truth. She did confide the other day that one of the doctors that she has worked with for quite a while came to see her often and finally told her the other day that he was definitely interested in her as a woman. 'I've watched you every time I've been into the ICU and we exchanged smiles, but nothing more.' She made him aware that she did notice that he wasn't a 'skirt chaser'. He said no, I've had opportunities, but I'd rather choose who I want, rather than to have someone thrust on me. That's pretty much how I feel."

"I do have some rather unsettling feelings for you; frankly, I'm afraid to fall in love. I don't really know if I can love, or do anything right, except nursing. I do know without anyone telling me that nursing is my true calling in life. I love the ER and feel I'm making a contribution to my patients and that I take very seriously."

"I do know that I think of you a lot! You really are kind and thoughtful; I noticed that when you excused yourself from talking with me to check on Carl, when Grace was brought in. I appreciate that quality of loyalty and concern. I would like to see you as often as you are interested, but know this; I will NEVER push myself into anyone's life. I don't want to ever make a mistake like I made in the past. So, I hope my bluntness has not offended you or make you think badly of me; but that's who I am and what I stand for. I'm much to untrusting for a decent man that I know you are and I felt like I needed to make you aware of that as well, in the event you have any interest in me or not."

David said; "I'm definitely interested in you as a woman who is honest and does her work with genuine interest in the person for whom she is nursing. I know my own feelings, and I frankly believe I'm in love with you as a person and woman. I don't want to frighten you away or make you unhappy in any way. Whether you think you can love makes no difference in how I KNOW I feel. If I'm not a nuisance, I'd like to see you as often as possible. I think you will find trust easier than you think now; I know I have."

Sheila said, "Well, David, let's see how things go and you know I don't really mince words; I will tell you if you do something I can't take and I EXPECT the same from you. Can you believe that and am I acceptable to continue seeing?" "You most definitely are the woman I'd like to know well."

"How far do we need to go before I turn off to the Indian Places? I've talked so much and haven't been paying attention to anything but you." Sheila started laughing and said, "I guess we did get a little deep for one trying to drive, but I enjoy talking and not being told to shut-up. We have about fifteen miles until we get to the first village. I'll pay more attention too." She impulsively reached over and kissed David on the cheek. "Now, I'll start paying attention to roads with you." David glanced over and smiled, she was sitting like a little girl looking out the window and watching for signs. He felt his heart beat more quickly and he had no doubt how he felt about Sheila. He could wait as long as it took for her to gain confidence in herself.

In mere minutes they were at the turn-off exit to go to the first place that Sheila had mentioned. They got to the small village, parked in a parking lot, and walked up and down the streets and looked in many small stores with exotic fronts. The Indians were friendly, but savvy with visitors. They noticed the red-haired girl and her companion, a tall, rather olive skin and dark, short hair. He stood straight and tall, while she began to notice every thing. He stood by patiently and commented on the things she pointed out. He glanced over at the history corner and spoke softly to her and said he was going to check the books out. She found a little Indian maiden that she wanted and followed him over to the history corner. David was looking at two books; one on the history of the area and one on a specific tribe. They looked some more and Sheila got a clove candy stick and David paid for everything and they left the store. Sheila offered David a part of her candy stick, but he declined with a smile.

David noticed the Indian men checking out Sheila, who wouldn't; her hair shone like red sunshine and her eyes seemed to dance. They looked green at certain times and then blue at other times, dependent on the light. At any rate, she was a beautiful woman with a really nice figure and he didn't blame other men looking at her, he did too. But as far as he was concerned, his stance and expression made other men know she was his companion. David realized that humans are much like the lower animals in staking a territory or mate. He prayed to himself and told God how great HE is and thanked Him for meeting Sheila and asked Him to bind them if it was His will David told the Lord; I think she is wonderful, but You already know that, so make me aware (clearly) of Your will.

David and Sheila continued down the street, looking at everything and occasionally buying an Indian snack or trinket. Soon, David said, "Sheila, don't you want to find a place to sit down and have lunch?" "Now that you mention it, I am a bit hungry and would love some coffee." They went back to the car and drove on toward another village and saw a restaurant and went inside to have lunch. They were seated quickly and it felt good to sit down. David had not realized he was tired, until he sat down. Sheila said, "David, I'm tired, but not like with work. I've walked a lot and frankly, I'm ready to sit a while." "Me too," he laughed.

They were brought menus and water and it seemed so many things were on the menu; especially for lunch. David told Sheila to order what she wanted. She looked closely and said; "I'll have the venison steak sandwich and some Indian pudding and coffee." David said, he would have the same, but would rather have a slice of coconut pie with coffee. They talked about the wonderful morning and then their food came.

"This is really tasty," Sheila said. "How is yours?" "Very tasty," he mimicked back. Sheila started laughing, "You are a sweet man; oops, I guess I shouldn't say sweet man, but I think you are terrific." "Thanks," David responded, but his heart was about to burst. He could not believe someone as open and frank, as Sheila would tell him he was terrific. He prayed (God if this is a sign from You, thank You, and if not make me aware; it sure sounds fine to me).

They continued eating and the food was good and the dessert came and Sheila offered David a bite of her Indian pudding. She fed him a bite and asked if he liked it; "Yes, it's really good with quite a few spices I've never had. Taste this coconut pie; it's not the usual." He fed her a bite and she said; "No, it's not, wonder what spices they put in coconut that makes it more than coconut pie?" David replied, "I don't know but it is darker with a different sweetness than most coconut I've eaten." Sheila said; "I'll bet its cinnamon and maple syrup or molasses."

They finished their meal and had another coffee and Sheila asked the waiter if the chef gave ingredients to his or her coconut pie. "I'll check and see," he said. In a few minutes a nice looking Indian woman came from the kitchen and asked Sheila if she was the one who wanted the ingredients to her coconut pie. Sheila said, "Yes, if you give them out." The woman smiled and handed her a card with the recipe already printed, as well as their address and a picture of the finished pie. "Thank you. I love to cook, but rarely cook something special just for myself. The sandwiches were also delicious, as well as the Indian pudding." The lady pointed to the back of her restaurant and said; "You might find a small cookbook you like over there." She smiled and went back to the kitchen. Sheila asked David, if they had time for her to check the cookbooks out. "Absolutely, we take all the time we need. I spotted a small booklet that I'm interested in over there too."

They looked at the books and cards and bought a few. Sheila said, "Excuse me, I'd better visit the bathroom before we get to the next village." David said he would too. Sheila came out and found David waiting on her; he had damp hair on his wrist and forearms. He had rolled his shirtsleeves up some time ago; she thought at least he washes his hands. She smiled at him and asked if they were ready. "Yes, the bill has been handled and we can now drive on the next village." Sheila said; "I did not mean for you to buy me the cookbook and cards, David, I'm not without funds and that is unusual for me." "Well, not today," David replied.

He thought to himself; that husband of hers must have done a 'real number' on her, that she couldn't trust him to buy her a little cookbook or trinkets. David opened her door and they were soon on the way. Sheila said" "Thank you David, for a wonderful lunch and the presents. That was really nice of you." "I'm just very glad I could get something that you picked out and would really enjoy. Do you really cook? With your hours, I'd think that would be hard to do." "I do cook," Sheila replied, "But rarely for just myself. I'll sometimes have some of the nurses over and we will have a 'brunch' before going to work. Sometimes it is the only food we get that day. It can get hectic in the ER and we grab what we can if the need arises, but mostly we live off coffee for the entire shift."

David said; "Well you sure do have a pretty figure, but I hope you won't ruin your health with that routine." "Oh, we are all accustomed to the routine." Sheila was quiet a few minutes and then said; "We are almost at the next village. I'm just as excited as a girl about each village. I guess that sounds silly to you, but I do enjoy day trips, especially areas like this." David replied, "That's not silly at all, I'm just glad I got to share the experience with you."

They got to the next village, but it was entirely different than the previous one, in color and construction. It was almost round with sidewalks around the entire village. David said, "I haven't seen one like this before, it's quite beautiful. The colors are so bright and the shape reminds me of old westerns movies in which the wagon trains formed circles for retiring at night." Sheila said; "Yes it does, but they are full-bloodied Indians, but I've forgotten the tribe's name."

Again they parked the car and went to walk around the village. This time David was excited. He saw old weapons, books of their history, and pictures of the head-dresses their Chief wore. Sheila was looking at the different types of dolls and cookbooks. They continued the walk around the entire village, stopping at many of the shops. Sheila saw a quilt that was exceptionally beautiful and pointed it out to him. "I'm amazed at the workmanship that goes into making quilts." They went on further and David said, "Excuse me Sheila, but I saw a public bathroom back there a way and I'll be back in a few minutes." He did indeed use the bathroom and then went back and bought the quilt for Sheila.

When he caught up with her, Sheila was looking at several things. He said; "I'm back. What have you been doing since I left?" Sheila said, "Oh just looking at everything and noticing the people. They look different from the other tribe as well. Their features are courser with big bones. They are nice looking but in a different way." "God likes variety, doesn't He?" David and Sheila completed their walk and went back to the car. David let Sheila in and dropped some things in the floor of the backseat. She assumed he had carried the books and stuff they had gotten.

When they got in the car, David said, "Now where?" Sheila said there was only one more village that she knew about, but it is a lot farther away; probably sixty miles. "That's fine." They started for the last village and Sheila began to tell him again how much she had enjoyed their day. "You haven't yelled at me once. You really are a nice man." David laughed and said, "Well I think so." They both started laughing and David felt himself relaxing more and more. Sheila was a darling.

They had traveled about sixty-five miles and came to the last village they would visit today. Again, it too, was very different from the other two. Beautiful, but still had a distinctly different appearance. They got out of the car and this village had sidewalks that looked like pine wood. The store fronts were labeled in the Indian Language with the English language underneath.

They both commented on that difference and began their walk. It was both pretty and ugly at the same time. Sheila did not remember it having a 'dark side', when she and her girlfriend came before. However, they went into the shops and again bought a small history book and checked to make sure it was in English. They saw some very old weapons, farming implements, and head-dresses their Chiefs wore. The farming implements stumped David. He did not remember until he thought for a moment, that Indians grew corn and other vegetables as well. They had some dried venison, and dried string beans, which he had never seen. He ordered some of the dried string beans and the dried venison. The man at the cash register told him that he might need instructions on how to eat these products. "We have a small cookbook our women-folk put together, but it is bound with leather and leather cording holds it together." Sheila said, "Where, I didn't see those?" The cashier told her where to look and sure enough there were several small books of women's work and cookbooks, bound the same way.

Sheila said, "David, I must have these, but you are not to pay for them. I can do this myself; there are also some kind of gourds that I want and dried squash I would like." David came over and said quietly to Sheila, "I know you want to purchase these things for yourself, but please let me do this for you. I really want to." Sheila looked straight into his eyes and in a few seconds said, "Thank you, David."

They continued to walk around the village for a while and Sheila said, "David, I did not realize the time, it's almost dark and although I'm off and can sleep in, you probably have to work. We better go home." David smiled at her and said; "Don't you remember that I told you the Captains had given Lucas, Carl and me this next week off?"

"Well I guess I forgot," Sheila said. She seemed to relax after that and they continued on until they had seen everything they wanted to see.

Then, David said; "It's time for dinner and my stomach is pinching." Sheila laughed and said she hadn't heard that saying before. She said; "As a matter of fact, my stomach is pinching a bit too." They got in the car and started home. David had spotted a very good restaurant a few miles from this last village, so he planned to stop there and have dinner. He was really excited to have spent so much time with Sheila and he had no doubt that he was in love with her; however, he would give her as much time as she needed to decide he was trustworthy and that she could be sure of her own feelings.

They stopped at the restaurant and went inside. They were seated promptly and given menus and water. Sheila drank about half her water and looked at David and said; "I drink a lot of water." They looked over the menu and David said, "Please make your choices, Sheila." She ordered surf and turf, green salad, and cucumber salad as well. David ordered a steak, baked potato, turnips and green salad and some corn muffins. The waiter took their order and David said; "I told you my stomach was pinching and I'm planning to order dessert as well."

Sheila laughed and reminded him that it wouldn't pinch much, after that dinner. She told him what a wonderful day this had been and she did not remember having so much freedom and fun in a day. David smiled sweetly at her and said, "Me too! It's been a great day and I've enjoyed every bit of it". I'm sorry it will end soon, but could we plan something for tomorrow or will you be too tired? I'd like to take you to the Navy Museum, which isn't far, but it is in the opposite direction." Sheila said, "Yes and no, I won't be too tired. That's something I've never seen." "Okay, let's plan on me picking you up about nine o'clock; it will be late when we get home." "That's great," Sheila replied.

The food came and it was great. Then, David ordered dessert that was coconut and pineapple cake and asked Sheila to order a dessert and so she ordered a slice of chocolate pie. They both had coffee and water with lemon. Sheila said; "I need to visit the bathroom before we get on the road." David said, "I will as well." When Sheila came out, David was waiting for her. He smiled at her and they went to the car and left for home.

It was dark by the time they started home, but David felt wonderful. He had truly enjoyed his day with beautiful Sheila. Sheila was quiet for a little while and then she said; "David, I really enjoyed today with you. Did I do anything wrong or that embarrassed you?" David looked over at her and then back to the road and answered; "Absolutely not; I was just thinking how very much I enjoyed being with you today. I felt like a kid in a candy store, with the best choice around, maybe not the best analogy, but I truly did have a wonderful day." Sheila said; "Thank you; David, I really had a wonderful day." She was quiet for a while and David glanced over and she was asleep and resting easily or she sure seemed to be. He continued driving and pretty soon they were back at her house. I had been about a two-hour drive from the restaurant and she had slept most of the way. David stopped the car and reached over and kissed her lightly on the lips. She awakened and looked at him shocked; "Did I bore you with the sleeping? I don't understand how I slept through our trip home." David said, "I thought you looked like an angel asleep and it did not bother me at all; in fact, I was glad to see you that relaxed."

They got out of the car and David opened the door for her and turned around to get the packages out of the car. He brought them in and asked where she would like them? Sheila said; "David, we did not buy that much stuff." He answered, "Well I did and I want to know where to put it." Sheila looked in the large bag and said; "David, where did this come from, I was with you the entire day." David said; "Well not when I went to the bathroom". "Well no, I wasn't. David I never expected this quilt in a million years. You didn't have to do this." "I don't do anything that I don't wish to do, Sheila. I knew you liked it, and I bought it for you." Sheila reached up and hugged him and kissed him until he could hardly breathe. He raised his head and still hugged her; but said; "We better stop before I make a total fool of myself; you are so wonderful I'd like to kiss you forever, but I will lose control and I don't really want to humiliate myself." Sheila said; "Well, I was getting a little carried away myself. I certainly haven't kissed anyone like you before. I like the way you hold me and kiss me. You seem so gentle and like you might break me. I'm pretty much unbreakable or some of the ER patients would have done so long ago," she said, laughing. "Well, could we put the bags on the bed in the other room and I'll separate the things you got and have them ready for you tomorrow. That is, if you are still interested in showing me the Navy Museum." "I'm definitely interested and will see you in the morning at nine o'clock." He bent down and kissed her and said, "Good Night, fair one."

David went home and thought about Sheila a long time; how her eyes shone when she got excited, how her hair looked in the sunlight, but most of all how she spontaneously hugged and kissed him. Wow! David you better learn to control yourself better; you almost humiliated yourself. Then he thought about her dead husband. What kind of man could humiliate her like he did, or strike that smooth beautiful skin? He must have been 'nuts'.

David decided he would press a little harder tomorrow, tell her that he really did love her and would like to spend the rest of his life with her.

That might scare her, but it was definitely true. She certainly did not have to make a decision of any kind; he just wanted her to know.

The next morning promptly at nine o'clock her doorbell rang and Sheila used her peephole and let David in. He was dressed casually as she was. She had another pair of slacks on and another light weight sweater. She kept low heels on, which David thought was brilliant. They went to the car and David said, "I thought we might have breakfast before we see the museum. It is rather large and there is a video that shows the beginning of the Navy."

They stopped at a breakfast restaurant and ordered a good breakfast, because David said we might have a late lunch. "That's fine, and good morning, David." David said; "It seems I forgot my manners again; good morning my beautiful sunshine girl." She laughed and said, "Thank you kind sir." Their water and menu had been left with them, along with a pot of coffee. Sheila ordered scrambled eggs and a sausage biscuit. David ordered eggs, ham, hash browns and French toast. Their breakfast came and they ate well. It was good and the coffee was very good.

When they had another coffee, they got up to leave and head for the museum. Sheila told him she was going to bathroom; David said he would pay the bill and meet her in a few minutes. They got back into the car and got to the museum. Sheila said, "I had no ideas this place was here and it is really neat." They went inside and saw the various vessels from very early in The American Navy up to the new ones of today. David told her all about each vessel, whether one above the water or those that went deep undersea. Sheila asked him if he had to learn all that; "He said, "Well some of it, but I really enjoyed learning about the navy and what was possible with sea going vessels. I studied a great deal and planned to go up the chain of command. Well, that will not happen now; but I still enjoy seeing them. The video starts in about five minutes and I think you would enjoy seeing that, if you would like to." "I sure would," she said. They went into the theater and took a seat. It wasn't long before the video came on and not only were the sound effects great; the history was extremely enlightening. When the film was over they went into some of the stores that housed maps and books regarding the navy. David was looking closely at one of the maps and Sheila was looking at other things, but noticed how intensely David was studying it. When he went on to another section and to the bathroom, Sheila bought the map and planned to have it matted and give it to him. It was in a fairly small bag and so David assumed she had found a little boat or ship she wanted. He said, "Well have you seen all you would like to see today?" Sheila said; "I've seen all that I can absorb today." David told her that he hoped it hadn't all bored her, and of course it definitely had not bored her.

"David, since you love the ocean and Navy so much, why did you leave?" David said; "Sheila, there are some things that happen in war that I haven't yet been able to talk about, except very briefly with Carl and Lucas. I'm not trying to be secretive; but I can't bring myself to think about some of the things that happened in fierce battles, let alone someone as precious as you are to me." Sheila said; "I guess I understand somewhat from some of the patients who come into the ER. The world is full of meanness, isn't it?" "Yes, it is, but there are some wonderful people too."

"Are you getting hungry?" "Well, now that you mention it, yes my stomach is pinching a little," laughing the entire time. David looked at her and began laughing as well. She was a beauty to behold and 'bright as a nickel in the well water'. "Then let's start looking for signs that will show us where some restaurants are located." "Great!" They saw a restaurant sign about the same time and David turned off the exit and they stopped at the restaurant and went in. They were seated quickly and the menu and water was brought to them. They looked at the menu and Sheila ordered a grilled chicken salad on sour-dough bread. David ordered a large steak sandwich with stewed apples and tomato slices. They both had iced tea and sipped the water and began to talk some more.

When the food came, they ate and continued to talk about just about everything one could imagine. They seemed like old friends who were very comfortable with one another. They completed their meal and David ordered coffee and a slice of chocolate cake; Sheila ordered a small slice of cherry pie and coffee. "David, I don't normally eat like this. I'd weigh two hundred pounds." "Well neither do I normally eat so much, but I've been anxious to be with you and to eat with you and do anything with you. You are a joy to be with."

Sheila didn't know what to say, so she changed the subject to something mundane. David knew she didn't believe a word he said, when he brought up feelings. She must have been through a lot to make her so untrusting and almost fearful at times.

They finished the meal and got up to leave. As usual, Sheila had to go to the bathroom and David did as well, but he was waiting and smiling when he saw her come back. They left to see some other naval sites and where they were trained, but they didn't stop and walk around. David said; "They might be in maneuvers that did not allow civilians in." "Well, that makes sense," Sheila replied.

David said; "I guess we had better head toward home, but I don't want the evening to end." Sheila said; "It doesn't have too, you've seen my house a couple of times, but I haven't seen where you live and I'd like to." "You would?" David asked clearly surprised. "Yes, I would." "Okay." David was really glad he had tidied up the house this morning before picking Sheila up. So they began to drive and in about a half-hour, David said, "We'll have to turn off here to see where I live." "Fine," Sheila said. They got to David's house, which looked more like a cottage than a regular house. Sheila liked the look of the place. They went inside and the entire house was ship-shape clean. Sheila was actually looking for an area that he might hang the map after she got it matted and framed. They checked each room; two bedrooms, a living room and rather large kitchen. "Do you do much cooking, David? I do enough to get by, but our Captain told all of us to 'bone-up' on some cooking skills; not fancy, just good well-seasoned food, because all three of us take our turn doing cooking duty. Carl nor Lucas had a problem with that and frankly, I think I can do enough to get by the hungry men, especially after a drill or actual emergency."

Sheila said; "David, it's getting late, perhaps we had better take me home." David said, "Okay, but I'd still like to visit a while." "That would be great." They drove to Sheila's house in about twenty minutes and David opened her door and went back to get her small package. He asked where she wanted him to put this and she replied, "Just put it in the other room, like the things from yesterday." "Okay."

Sheila said; "I know we only ate a short while ago, but I'll be glad to fix you some supper if you are hungry." "Thank you, but I'm pretty well still filled." Sheila came over and gave David a hug and kiss. He hugged her and kissed her until he drew his head back and took her arms very gently and took one step back. "Sheila, you are the most desirable woman I've ever seen." He noticed that Sheila stiffened and she had her eyes closed. "Sheila what is wrong, my darling." Sheila opened her eyes and said, "Aren't you going to beat me or rape me?" David kept his eyes straight on her and said, "Sheila whatever gave you such an idea?" Sheila saw that David was in shock; she said, "David that's my previous experience and I didn't mean to insult you. Please forgive me." David took both of her arms and said; "Look straight at me Sheila," she did and saw shock and hurt in his eyes. "I am not the kind of man who would ever abuse any woman. I never have and I never will."

"Did your husband put this kind of fear in you? I've noticed it before, but was unsure why." Sheila started to cry, not cry, but sob so violently, David was afraid she was losing control of herself. He picked her up and sat on the couch with her in his lap and hugged her until she could stop sobbing so violently. She was still crying and looking for a tissue and turned her head away from David; who had pulled a tissue from the box at the end of the couch. "Turn around towards me, Sheila." She did and he gave her the tissue. She wiped her eyes and nose and noticed his shirt was soaked. "David, I'm sorry I wet your shirt; I'll be glad to wash it and dry it for you."

David said; "No need for that; what I want to know is whether you honestly believe that I would injure you in any way. I don't speak lightly about the fact that I love you and really want to spend the rest of my life with you. However, I know now, you are in no shape to make any decision and I will gladly wait as long as I live for you to decide to trust me enough to love just a little bit. It breaks my heart to see you this upset, especially since I have a pretty good idea who put this fear in you."

Sheila said, still crying, "David, being beaten, or shaken or slapped and talked badly about how sorry I was about sex; well I figured I must be. He never cared one way or the other, if he wanted sex, he simply got sex. I don't mean to speak ill of the dead, but that is the truth. I'm really not sure I'd be any good at sex or not. He was the only experience I've had. Please don't be angry with me; when you took a step back from me, I waited for a slap and cursing and a rape." David said, "Look at me my dearest Sheila, it takes two to make love. Sex is just sex. You know that I want you very badly, but not now, at this time. You have to come to believe I would never hurt you or injure you in any way. I want to marry you and then and only then will we make love, - not have sex, make love with one another with gentleness and loving kindness. Do you believe me?" Sheila looked at him for several seconds and finally said, "Yes, David, I do believe you. I enjoy the way you hold me and kiss me; you aren't at all rough. I cannot help what happened in the past; it has definitely affected me in the present."

"I would like to get used to being held and kissed by you. You feel good to me, but I in no way mean that as a tease. I would have sex with you in a minute now; but I honestly don't understand, when you say make love. Of course I know the mechanics, but the feelings that are supposed to go with it are missing or I've simply decided there is no such thing as real love. I know this, I enjoy being kissed and hugged by you. I also think about you so much and have even dreamed of you; I awake and wonder if you really mean it or wishful thinking on my part. There is definitely some deep feeling I have for you that is warm and comforting. A while ago when you stepped back from me, I had flashbacks of what comes next. When you simply looked shocked and hurt, I could not control myself. I've told you the truth, David, even with the real possibility that you might think I'm not worth the effort."

"Dearest Sheila, if you have some deep feelings for me that you can't express; except as warm and comforting, then that is the beginning of genuine love." "David how do you know so much?" "I told you, I know what love is. It was demonstrated by my parents and I simply grew up knowing the difference between sex and love. I nearly lost all feeling except anger in my last tour of duty. But my feelings are back and real. I do love you and want to marry you. Anytime you want to be hugged and kissed, I love that; however, I'm afraid I'll lose control and embarrass myself with an emission. You are a nurse and you know what I'm talking about; it is not you, it's my fear of embarrassment or disappointment by you." "David, was that all that happened a while ago? You didn't seem angry nor did you shake me or slap me, but I did not understand. If you are still willing to put up with me, I would like to see you as often as possible and I really do enjoy hugging and kissing."

David said "Is that why you became so stiff; of course it was; but you never have to worry about any such behavior from me. I enjoy kissing and hugging you very much and I'll say to you, let's stop a minute and you will know why. Is that a deal?" "That's a deal," Sheila said, finally smiling. "Are you able to sleep tonight or should I sleep on your couch, so you won't feel alone or afraid?" Sheila said; "I can sleep, but I would like to have your phone number, in case I do become fearful. Would that be all right with you?" "Absolutely and here is my card and number where you can reach me at any time. I would be honored."

"Now, what would you like to do tomorrow; unless you are worn out from our previous two days? We could go to the park or simply hang out around this area and get to know more about the geography." "I've done very little sight-seeing since I've been working." David said, "In that case let's just hang-out and see the local sights. I'll pick you up about nine in the morning if that's okay." "That is very okay." David stood up and Sheila stood up with him; they did hug and kiss goodnight, but no further incident of shock and fear. They spent the next day sight-seeing and walking in the park. They ate when hungry and stopped and rested when they chose. When they got back to Sheila's house there was some heavy smooching and David did exactly what he said he would. He told Sheila in a very husky voice, "We better lighten up a bit." She said; "Yes, I think you are right, because I might attack you." David laughed out loud and they kissed goodnight and he went home and thought about the three days they had together. He knew he was in love with her. He also thought she was beginning to love him. He knew she was no longer afraid of him. There had been times today when she would reach for his hand and hold it close to her body. That simple spontaneous act spoke volumes to him. He thanked God for His goodness and for Sheila and the progress she seemed to be making.

Sheila stayed inside and locked the door after David left. She thought about all three days and she realized that there were real feelings inside her; but she not know, if that was the beginning of love or not.

She waited about thirty minutes and decided to call David and ask him if what she was still feeling about him could possibly be the beginning of love---she simply did not know. She said; "You probably have to be at work early, but could you talk to me about real love?"

David smiled to himself and said; "I'd be thrilled to talk to you all night. I know the difference in real love and sex or lust. My parents demonstrated true, genuine love for one another, and that, meant wanting the very best for the other one. They did not often tell one another they loved them except through a card or some small thing the other liked; and each one of them would give something like that to the other.

Did that help you any at all?" "David, I think so, because I've never had feelings like this for anyone. My parents were killed and I was reared in foster care. I don't have experience with what you are talking about, but you seem so sincere and you haven't jerked me, slapped me, or raped me; and I know you could. You are a big man and it would be very easy."

"I distinctly remember about age twelve, that I would never let anyone close on the inside of me; I never have; perhaps that is why my husband didn't like me."

David said; "No, Sheila, you've had so much hurt and been unable and unwilling to let it show; you think that caused that sorry man to mistreat you. You are in no way responsible for anything anyone has done; I believe something happened to you as a young child, that you can't allow yourself to remember and that is why you think you can't feel. My guess is that you were abused as a small child and did not understand and felt guilty, but you did not know why."

Sheila was quiet a few minutes and then said, "David, do you still think I am worth seeing again?" "Yes, dearest Sheila, I know how I feel and it is genuine love for you; you are definitely a wonderful, worthy person and I want to see you as often as I can." "David, do you believe in prayer and that God loves each of us?" "Sheila, yes I do believe in prayer and I know God loves all of us. He sent His only Son to die on a cross, as a sacrifice for each of us who believe in Him. He has done the same for you, if you can believe. Do you have a Bible?" "No, but I've thought of getting one, but I don't know how to read old English."

David asked if he could come back over to see her. She said; "I wish you could, but you will have to go to work and you need rest, but maybe after work you could come see me. I will take another day off; I think what you said is very important." "Sheila, I told you that I have the whole week off and I want to see you now." "Thank you, David."

David hung up and quickly looked for a new Bible that was easily read and understood. (David has originally thought of becoming a minister before he went in the Navy, but knew that was no longer possible). Then he brought himself up short and; asked, Dear God, I still know I can serve You just where I am, but this deep instinct to study and know You is very sharp at times. Please make me aware and how to do the Chaplain work if it is of You.

David quickly found the Bible he was looking for and signed it: 'To Sheila, a Woman of Integrity and a Joy to be Around, I Love You, David'. He got into his car and quickly drove to see Sheila. He rang her doorbell and again, she peeped out through her peephole and let David in. He reached out his open arms and she walked inside them and he hugged her very gently. He kissed her gently and asked if they could sit down. Of course, they could.

David handed Sheila a Bible that was fairly small, but with a red cover. She was not sure what it was for a minute and saw Holy Bible on the front. David said; "I've had this for some time; look at the inscription on the flyleaf." She did and said, "David, why did you do this?" He told her again very plainly; "Sheila, I love you and want to marry you. I most of all want you to know how deeply the Heavenly Father cares for each of us."

Sheila said; "Where do I start reading; is there any particular area I should begin?" David said, "Sheila, I want you to start in JOHN, and ROMANS, but tonight I want to explain something to you."

Sheila said, "Okay, explain." David smiled at her and said; "You remember in nursing school the 'Sisters' were strict about your shoes?" "Yes," she said. "Well did they not teach you about God?" "They tried; but some of them were as mean as the devil, excuse me, they were not very nice; so I didn't pay them any attention, I pretended to read along, but I'd be studying anatomy or chemistry or some other subject that I was more interested in learning."

"Well, Sheila; God is our Heavenly Father who is also The Creator, Our Provider, Our King and Savior. You see God created the first man, Adam, and all the rest of creation, the sun, moon, stars, seas and every form of life, creature, grass, trees, mountains and each one of us. But before any thing else was done, HE caused a deep sleep to fall on Adam and took one of Adam's ribs and fashioned a woman. She came from Adam's side, to be a helper to work with him to provide for family and others. She was equal to Adam in every way, except Adam tended Garden and she stayed fairly close by and worked with him. They also played and talked with God every evening. God came down and talked with them and that 'must' have been a remarkable talk; (My belief was the God in that setting was Jesus, pre-incarnation as our Savior)."

"However, one day Satan (disguised as a serpent, which must have been beautiful and walked around in the garden); (the reason I believe he could walk is that archeologists have found snakes with legs in ancient digs). Nonetheless, he came to Eve in the Garden of Eden and asked; "Did God say you can eat from the trees of the garden?" "Yes," Eve said, "Except we cannot eat from the Tree of Knowledge of Good and Evil, because in the day we eat that, we will die." Satan said, "You will not die, God knows that when you eat of the fruit of that tree, you will become like Him." So Eve looked at the fruit and saw it was pretty and would make her wise, she took and ate and gave some to her husband who was with her. Immediately their eyes were opened and they noticed they were naked and made fig leaf clothes to cover themselves. They hid in the Garden when God came down for His usual fellowship with them

God asked where are you, Adam? (God did not need the information) but Adam and Eve needed to admit what they had done. So God told Adam because he disobeyed that he would till the soil with the sweat of his brow; He told Eve she would have pain in childbirth; and He told the serpent that he would crawl in the dust forever. God then put them all out of the Garden and set an angel with flaming swords to guard the Garden.

Prior to this, God knew that one day He would make mankind, and that man, with 'a free will' would disobey which is sin. So the Heavenly God Head (God the Father, God the Son, and God the Holy Spirit) would one day need to pay the price of sin for all mankind. Therefore they determined that Jesus, the Son of God, would be the perfect Sacrifice to take sin from mankind, if they would believe Him. God through His Son's death on the Cross paid our debts and enabled those who believe this to be his own sons and daughters (joint heirs with Christ) and would live with Him forever. Those who chose to disbelieve on the Son of God would end up in hell (by their own choice to disobey). God made hell for the devil and his fallen angels; not for humans, but if we choose not to believe, then that is where one who disbelieves will end up forever.

David stopped talking looked at Sheila who was looking directly at him. She had seen the beauty of his face when he talked about God; almost like he was talking to a dear friend. She said; "David, I think I believe in God, well I don't 'think that', I've seen too many things that humans can't do, there must be a God. However, I've never heard or don't remember having things explained like you just did. David, you know God as a friend and father, don't you?" David replied, "Yes, I certainly do."

Sheila looked down at her hands for a long while, and David simply waited. When she looked up, she noticed that David was smiling so sweetly; "David could you show me how to have whatever it is that makes you so loving?" If this is Jesus, will you tell me how to talk to Him and God?"

David took both her hands very gently; he prayed a simple prayer and talked to the Father to open the door of her heart to understand that He loved her, no matter what she had done in the past. He quoted: John 3:16 and she shook her head; then he opened her Bible to Romans 10:9-10 and read that to her. "Sheila, do you believe that?" Sheila looked at him and smiled a very relaxed smile and said; "Yes, David, I do; but should I not thank God for all He has done for all of us?" David held her very gently and prayed out loud: "Dear Heavenly Father, You know our heart and everything about us. Please accept our deepest gratitude for Your Mercy and Sacrifice and Love for us; 'Your children'. Lord, I thank you for Sheila, help her to grow in the nature of You and develop a far better understanding of Your love and protection. Help her to open her heart to You and Your will for her daily life, and Father, please let her know, without doubt or fear, that I love her too. Lord, You know I've prayed for Your will and You know I want to marry her and for us to walk daily within Your will. Thank You, Heavenly Father."

Sheila had been held so gently by David, but she also felt inside a warm relaxation and it seemed like the heaviness was gone. Sheila relaxed in David's arms and said; "Thank you, David, and I also believe and thank God for His Love; I feel inside warmth also like the heaviness is gone. Is that a real feeling from God? I mean to feel lightness inside, deep down here, she took David's hand and placed it below her breast but almost touching them?" David said, "Yes, I believe it is God allowing you to feel His touch."

Sheila felt so relaxed and warm in David's arms. She asked him if he really wanted to marry her even knowing her background. David said; "I really want to marry you, because you really can understand love much more accurately and I believe you feel some love for me." "Oh, I feel a lot of love toward you for several reasons; you explained God to me in a way I understand that He is my Father now and I am His daughter; also for just not giving up on me."

David asked her again to marry him and she looked straight into his eyes and said, "Yes, I would love marry you." David could see a new light in her beautiful eyes and hugged and kissed her. He asked; "When would you like to get married?" Sheila said; "David, I love you and I want to marry you, but I'm so relaxed and a bit tired; could we just lie on my bed and sleep a while? I'll be much more logical after some rest. Also, I'll just wear some sweat clothes instead of a gown, because I don't want to act as a tease and that will enable us both to rest well."

David began to smile and then laughed out loud. "Oh my darling Sheila that demonstration of love and trust has made me so happy. But if you need your gown to rest easily, I promise not to do anything but hold you." "Then let me get into sweats because they will keep me warm too."

David said, "Go ahead and change sweetheart, we will sleep a while and talk about all this wonderful news tomorrow."

Sheila put her sweats on without a bra and they went to lie on top of her bed. David wrapped his arm around her waist and they both relaxed and went to sleep.

# Lucas and Molly Decide To Prepare To Move

Lucas stopped talking and sat watching Molly feed Luke. He said, "My dear Molly, I did not mean to give you orders, I realize you have about all on your plate that you can handle now." Molly told Lucas that was a great idea because she too wanted them to be able to settle in their own home. "The moving won't be too difficult, but it will take some lifting on your part; like Luke's crib, chest of drawers and our personal chairs, etc. Michael won't care what I take from the house, because he and Lucy will want to get some furniture the two of them want and maybe paint."

Molly told him that she was to see the doctor in two more days and wondered if he would be able to take her. "Of course I will, the Captains gave David, Carl, and me a week off to get our personal lives in order. Besides, the recruits told them they were 'busted'. Those teachers must have been in the same unit; they act without talking much and we get worked to within an inch of our lives."

Molly said, "I don't doubt the boys feel tired. They are not used to such stressful routines." "No, they aren't, but all the Captains put us in charge of bringing them into a well-oiled machine and we intend to do that."

Molly had finished feeding Luke and talking to him and he was ready for a nap. She stood up and put him in his crib and rubbed her bottom. "What's wrong, Molly?" "Oh, just my bottom gets a bit sore sitting in the rocker without a pillow. I'm really fine."

Lucas took her in his arms and began to massage her bottom and hug her and she began to kiss him. He said; "Oh boy, we better stop this for a while." Molly said; "Okay, but I love you." Lucas smiled a real smile at Molly and said, "I love you, too!"

Lucas brought some boxes in and Molly began packing them, as well as, Luke's toys and some sheets. Lucas said; "Why don't we go over to our new home and see if you like it?" Molly said, "That's a great idea and I'll have some idea where to place things. I also want to look at the kitchen."

"Well, let me get these things in the car and we will take Luke for a ride to see his new house and my beautiful bride to insure she really likes it." Molly could feel that Lucas was afraid that she might not like the house, but she knew better. She intended to point out everything she really liked and make him aware that she loved him and her new home.

Lucas loaded the car with all the boxes and several other things that belonged to him; that he knew Lucy didn't want. They drove about twenty minutes and came to the house. It was set off the road in a group of trees and shrubs that had been neatly trimmed. It looked like it was made of cedar, but Lucas said, "No, it's made of 'heart pine' that will last many, many years." Lucy looked up at Lucas and said; "You know, that looks like us, I love the setting and the house. "Could we go inside?" "Of course we can and I want your opinion on where our bedroom will be and how you think we can make a smaller room for Luke."

They went inside and it was what Molly had imagined. She only remembered a little of it when she was over there with Lucy, because she was sick. Molly knew that Michael wanted the house they grew up in and it seemed that Lucy also knew that Lucas wanted the house they had grown up in.

Brothers and sisters might fight some, but they were so close, they could sense the other's feelings almost any time the other was hurting or confused. She knew Lucas and Lucy were the same way.

They went into the house and there were two large bedrooms, with an open space (what is now called a great room), but when the house was originally built, it was a 'shot gun' house, with a hall all the way down to the kitchen. The kitchen was all along the back of the house and Molly immediately fell in love with it. There was a room off the hallway to the right and left, but she stayed in the kitchen a good while, while Lucas held

Luke. "Lucas, I really like this house, the kitchen is what I would have planned had I been going to build it." Lucas said; "Well let me show you the other two rooms. One is rather small and I thought we could put a bathroom between it and our room. The room would be smaller, but it would be ideal for Luke." They went into both rooms and Molly almost jumped up and down, but thought better of jumping when her tummy hurt. "This is perfect, my dear Lucas." Lucas held her close (well as close as possible with Luke in his arms), but then lay Luke on the couch and really hugged and kissed Molly. "Do you really think you can be happy here?" "I know I'll be happy here. Could we go bring some other things over and clear the refrigerator and fill this one? Before Michael and Lucy get back we will fill their refrigerator and freezer and have all the beds made and ready for them to occupy. That way, we can work on our house by cleaning and dusting some and making a list of items we need. I know there are bed linens, but I don't know who they belong to." Lucas said; "I don't think that matters. Did you see the washer and dryer and the stove and ovens?" "Yes and they too are perfect."

"Well, let's get back and empty out the refrigerator and freezer and I'll put the linens over there into the washer and we can dry them and put them on their beds. However, the food and frozen things will need to be put in this refrigerator and freezer before we can do all that." "You are absolutely right, love. When we get back, I'll dust the furniture and make everything clean and ready for occupancy. You will need to take the linens and clean them. It won't take long to accomplish that. I'm so excited; I can hardly stand it, Lucas."

# Carl Decides to Tell Sarah How He Feels About Her

Carl was also glad the Captain had given them all three the week off. He hadn't heard from Lucas or David, but he assumed they were taking care of their own business. He knew Lucas and Molly were getting to know one another and the baby, but he didn't know where David was or what he was doing.

Carl decided to go see Sarah this morning and spend as much time as possible with her. He also wanted to see Grace and Karla. He went to see Grace and Karla first to find out when they could come home for sure. They were almost ready to go and Grace said, "We are waiting for the final check-up and then I was going to call you to take us home." "Well, I'll be in the hospital and you can call my private phone and I'll be up to get you both." Karla still had a soft cast and again, she asked him to sign it too. He did and drew a tiny monkey on the cast and wrote, 'love You Bunches' with a tiny bunch of bananas beside, love you bunches, 'Uncle Carl'. Karla smiled and said, "We are going home today and that's why you drew the monkey and bananas." "Yep. See you in a little while."

Carl left and went to see Sarah. She looked a little better without so much swelling. He smiled at her and she smiled back; "Guess I look pretty bad with blue, green and black eyes." Carl said, "Guess you do not; I like blue, green and even black, but not on your face. I wish I could get hold of the bastards that did this; excuse me, the men." Sarah laughed and said,

"That word is not considered so bad in today's world. I hear it a lot at the restaurant."

"Carl did I dream it or did you tell me not to sell my restaurant at this time." "Yes, I told you that, especially when I realized you want to keep the restaurant and go to school to become a chef." "Did I tell you that?" "No, Dr. Knowles told me while he was visiting my sister, Grace."

Sarah said, "Well it's true, I want to go to school, but I am afraid to stay at the restaurant at night. I don't know if they have caught the men who beat me or not; however, it might happen again and I guess I'm a coward. I'm afraid to stay alone, especially at night."

Carl said; "Don't you remember that I said you can stay at my house with my sister and niece, if you can stand Karla's constant questions and talking. She is a dear and I love her, but sometimes she gets too nosy and I finally said to her one evening; Karla, you know I love you, but you must remember that adults like to talk to adults sometimes. I know you are really smart and kind, but you are still rather young to try to converse with every person, especially adults. Sometimes, they want to talk to each other; like your mommy and daddy did." Karla said, "Yes, that makes sense; since my daddy died, mommy has had no adult to talk to but you and Dr. Knowles. He really likes her you know." "Yes, I know," Carl replied.

"She might forget and begin to ask you questions and talk 'a mile a minute', but just tell her you need quiet a while and she will simply read or say that's best for you."

"I've already told both of them they might have a house guest who would stay in my room and I would stay in her apartment behind her restaurant." Grace looked at me for a moment, and said, "That will be wonderful, Carl." "So when you are ready for dismissal, I would be honored if you would take my offer seriously." "I do and thank you, Carl. I have a key to my restaurant in my purse and I believe the bed is made fresh, although I can't remember for sure. At this moment, I don't know where my purse is, or my clothes. Dr. Knowles has done another MRI on my face and head and said, I could probably go home tomorrow, if all goes as he thinks."

Carl said; "That's great, because Grace and Karla are being discharged today and it will give me a chance to get them settled and insure my room is clean for you." "Carl, that is wonderful of you and your sister, but you don't have to do this. I'll find somewhere to stay for a while until I get over the anxiety. I do intend to go to culinary school, but that might take a few weeks." Carl looked straight at Sarah and told her; "It is NO trouble, in fact, to be absolutely honest with you; I have real feelings for you. I don't say that lightly or out of sympathy or anything else. I've noticed you for a rather long while and observed how you treat people and I am very interested in you as a woman who is beautiful, as well as deeply caring for others. I am not a man who talks a lot, but when I say something, I mean it." Sarah said, "In that case, I would be very thankful for what you are offering."

"I would never intentionally make you mad or be in your way or anything like that. We hardly know one another, at least I don't know much about you, except you are very kind and helpful to me. I just don't know why, but I do appreciate you for helping me. I'd like to get to know your sister and niece, because I don't have family left. It gets a bit lonely at time, except for my customers. I enjoy conversing with them, but I keep my distance from most people."

Carl said, "I've noticed that too; but we will get to know one another, but there are some things I'm unable to speak about. The major one is my service in the army. I don't even like to think about war and certainly don't wish to talk about it." Sarah said, "Thank you for your honesty, Carl, there are things I'm afraid to speak about as well, but I am not a person to pry into another's affairs. You are so kind and good to me, I will always appreciate you." Carl said; "Well, let's just make a deal to take this relationship, one day at a time and see what happens. I meant what I said about having real feelings for you, but we must both grow toward one another day by day. I also have a small farm and can, if you wish, grow any vegetables or herbs you might need for school and your restaurant. I can also help in the restaurant after work, if you like. Just think about what I've said and here is my card with name, address, and phone number. You can reach me day or night with this phone number."

"Will one of the nurses find your purse or tell you what might have happened to it and to your clothing? If you wish, I'll get whatever you need, but I don't know your size." "That's fine, Carl, but when I find my key, I'll give it to you and my clothing is in my apartment behind the restaurant. Do you mind looking in that closet over there to see whether my clothes or purse are there?" Carl went to the closet and found her purse and some shoes, but no clothes. He handed her the purse and said, "The police probably have your clothes for examination for any DNA they might find that will help identify the men that did this. Who knows but what this may be a pattern these men are performing, especially on unsuspecting women."

Sarah looked in her purse, her wallet was gone, but her key had been hidden in a concealed pocket in her purse. She opened the pocket and sure enough the crooks hadn't seen that pocket; she handed Carl her key and said, "Just, when you have time, pick up some underwear and anything hanging in my closet. I'll wear anything you bring, at this point it doesn't have to match, and I'll need some gowns and a robe." Carl said, "I'm going to check on Grace and Karla and hopefully be able to take them home in a while. Then I'll go by the restaurant and get your clothing and bring it back to you." "Take your time and know I really appreciate this. Thank you, Carl." Carl smiled at her and said, "Most welcome, Sarah."

Carl went back to Grace's room and Karla's to see when they might be discharged. Karla said, "Uncle Carl, they are so slow around here. I've read half a book since they said we could go home. Dr. Knowles is in talking with mommy, and I guess they are making arrangements to go home." She motioned for Uncle Carl to come closer, "You were right the other day when you said, grown-ups need to talk with each other some of the time. They pushed the door closed and I couldn't hear what they were saying. Don't you think it might be grown-up talk?" "Yes, Karla, it is, but you must understand that in no way means your mommy nor I love you any less."

"Grown-up talk sometimes involves kissing or hugging and most of the time they don't want others knowing." Karla said; "Do you have a grown-up friend that you like to talk to like that?" "Yes, as a matter of fact, I do, but she does not know it yet. She is going to be a house guest for a while and she will use my bedroom. I'll be sleeping at her apartment, because some bad men hurt her the other day. She is afraid to stay alone at night, so I checked with your mommy and asked her if it would bother her for Sarah (that's her name) to stay in our house for a while. Karla, I want this information to stay between you and me; about the hugging and kissing stuff, and especially regarding my feeling about Sarah, because she doesn't know." "Okay, I understand Uncle Carl, but you still love me too don't you?" "Karla, no matter what ever happens, I will always love you!"

Carl told Karla he was going to see Grace to find out when they could go home; but I will knock on the door first. Karla started laughing and said; "Uncle Carl, you are so smart, you think of everything." "Thanks, Karla."

Carl knocked Grace's door and momentarily, Robert opened the door. Carl said; "Hello you two; when may I take my loved ones home?" Robert looked at Carl and said; "They are my loved ones, as well. You might as well know, I've asked Grace to marry me and she agreed; but we will wait a while until Karla can get used to me being around more often." Carl looked at Grace and asked if she was sure of her feelings. "I certainly am, I've known Robert and worked with him quite a while, so I'm fully aware of my feelings."

Carl looked back at Robert and said; "Then that is fine, but don't ever hurt either one of them." Robert looked shocked and hurt; "Whatever made you think such a thing, Carl?" Grace spoke up and said; "Robert, he is playing big brother and protector;" she looked at Carl and said; "You hear me well, big brother, I am old enough to know my true feelings and you don't have to be so protective; do you understand me?" "Oh, absolutely, love." He turned back to Robert, reached out his hand; and Robert put his hand out. They shook hands and Carl said; "Welcome to the family, and I really mean that."

"Grace is right; sometimes I step on people's toes and don't realize I've hurt someone's feelings until Grace 'tones me down'. Please accept my apology for what I said to you." Robert shook Carl's hand firmly and said, "You are forgiven and I probably would be the same way if the roles were reversed."

"By the way, Sarah will be Grace's house guest for a while and I'll be sleeping at her restaurant. She is afraid to stay there at night and you well understand why." "Yes, I do; and Carl, forgive any intrusion, but do you have feelings for Sarah?" "Yes, I do, but she does not have any idea of my feelings. She just thinks we are being nice. I would prefer to wait a while until she is stronger emotionally and physically to speak with her about my personal feelings." "I understand," Robert replied.

"By the way; Grace and Karla have been officially discharged. I held up the process to talk more with Grace."

Carl said; "Karla told me they were very slow around here, she had read half a book waiting to go home." "Well, you will need to go down and sign them out, but they are free to go. I'll probably see all of you sometime tomorrow."

"Sarah will most likely go home tomorrow, because I removed the packing and the MRI that I had done last evening is still negative." "Thanks," Carl said; "I'll finish up and take them home, and ensure they get dinner."

Robert had helped Grace pack her things and then went and asked Karla if he could help her pack. Karla said; "That would be very nice; thank you."

Carl came back in a few minutes and they were all packed and so he took everything down and the nurses brought Grace and Karla down to the car. They got home and Carl ordered dinner for all of them. He went to pick it up and brought their dinner home and they all ate. Karla told her uncle that she sure enjoyed a good hamburger for a change. Carl laughed and said; "Me too. Now you two ought to get ready for bed, you are probably going to enjoy sleeping in your own bed tonight." "I think so, too," Grace replied.

Carl told them he would see them in the morning, but he was going to Sarah's apartment and pick up some clothing, a robe and gown. She said it did not matter what I chose, she would wear it. So that's where I'll be for a while.

Carl went to the restaurant and looked around again. There did not seem to be anything else out of place. He went back to Sarah's apartment and it was as neat as could be. He looked in the closet and found clothing that was set up for matching. He took two outfits and then looked in her chest of drawers to find her underwear. He got two pair of panties, two bras, and two gowns with her robe. He left those things in his car and went back to the hospital and told Sarah what he had in the car. She asked him to bring one set of underwear and one outfit and she would wear that tomorrow to go to his house. "I'll sleep in this hospital gown tonight. I don't know exactly what time, but Dr. Knowles said in the morning." "That's fine," Carl said, "I'll see you in the morning." He reached over and kissed her on the cheek and said, "Good night."

# Carl Brings Sarah To His Home

Carl had talked with Sarah the night before he brought Grace and Karla home yesterday. Grace already had checked on a nurse to visit three times a week. Grace and Karla had settled in and he went back to the Restaurant to gather the clothes that Sarah told him she needed and took them to her. He brought several other outfits and underwear to his closet and chest of drawers. He took his things in a box to her apartment behind the restaurant.

Today he would bring Sarah home to settle in and meet Grace and Karla. He went to the hospital when she called him and had prepared his car for her to be comfortable. The nurse brought her down in a wheelchair and he took her things from the closet and went to get the car. He pulled around to the front of the hospital and they were waiting. He got out of the car and helped Sarah into the car. They then started home and arrived in late morning.

He brought Sarah into the house and took her to meet Grace and Karla. They all took an immediate liking for one another. Karla said; "Uncle Carl, if you will bring my crutches, I'll show Sarah her room." So Carl got her crutches and allowed her to show Sarah her room. He looked at Grace and said; "Thank you, sis, I have feelings for her and have for a good while, but she doesn't have a clue; she thinks we are being nice because she got beaten so badly. I've tried to make her understand that I want to do this."

Karla was chattering away to Sarah and said, "Uncle Carl told me that you and I had the same surgeon. You can see my face is almost well, but not quite yet. Yours will be well soon, too. Does your face hurt?" "Well, a little bit," Sarah told Karla. "Mommy still has pretty bad headaches, because her skull was fractured. The doctor told me that she would be all right and you probably will as well."

"Uncle Carl got me a digital reader the other day and I'll show you how it works and if you want to, you can read anything you want. It is not just for children, it is also for adults. It makes mommy's head hurt too much to try to read it, but she knows about it, but doesn't want me to read too much to her right now. Uncle Carl said you might want to go to chef school in a few weeks, and I looked up some books on chef schools for you. I've written them down and when you feel better, just let me know and I'll get them for you." Sarah said; "Karla, that is so sweet of you; I had very little idea that Carl had told you all about my school ambitions." "Well, I'm almost six, but I've been reading a pretty good while. I just learn easily, even though mommy sometimes says that I should let others join in the conversation."

Carl came in about that time and said, "Karla, your mom is right this time; Sarah needs to lie down a while and rest some. You can go with me to get lunch if you will. You know your memory is better than mine sometimes." "That's true so I'll simply go take mommy's order, and Sarah's order and you know you and I like good hamburgers." "That's true, now off you go. I need help with this stuff."

Carl told Sarah; "I love that child so much, but she is so smart and talkative, it does get a bit much, especially if one is unwell." "Oh Carl, she is so very dear, she offered to help me look up some schools I might want to attend and has even written them down. I really appreciate that so much." By this time, Karla was back with her crutches and a pad; "Well, what would you like to eat Sarah?" Sarah answered and asked what she would be having; Karla said, "Uncle Carl and I will have hamburgers, but mommy wanted a BLT and some juice." "Well, Karla, at the risk of being a 'copy-cat', I'd like a hamburger as well." "Good; now would you like a soft drink or juice or coffee?" "Thanks, Karla, I'd like a soft drink." Karla beamed at Uncle Carl and said; "She likes good food, like you and I do."

Carl said; "Yes, now we had better go get it so we can eat before all of you take a nap." "I'm ready," Karla said. They went to the car and Uncle Carl picked Karla up and put her up front with him, but insisted she wear a seat belt. "Oh I will; Mommy said; never forget your safety issues, so I'm pretty careful."

Carl was thinking about several things: 1) How glad he was to have a week off; (2) How he had deep feelings for Sarah and knew very little of her background (3) Would Grace really consider marrying Robert Knowles; it seemed likely and (4) Could he really relax with Karla not being around?

He snapped back when he heard Karla say, "Uncle Carl, we almost missed the turn-off." "So, we did, I'm sorry to almost miss the turn-off, thanks for telling me." Karla said; "Uncle Carl; you know I'm almost six (actually six days from now); are you worried about something?" "Karla, I was thinking about several things, but I'm not worried. Now, do you have the list of things to get?" "Yep, got it right here, but you know I've already memorized it." Carl smiled at her and said, "I thought as much."

They got out of the car and got the sandwiches and drinks and he carried them, but as they got close to the door, he asked Karla if they should get some dessert too, for later on. Karla said, "I like ice cream, but I don't know if mommy's head would hurt or if Sarah's face might hurt, tell you what; let's just get a chocolate cake." "Good idea," Carl said. They got the cake and Carl took everything and Karla managed her crutches very well. He put the lunch in the back seat area and helped Karla buckle up. They went back to the house and found Grace and Sarah sitting in the living room, just chatting away.

Carl called; "Soups on" and Karla mimicked him, "Soups on," and Grace and Sarah started laughing and went to the kitchen. They thanked God for the good food and family and friends. Grace ate about half of her sandwich and looked at Carl and said; "You had better call Robert, and Sarah, can you see well enough to help me back to bed?" "Of course," Sarah said; they got Grace settled and Sarah said, "Grace, what happened?" "I'm not sure Sarah, but I suddenly got a severe headache and my vision is blurred. Please don't tell Karla except mommy got a bad headache, at least until Robert can get here."

Carl was on the phone in thirty seconds with Robert on the phone. He said, "Robert, please come out and check on Grace; I don't know anything except she held on side of her head and asked Sarah to help her to bed. Are you able to come quickly or should I call my squad." Robert said, "Carl, if you will let me off this phone, I'll be there in ten minutes; I was already on the way to see her and I have my bag in the car." "Okay, thanks Robert." Robert said, "I'm calling the neurosurgeon to come to the house now, as well."

"Uncle Carl, should I go sit with mommy and Sarah?" "This time Karla, I think we should let Sarah stay with mommy and I'll just go check on them. When the doctor arrives, please show him to mommy's room and finish your lunch." "Okay," she said.

Carl went into Grace's room and Sarah was holding her with Grace's head on her shoulder. She asked Carl to get a very cold cloth to put on Grace's head. He did and it seemed Sarah knew what was needed more than he did. Grace's eyes were closed. Carl spoke softly to Grace and she said, "I can hear you Carl, but did you get in touch with Robert?" "He said he was already on the way to see you, and he is calling a friend who is a neurosurgeon to come out too."

Grace said, "Carl, if I have something really bad, promise me you will take care of Karla, Sarah will help you any way possible, but I think you knew she would. Thank you and Carl, try not to worry so much. Please don't go back to your desert; I need you here with Karla." Carl said, "Sis, I'm not even close to the desert; trust me, since Sarah said she would help out, I feel on a more even keel. No one is upset; I told Karla that mommy had a real bad headache and Sarah was a grown up and could help mommy more than he could right now."

Carl told Karla to bring the doctor to your room and then to rest awhile; that Sarah or I or both will be close by. About that time the doorbell rang and Carl could tell that Karla was on her crutches and was already at the door and inviting him in. Karla said, "This is mommy's room, but be quiet, her head hurts really bad." "I'll be quiet, Karla, but another doctor, named Dr. Pierce is close behind me; would you please let him in and show him your mommy's room?" "Yes," Karla answered.

Dr. Robert was checking Grace's eyes and face. He said; "Grace, can you see?" She said, "Yes, but everything is fuzzy." "Well, Daniel Pierce is right behind me and Karla will show him your room; however, she will also tell him to be quiet, mommy's head hurts a lot." Grace smiled and said; "Robert, this nice lady who is helping me keep my head up is named Sarah." Sarah looked at him and said; "Thanks for putting me back together." "Sarah I just recognized you. You look much better and I understand from Grace you will be a house guest for a while. That's a good idea." Sarah smiled and said, "Thank you."

In a moment the doorbell rang and they could hear Karla tell Dr. Pierce that she was expecting him; come in and I'll show you mommy's room, but you must be quiet because her head hurts a lot. "I will Karla, Thank you."

Robert said; "Daniel this is Carl, Grace's brother and he can get an ambulance or chopper in moments if needed." Dr. Pierce looked at Sarah and said; "Young lady, let Robert take your place; you look like you need to lie down." Robert said; "I'm sorry Sarah, I should have paid more attention, You and Carl go take a rest and I will let Carl know of anything we might need." Carl said; "Thanks."

Carl took Sarah's arm and helped her to his room. He told Karla to go take her rest now. "I'll be here if the doctors need anything." "Okay," Karla replied and let out a big yawn.

"Sarah; I'm certainly not a good host, please forgive me, but I hadn't noticed how fatigued you are." "Carl, please know this, I'm fine, except a bit tired, but you are very pale and I'm afraid for you. Please lie beside me and rest if you can; I'm not sleepy, just tired." Carl looked at her and said; "Sarah, I am afraid and I hate to admit that, but Grace is my sister and I'm afraid they will have to do surgery on her. I would like to lie beside you, and if you don't mind, may I hold your hand while resting?" Sarah took his hand in her rather smaller hand, but it was warm and comforting to Carl. He could feel himself begin to relax a bit. Sarah rubbed his hand and arm and it felt like a gently massage. He hadn't realized it, but he had one arm around Sarah, but he heard footsteps and sat up straight and rigid. Sarah said, "I think it is one of the doctors, Carl." He looked at her rather strangely for a moment; and then said; "You are probably right; thank you Sarah, I felt like I was relaxed because of your gentle massage. I'm fine now."

Carl opened the door before the doctor could knock. He said; "How is she, should I call my squad or a chopper?"

Dr. Pierce said, "I think she will be fine, but I need her to go to the hospital for another MRI. Could you perhaps have a chopper that could have a number of pillows to hold her up and I'll meet you at the hospital." Carl called Lucas. "Lucas, I need a real favor; Grace has had some sort of set back and the neurosurgeon and Robert have suggested she go back to the hospital on a chopper. They wanted something to keep her head upright; but I can fit in the chopper and hold her head up. I know you have the week off too and Molly may need you, but I don't know a pilot I trust like you."

Lucas said, "Is there enough room to land my chopper at your place?" "Yes, but we will need you to land on a slight elevation with grass on it." "That's no problem; I'll be there in about seven minutes." "Sarah will look after Karla while I'm gone?"

Lucas told Molly that Carl's sister was in trouble and he needs me to chopper her to the hospital. I can land it on a small hill with grass covering it. Molly said, "Darling, I'm fine, and so is Luke; and you do remember if needed, I'll call 911." Lucas bent down to kiss his wonderful wife and asked her to pray for Grace and Carl. She said, "Of course, now go. I love you."

Lucas got the chopper up in about one minute; he always ran a quick check on all parts. He got to Carl's and landed on the hill. He was going to help Carl bring her out, but two doctors were helping him. Carl got in at the end of the patient section and they placed Grace in the patient's space and there was enough room for Carl to hold his sister's head up. They got to the hospital before the neurosurgeon did, but a neurosurgical partner was already there. He told the ER staff what type stretcher he needed and reminded them to call all OR staff in, as well as the x-ray crew. They were already there on stand-by. Very quickly Dr. Pierce and Robert came into the ER and went with Grace for an MRI. Robert said, "Carl I'll hold her head through the MRI and you can take a little break. I will let you know anything and everything that happens." Carl looked at him and shook his head yes, kissed Grace on the cheek and left.

He found Lucas still in the ER and told him all he knew at the moment. "They are doing another MRI and Robert will keep me posted. We were sitting at the dinner table, having lunch and Grace had eaten about half of her sandwich and put her hand to her head and asked Sarah to help her to bed and help hold her head up. Sarah is a God-Send; she isn't feeling the best, but she is with Karla and I'm at ease about that."

"What is eating my inside out is that Grace looked at me and said; Carl, if something serious is wrong, look after Karla. She didn't think I saw her fear, but she can't see well Lucas. Karla is taking a nap and Sarah is with her. I will forever be in your debt, Lucas, and I don't know how to thank you." "Carl, listen to me, Molly and I have been praying since you called and I don't think God will take Grace away from her little girl or big brother. You owe me nothing except to be my friend, and I don't ask that lightly." Carl shook his head and said; "Nevertheless, I do thank you. Now you better get back to Mollie and tell her how much I appreciate her prayers. I'll keep you posted on Grace." He turned and went back toward the x-ray department and Lucas took the chopper home and gave it a good inspection.

He went in to see Molly and told her what had happened. Molly said; "I feel at peace about Grace, but we still need to pray for Carl." "I do too, Molly. He said that Grace looked at him and said, 'Carl, please don't go back to the desert, I need you to care for Karla if something serious happens to me'. That is about the only time I've seen Carl's mask slip." "Yes, my dearest, we all wear one; not one of us could stand for anyone to see too deeply inside."

"Do you think I should give David a call? I know David is a praying man. I heard him one night (he doesn't know) and he was talking to God like his best friend. He said, Father, You know I wanted to be a minister for You, but You also know that can't happen now; however, thank You for the job as a First Responder, I can still be of service."

Molly said, "Lucas that is a wonderful idea and you can bet he will pray without letting the world know what shape Carl is in." Lucas picked up his personal phone and called David; there was no answer, so he called the cell phone they all carried. David, said, "Hello, how can I help you?" Lucas said, "David, I'm asking you to pray for Carl. His sister took a backward turn and he is really afraid. The woman he is so interested in is staying at their house and watching Karla. He isn't worried about them, but he really is about Grace. He called me to chopper her to hospital; her dear friend (who I think will be her husband) was on the way over when Grace said;

'Carl, I think you had better call Robert'. A neurosurgeon followed Robert to the house and that's when Carl called me to use the chopper."

David said, "Consider it done.  God will not let Grace leave her little girl or her big brother.  Carl is a believer, but feels unworthy to ask God to take care of everything. I've known him a bit longer than you have and he was so traumatized in the desert; he still has severe flashbacks.  His fear often comes out as anger. I'll pray now, are you and Molly all right?" "Yes, thanks David."  He hung up and told Molly the same thing that he told her when he called me that night.

# Carl Goes Back to the Hospital

Meanwhile, back at the hospital, Carl began to feel more relaxed and not very fearful at all. God I thank You for taking care of Grace and the surgeons. Lord, You are our Creator and the Lover of our soul. Thank again for caring for Grace and thank You for Lucas and Molly. You are God Almighty and there is no God but You. I praise You.

In a rather short time to the surgeons, not the neurosurgeons, and Robert came out smiling and gave Carl a bear hug. "She is going to be fine; praise the LORD!" He was almost crying when he told Carl that there was a slight bleed and keeping her head up was the best thing he could have done. "I know Grace is the best nurse and woman I know, but you didn't argue with her, just did what she asked. Thank you, Carl."

Carl actually smiled and asked; "Well if she will be all right, what did you all do to make her all right?"

Daniel and his partner put a burr hole in the perfect place and could actually aspirate the small clot. "She will have to stay in the hospital for a few days to insure another clot doesn't form, but, I've hugged her and she asked how you were doing. I told her I didn't know, but I would come find you so you two can see one another." Carl said; "Well, let's go see her." "I forgot to tell you that her head is in what you might think looks like a medieval torture instrument, but it actually only looks awful. It is doing a job."

By the time they got to Grace, her face was a bit swollen, but she looked beautiful to Carl and he knew his sister was a fighter. "Carl, it wasn't so bad after all, thank God. I'll be up here for a few days and you and Robert must make some arrangement for Karla to see me. I really don't want her to see the 'bonnet', but she will probably find it most interesting. Now, give me a kiss and go tell Karla and Sarah all about it." He dutifully kissed his sister and said; "Yes dear." Carl left the hospital and felt such relief and gratitude. He got home and told Karla and Sarah everything that he could remember about Grace. He said, "She looks great, but her face is swollen a little. Sarah, the doctors told me that you holding her head up kept it from having a larger bleed. Thank you."

Karla was trying to dance around, and asked quite quickly when Uncle Carl finished talking with Sarah when they could see mommy. "Sarah and I did everything you told us too and Sarah did more; she cleaned the kitchen, but she let me help a little. So we both want to see her and tell her we have missed her, and that I've been good, and so has Sarah."

Carl said; "That you have, but we'll have to wait for Robert to get it arranged." Karla said; "Well I hope it isn't too long, because Sarah and I want to see her, don't we Sarah?" "Yes, but, perhaps Uncle Carl and I had better make her room neat and tidy and change the linens. I can then wash them and take a rest with you. You have been up on your crutches a pretty long while, you know." Karla; said, "Well I'd be glad to help, but my head hurts a little bit and my legs are tired; would you want to rest with me or on Uncle Carl's bed?" Sarah answered; "I think I'll rest in the other room, but thank you so much." "No problem," Karla answered.

Carl looked closely at Karla and realized she was tired and probably need a dose of the medicine the doctor had prescribed. He told Karla that he felt like she needed to take some medicine and rest and he would rest on the couch after he and Sarah finished with mommy's room. "That's fine," Karla replied.

Carl gave Karla a dose of medicine and picked her up and took her to her bed. She said; "Thanks, Uncle Carl, I think I'm sleepy and I know Sarah must be too and the doctor said he would call you, didn't he?" "Absolutely, and I'll get you up." "Well, good evening," she said. It seemed only a few minutes until she was fast asleep.

Carl went out and told Sarah; "We'll have plenty of time to tidy Grace's room. I'm as near exhaustion as I can remember being. Would you mind if I lie beside you and rest with you?" "Carl, of course not, I like you being close, it makes me feel safe." They both lay down on Sarah's bed and Carl turned over and kissed her and she kissed him back. He looked a bit surprised and held her very gently and closed his eyes. He was tired, but he knew Sarah was near a breaking point too; She said, "Thank you, Carl," but Sarah doubted he heard her. He was really 'on the edge', but oddly, she felt more relaxed and comfortable just lying with him.

In a few minutes, she heard Carl sound asleep and she was gently massaging his arm and hand. He seemed relaxed and really asleep. Sarah lay with him for about an hour and she dosed off, but Carl was still asleep, as well as, Karla. They all rested approximately three hours. It was getting a little late, but Sarah was afraid to move out of bed and begin any dinner. She might awaken Carl and she knew how much he needed rest. She thanked God for this good man and for what they had all done for her. She felt 'at home' with all three of them. She definitely wanted to get to know Carl more, but that would be on his choosing, if he ever did.

In about ten more minutes, Carl's phone rang, and he put his hand in his pocket and said; "This is Carl." He then realized his other arm was around Sarah and seemed a bit shocked. The doctor told Carl that they would be able to see Grace a little while tomorrow. She needed to stay fairly quiet tonight and maybe for a few more days. She told Robert to tell Carl to make sure that Karla was all right and was fed well. Carl told the doctor to tell her that he was already doing that and he expected Grace to be obedient and obey the doctors. Sarah could hear Robert say; "Boy, I bet the two of you were always looking out for one another, but Grace says you are bossy." "Tell her I am still bossy and that I love her and we are all fine here. Call me when we can see her tomorrow."

Carl reached over and hugged Sarah and asked, "Did I lay on you or just have my arm around you." "You kept your arm around me and I felt safe and comfortable. Did you, Carl?" "You know Sarah, I really did rest and I appreciate you staying with me. Are you in any discomfort?" "Absolutely not; what would make you think such a thing? Oh, Carl I'm sorry for the way I look, but it seems to be fading and nothing was broken except my nose and it is straight now." Carl interrupted her and said; "You look beautiful to me and I don't want to frighten you away, but I'm fairly sure

I actually love you. I've looked at your behavior with all your guests and with Karla and Grace. You don't seem afraid of me, although you realize I sometimes have severe flashbacks of the desert and I would never want to hurt you or frighten you."

Sarah said, "Carl, I'm not in any way afraid of you, in fact, I'm a bit embarrassed because I have rather deep feelings for you as a man who is caring and good. Who took a perfect stranger into your home and Grace and Karla and you have made me feel very comfortable and not at all like I'm intruding."

Carl felt his own heart melting even more; he already knew he loved Sarah, but was waiting to ensure she was ready to know him better and was emotionally strong. He had dated plenty of women, but he kept everything on a very superficial level, even sex. He did not feel by Sarah that way. He glanced at his watch and asked Sarah if she remembered if he called Lucas? "I simply don't remember. But, I believe you did, however, it wouldn't hurt to let him know how she is doing. "I'll go check on Karla." Karla must have been one tired little girl; she was sound asleep. Sarah went into the kitchen and looked in the refrigerator and freezer to see what she could prepare for supper. She found some pork chops, frozen beans and corn, and the makings for a salad.

She also saw a chocolate cake (must have been from last night). She put the chops out and baked some sweet potatoes, and started to make some biscuits to bake later. She put the chops in some buttermilk with plenty of seasoning and let them soak a few minutes until they were thawed. Then she opened the small bag of corn and beans and mixed them together, pepper, salt, butter and a few other spices that she enjoyed with them. She thought Karla would really like that. Maybe Carl would too. Grace kept a well-stocked kitchen and still had some fresh vegetables, so Sarah made some cabbage slaw.

She got some flower for the biscuits and to cover the chops for frying and measured out the ingredients for biscuits. The potatoes were almost baked and the chops were almost thawed as well. She knocked gently on the door of Carl's room; he had lay back across the bed and seemed asleep. She went into the room quietly and planned to ask him if he was hungry, but she turned around and was about to leave, when he said; "Come over here, Sarah," and she did. He stood up and put his arms around her and kissed her gently at first and them more deeply. "What did you need sweetheart?" "Nothing," Sarah answered, "I am making dinner and was going to tell you what I'm making, but I thought you were asleep. Karla is taking a long nap, because I've already checked on her." "Well, I would appreciate dinner, but I'd really like to hold you a while and maybe a little hugging and kissing." Sarah smiled and said; "That would be very nice." Soon Carl felt himself about to lose control. He said, "Maybe we better go check on the cooking." Sarah smiled and said, "Yes, we'd better."

They held hands and went to the kitchen for her to finish dinner. He washed his hands at the kitchen sink and said; "I'll set the table." Sarah began the biscuits and put them in the oven, and took the sweet potatoes out and laid them on a rack to cool. She then made the slaw and put it in a bowl. She checked the corn and beans and although they were done, she simply turned them off. She then dredged the pork chops (she already had the oil hot) and fried them. They smelled wonderful. She then peeled the sweet potatoes and sliced them and put a few cherry tomatoes around the platter. Then she put the corn and beans in a bowl and checked the biscuits. They were almost browned and ready to eat.

# Lucas and Molly Prepare To Move

Carl had called Lucas and told him about Grace and thanked him again. Lucas awoke the first time the phone rang and answered; Lucas here. He sounded hoarse and said, "Carl, I've been sound asleep. I guess I'm tired more than I thought." Carl said; "I just wanted to tell you about Grace and thank you again." Lucas said, "No problem."

About that time, Luke made himself known. He was definitely hungry and wet and not at all happy. Too bad, Lucas thought to himself. He got a damp cloth and changed him and put fresh pajamas on him, but he never stopped yelling. Molly had stretched and got up to go to the bathroom. She washed her hands and breasts and got back onto the bed. "Thanks, Lucas." She took the baby and he latched onto her breast as though he had never had anything to eat. He finished the first and Molly transferred him to the other breast. When he finished, he just quit. He began to look around and finally Lucas said; "Did you get enough to eat big boy?"

It was later than Lucas thought and he knew he and Molly needed to have dinner. He went into the kitchen and ordered a nice dinner to be delivered as soon as it was ready. He had already checked to see if Molly had lemon sorbet, she did, but he ordered another box. He and Molly played with Luke for a little while and Molly said, "Lucas I need to go to the bathroom for a quick wash, would you watch him while I'm gone?" "Absolutely my love. I love you. I've already ordered dinner, sweetheart. I know neither of us should cook tonight." "Thank you, love."

The food came and Molly and Lucas ate and it was delicious. Lucas showed her that he had more Sorbet and Molly smiled and said that sounds good, but a little later. They too had made a pallet on the floor for Luke to play on and use his rattle or anything he could hold. Molly was amazed when he picked up a small truck and waved it and threw it. "Lucas did you see that?" Lucas started laughing and said; "I sure did; he will be a big man like his daddy and Uncle Michael."

"It sure looks like it to me." They all three stayed in the living room and Molly said; "Lucas, what is today?" "It's Wednesday night." "Oh good, we can have another few days to get things a little more organized here. You also may need some sleep and I will too, while Luke sleeps." Lucas began to laugh and said, "Count on it my darling."

# David and Sheila Decide to Marry

David woke up and for a moment didn't remember where he was. Then, he felt an unfamiliar weight beside him and someone was touching him. He immediately became fully awake and realized his dear Sheila had slept all night right beside him. He wanted desperately to hug and kiss her, but knew that would frighten her. He got up and eased out of bed and went to the bathroom off her other bedroom. He washed his hands and face and wet combed his short hair with his hands.

He went back into the livingroom and sat on the couch and just waited until she awoke. He had decided to propose to her today and make her aware that he really loved her, no matter her past. He will remind her that God has forgiven anything she did in the past. He took this time to really talk with his Heavenly Father and thank Him for this new day and for salvation for Sheila. He asked God to please make him aware of the time and way to talk with Sheila in order to help her begin to grow in her Christian walk. He prayed for all the First Responders and for Grace. He was thankful that Lucas called him last night. He would go outside and call Lucas around dinnertime. That way, he would not interrupt them in working on their house.

In a few minutes, he heard Sheila moving about in her room. He heard her talking to herself, he thought and realized she was unaware he was there and she must be praying. He listened a while and she said, "Well, Heavenly Father, I don't know what to say except thank You." Then her tone changed and she asked herself; "Wonder what happened to David?"

David went to the door and said; "Did you call me?" David smiled at her and said; "I heard you talking and thought perhaps you wondered what was happening?" Sheila smiled and said, "Good morning or evening or whatever." "I think it is nearer dinner." Sheila asked; "David, did I ask Jesus into my heart last night?" "Yes you did, sweetheart." Sheila said; "I thought so, I'm at ease this morning and I know you slept with me, because, once I got up to go to the bathroom and you were fully clothed, lying right beside me." David said; "I sure did and I enjoyed it so much."

Sheila went over and gave David a big hug and kiss; and told him thank you for staying with her. David hugged her back and realized she had no bra on under her sweats. He said; "It's getting toward evening and I think we need some food." Sheila laughed and said; "Is you tummy pinching?" "Yes it is, and I bet yours is as well." "As a matter of fact, I'm just plain hungry." "Well why don't you get dressed and if you can stand me in wrinkled clothes we will have a good meal."

Sheila said; "Great, I'll be back in a few minutes." She went into the bathroom and took a quick shower and put on some make-up, dressed in slacks and another light sweater.

She had shampooed her hair earlier yesterday morning and only needed to comb it. When she finished she came out and David stood up and whistled. "You look great!" "Thank you, kind sir." David asked her; "Where she would like to go?" And she replied, "Most anywhere with real food." David helped her into the car and they went a way out into the country and found a nice restaurant. They went inside and the look was similar to a log cabin, but at the same time, modern. They had been seated and a menu was brought to them. Sheila looked at the menu and she wanted 'Surf and Turf', steamed vegetables and a green salad and extra water. David ordered steak and eggs, potato fries, and turnips mixed with kale. They ate and enjoyed it very much. David told Sheila to order a dessert and coffee and she did; key lime pie and coffee; he ordered cherry pie and coffee.

They both realized about the same time, that they had not talked very much at all. David said; "Sheila did I do something to offend you; you've been so quiet today and you usually are so bubbly and talkative?" "Oh no David, it seems my 'inside me' is so light and airy, I'm unaccustomed to this. I recognize that I really care about you, as a person and man that

I can trust. This is so unusual. I have to get used to not feeling fear or anxiety. I guess I am a little anxious, because this is so unusual."

David asked; "Do you remember that you asked Jesus into your heart last night?" "Of course; and He is still there."

"David, did you know that Jesus is real and He really does make me less fearful?" David asked; "Do you remember that I told you I really love you and want to marry you last night?" "Yes, but I didn't quite believe you or understand you; but you know, David, I think (no I'm fairly sure) that I love you too"! But, "David, suppose I make a mistake and you turn to hate me; I know Jesus is still here, but I think that would hurt me a lot." David said; "Sheila, there is no way you could make me hate you; you understand Jesus took my hatred away. However, I do have flashbacks of things that happened in the Navy and I definitely felt hatred toward those people at that time; but when I awake and realize where I am, I immediately ask God too remove my hatred and forgive my unforgiving spirit. He does too!"

"Have you finished eating?" "Certainly, I guess I was so busy talking to you, I forgot about food, but as you can see, one doesn't have to think to eat." She started laughing and so did David. "Well, I'd like to take you somewhere today and it is a surprise, but a nice surprise." "Okay, when?" "Now, Sweetheart."

David paid the bill and as usual, Sheila had to go to the bathroom. When she came out, David was waiting with a big smile on his face. They got into the car and David started driving along the country road, she saw a pretty lake, and David took that exit. They got out of the car and David took her hand and they walked down to the lake. He found a stump of a tree right beside the lake and sat her on it; he then got down on one knee and said; "Sheila, I love you and I'm asking you to marry me." Sheila looked at him and said; "I would like to marry you, thank you, David". David stood her up and hugged and kissed her for a good while, he then said, "I have to step back a minute, sweetheart." She started laughing and said, "Thank you." David asked; "When do you think we could get married?" "David, I don't know a minister, but I would like to be married by one, and I would like it very simple." David saw that the sun was just beginning to go down and dusk was fast approaching; he said; "Sheila, I have a wonderful pastor and if I call him, we could see him and the Church tonight or tomorrow." "That would be wonderful, David. I need to go to work tomorrow, so do you think he would see us tonight?" David took his phone and called his Pastor and asked if he and his lovely finance could come over to see him? The Pastor said; "Of course, David, come on over."

David smiled at Sheila and said; "Let's' go see him and you decide if you like him and we will probably get a chance to see the Church." Sheila kissed him and stepped back and told him to, 'let's get on the road'. She and David went back to the car and drove only a short distance until Sheila saw a small Church and a house beside it. They drove up into the driveway and David got out and helped her out of the car. He rang the doorbell and Pastor Jenkins came to the door. He immediately asked them inside and David introduced him to Sheila. They shook hands and he invited them to sit and talk to him a while. They did. David said; "Pastor, you know everything about me, but I wanted you to see the woman I love." Pastor Jenkins smiled at Sheila and said: "You must be a special young woman, in fact I know you are, because as David said; I know quite a bit about him. I would like to know you, as well." Sheila said; "Pastor Jenkins, I am a nurse who works primarily in the ER and met David when he came in and introduced himself. He is a First Responder and quite frankly, I did not know why he came to see me. David knows my history and loves me anyway. The most important thing is that David told me about Jesus and how He loves me and will always love me. I asked Jesus to come into my heart and cleanse all the hatred and fear away; you know what? He did! I awoke this morning feeling very light inside and clean. Can you imagine that?" "Oh yes, Sheila, I well know it too, just as David does." "Well what else do you need to know?" Pastor Jenkins said; "Nothing, except when you all want me to do this marriage."

David said; "Pastor, we've just a while ago decided for sure; I haven't had a doubt about my love for Sheila, but she has had some very bad experiences with her first husband. He was killed in Iraq, but she had already planned a divorce, because of his abuse. I know she hates he got killed as so many of our Service People have, but she made no secret to me that she did not believe in love; although, she knows there is a God. She had experienced things in the ER that only God could do. We do appreciate you talking with us, and I will keep you posted on a date; however, could we look at the Church or is it too late?" "David, It is only eight thirty; of course you can see the Church." They walked over the lawn and up to the small Church and Pastor opened the door. It was indeed quite beautiful. "Do you mean we can actually use this for you to marry us in?" "Sheila, our people are loving and kind and I don't need to ask; the answer is yes!"

David started to shake his hand and Sheila reached over and hugged his neck. David said, "My little red-head is indeed impulsive when she is not afraid of someone. Thank you, James. Good night."

David and Sheila went back to her house and he asked her to get a calendar and they could set a tentative date, but she would need to take a couple weeks off for preparations and a honeymoon. Sheila hugged him and said; "That's no problem, I work almost all the time, and when I ask for time off, it is always granted. Do you mind if I tell some of the friends at the ER and also tell Grace?" "If you don't, I'll be disappointed, not angry, I just want the world to know I love you and you have agreed to become my wife."

They looked at the calendar and Sheila said; "You know, I think these two weeks would be great. That will give my supervisor time for my replacement and I can look for a dress and some things I need. Plus, I can talk to the girls at work about a wedding cake and florist, since I don't have a clue. David, I didn't ask the Pastor about the Reception Room for a small reception. Do you think you could do that?" David said; "I don't remember much else about a wedding, so I'll need your help and definite input." "I've told you, I would like it simple, but I didn't even ask you what you want." David said; "I simply want to marry you anyway you wish. Remember that I have to speak with the Captains regarding time off, as well. I think after the three weeks of training that I'm committed to, for our new recruits, there will be no problem." Sheila said; "That will be perfect, five weeks from now." "Great," David responded, and almost kissed them both senseless. "Whoa, David." Sheila started laughing and said, "Whoa, Sheila."

# Lucas and Molly Move to Their New Home

Lucas and Molly had done quite a bit of packing and had already made the house ready for Michael and Lucy. They had filled the refrigerator and freezer with food and made the beds with fresh linens. They were now ready to tackle Lucas' house, but not too much tonight. Molly had to feed Luke and Lucas got the ATV ready for them to go on over to his house. He was sure he had made his bed with fresh linen and there were plenty of towels and bathroom needs.

When Lucas brought the ATV around to the front door, Molly and Luke were waiting. He noticed that Molly was tired and ready for food and bed. He phoned ahead and ordered dinner for them both, helped Molly and Luke in the car, and went by the restaurant to pick up their dinner. Molly looked at him and said; "Thank you, Lucas, I am tired and hungry and I know you must be, because I don't remember if I fixed us a sandwich or not for lunch." "You did, but we both need a good dinner and hot bath and bedtime. I'm a little worried that you look so tired." "Well, Lucas I am, but I will be glad to have Luke down for the night and have dinner. I would love a shower and I expect you would too. Then we can get a good rest tonight and begin again tomorrow."

Lucas said; "Molly, this is our house now and we can do what we want, when we want, and not be rushed. I don't expect us to be totally settled for some time, but we will get it comfortable and presentable before I have to go back to work. When I do go back to work, I expect you to rest morning and afternoon when Luke does. By the way, you are to see the doctor tomorrow; I had almost forgotten." Molly said, "Lucas, I had forgotten, so I'm really glad to be home, so we can take our time."

Molly put Luke in his crib and he was down for the night, or early in the morning. She put dinner out and she and Lucas sat down and had a good dinner. Lucas said, "You get your shower first and take the time you need. I'll shower in the other bedroom." "Okay," she said.

They both took a warm shower and Molly put her gown on and Lucas put a tee shirt on and soft flannel pants. They went to bed and Lucas held Molly and reminded her of how much he loved her. She replied, "Lucas I love you too and you feel good lying beside me. This bed is comfortable and I'm already relaxing, but I might need half of a pain pill. My stomach muscles are still sore and I want us to have a good night of sleep." Lucas said, "That's a good idea, sorry I didn't think of that before." He got up and got her half pill and glass of juice and they both lay back down. Lucas continued to hold Molly and rub her back and stomach ever so gently. She was soon asleep and had no idea that he had rubbed her tummy. He could feel the small incision line and realized she probably did too much stretching today. He held her close and they both went to sleep.

Luke woke them up the next morning fairly early; as usual wanting his breakfast and dry clothing. Lucas got up and got a warm damp cloth and wiped Luke down and put a clean diaper on him and some fresh pajamas. He didn't know what Molly would want him to wear when she went to the doctor. Lucas got a clean, warm and damp cloth for Molly to wipe her breasts down and she got ready to feed Luke, who was not happy to have to wait on his breakfast. Lucas started to laugh; "It seems our son is a rather impatient little guy, he likes his food." Molly smiled and said, "He's acting like he hasn't had food; he has almost emptied this one breast and shows little sign of stopping." She switched him to the other arm and breast and he continued to eat. He was soon finished and babbled at his mommy and got milk all over her face. Lucas smiled and got her another cloth to wipe her own face and Luke.

Lucas went to make some coffee and warm some muffins he had picked up yesterday for their breakfast. Molly came in with Luke in her arms and sipped her coffee and smiled at Lucas. "Thank you, Lucas for all the help and coffee and muffins. Everything is good. I'll need to change soon and get ready to go to the doctor. Do you mind holding Luke; he doesn't seem to want his crib." Lucas picked him up and they began to talk. Lucas told him what a good boy he was and Luke just babbled and seemed to agree. Molly smiled and went to get dressed for the doctor's appointment.

After she had dressed, put her hair up and put some make-up on; she came back to the kitchen. Lucas and Luke had left and were somewhere in the house. She went to the room that Lucas said Luke would like and he was showing Luke his new room. Luke seemed fine with any situation, now that his tummy was full. Molly decided to put a one-pieced outfit on him and prepared the diaper bag with some water and formula in case Lucas needed it before she got out of the doctor's office.

Dr. Corbin came in to check Molly and commented on how well she looked. "You don't seem to need any additional blood, but you know how you feel better than I on that deal." "I think I'm fine," Molly replied. "Then, let's check out your pelvis and stomach muscles." Molly flinched when he pressed on her stomach muscles. He said, "Molly everything looks great, but are your muscles still that sore?" Molly said; "Yes, but not from having Luke; Lucas and I have done some moving into our new home – no, I have not lifted anything, but I didn't rest much yesterday; however I slept wonderfully well last night. I mostly dusted the furniture and checked and made a list of the groceries we would need. Lucas has done all the lifting and heavier work, as well as, told me to rest. Well, I didn't think I needed to rest. Luke is eight weeks old and his doctor said he was just the right size for his age and height and was probably a full-term baby. He thought we had miscalculated conception; he is probably right." Dr. Corbin checked Molly real well and said, "Everything looks fine. You can have sex and resume some light lifting, but nothing too heavy; like over twenty-five pounds." "Thank you," Molly replied. He left and wrote on her chart and Molly got dressed and went to the exit window. "Dr. Corbin wants to see you again in six weeks. I'll give you an appointment card." "Thanks," Molly responded and went to the lobby to find that Lucas and Luke were doing fine. She said; "Lucas, I've got a clean bill of health and can now lift up to twenty-five pounds and most anything I want; however, I should still rest a while in the afternoons."

Since Carl had needed him to get Grace to the hospital in the chopper, Lucas felt bad about having to leave Molly. She had a clean bill of health for which he was grateful, but she still needed rest. He came into the house and went to their room. Molly was in bed and seemed to have rested.

"Molly, my love, I've neglected you some today and I'm sorry. I want to spend as much time as I can with you." "Lucas, we are married, that makes us one. By the way, I'm healed now and we can make love whenever we want." "Not yet honey, I have no protection to keep you from getting pregnant. It is much too early for another baby." "Is that what you've been waiting for?" "Well, yes, and to get somewhat settled in our home." Molly smiled and said, "The doctor took care of that while I was in the hospital." "He did?" Lucas looked strangely at Molly and said; "I haven't given you a pill since you've been home." "Darling Lucas, I should have told you, but you know I haven't been up to standards for a while, but now I am. The doctor inserted these measured doses of birth control under my left arm. Give me your hand," and she put his hand on the long strips that were under the skin underneath her upper arm.

"Does that mean you are ready, emotionally and physically?" Lucas prayed again for Carl and Grace and then he thanked God for Molly and Luke and for her thoughtfulness. Although she had been ready for several days, she did not think he was. He had tried very hard not to get carried away with kissing and hugging her. He showered and dried off and put on underwear and came out to find her making room in the bed for him. He smiled and lay down beside her and took her in his arms. She was so little, what if he hurt her? He couldn't take that chance; he said, "Molly I love you, but when it is time to make love, I need you on top, because I'm so much bigger than you."

"Darling you don't have to explain anything to me. Besides, what if you are asleep and I want you again; rather than waking you first I can simply get on top of you and start hugging and kissing you." Lucas started laughing; "You are sure of your feelings, aren't you?" (Molly had immediately striped his underwear off); "Yep, now give me a kiss." He did and held her so close and they kissed and petted for a good bit. He said in a husky voice, "Can I feel your breasts?" "Yes, but sometimes they leak and I haven't put a little pad on the nipples." "That's not a problem." Lucas kissed her deeply and fondled her breasts and kissed them. There was a drop of milk, which he simply took on his tongue. "Did you know your milk is sweet?" "No, but most new mothers who are breast feeding say it is." He started kissing her again and said; "Molly, could I lift you on top now?" "Yes, but I'll help."

Lucas lifted her up and hugged and kissed her again and again. "Are you ready, darling?" "Yes, how do I handle this?" He smiled at her and said, "Just sit down." Molly did and he felt so good and his stomach and chest. She said, "Which way do I move and Lucas showed her with her buttocks and his slight movement. Molly shivered and asked Lucas, What in the world was that?" Lucas said; "It's your orgasm." "Well, I know, as a nurse that women have an orgasm, but I haven't." Lucas hugged and kissed her and moved a bit more vigorously and she shivered again and she felt his release.

Lucas continued to hold her and massage her back and buttocks and her breasts. "Molly you are a gift from God above. Not only have you married me and let me be Luke's real dad, but you've shown more than you know. Luke's biological father hadn't a clue or concern with your feelings. That you could have an orgasm or maybe two shows me that you really understand love in every way. I thank you for that." Lucas kept holding Molly and kissing and massaging her and soon, Molly could feel his arousal. Molly said, "Lucas I love you and I want to do some kissing now." "That's wonderful, but don't move too much, I'm about as aroused as before." "Well, that is just okay, I'll move when I want to," and she did, and again an orgasm and release almost at the same time. "You little imp, I have no control when it comes to you. You are my dearest love." "You are mine too," and she laid her head on his chest. It wasn't long before Lucas felt her relax totally and he noticed the little imp was asleep. Lucas prayed; "Thank You, Heavenly Father for this wonderful woman and for Your Great Love for us all". Soon Lucas was asleep too. He had pulled up some cover and then they both slept a long time.

# Carl Takes Karla and Sarah to visit Grace

Earlier DR. Knowles called Carl and told him that Grace would be able to see her daughter and him, as well as Sarah about two o'clock. He told Karla and Sarah they could see Grace and might stop and an early lunch before going to the hospital.

Karla was so excited; she almost danced and remembered that her leg was still sore. Sarah smiled at Carl and said, "That would be wonderful." Her own face has much less swelling, but the black, green and blue were present, but fading. She and Karla would get dressed and be ready when he thought they might leave to have lunch and see Grace.

Carl said; "There is something that Robert told me that you and Karla need to understand. Grace has her head in a contraption that looks like a medieval torture mechanism, but it is to help hold her head upright." Grace told him that she didn't want Karla nor Sarah upset at her "bonnet, but that Karla might find it interesting. "Oh, I will, you know I'm very interested in things I've never seen." Carl said, "Yes, I know sweetheart, but mommy was a little bit afraid that if I didn't tell you both, you might be worried."

About eleven o'clock, Sarah went into her room to dress and told Karla she would help her get dressed as soon as she could. Karla told Sarah and Uncle Carl she could dress herself, but might need some help because she still needed the crutches to stand well. "Fine," Sarah replied.

As soon as Sarah showered and dressed, she put some make-up on, but she could not cover all the various colors of her face, however, it made her feel better. She had also shampooed and dried her chestnut brown hair. It was rather long, but she wore it in an upsweep, because there would be nothing worse that having a hair in someone's dinner. She had practiced this since opening her restaurant and it had become a habit. She wore slacks and a lightweight sweater and flat shoes.

When she came out to go help Karla, Carl said, "Wow, I didn't know your hair was that color, it is quite beautiful and you look great." Sarah smiled and said, "Thank you, Carl." She went into Karla's room and Karla had done a good job of bathing (a bird-bath, mommy called it) and had her panties on and her clothing on the bed. She was sitting on the bed and waiting for Sarah to assist with the dress and one shoe she wore. Sarah combed Karla's hair that was blond like her mother and Uncle Carl, but she had blue-grey eyes, "Must have come from my daddy," she told Sarah. They were both dressed and went out to meet Carl. When he saw them he began to clap and said, "I have a lunch date with the two prettiest women I know and will see the third at two o'clock." Sarah and Karla laughed and said, "Thank you, and may we say that we have a nice looking gentleman taking us out." "You may," he laughed.

They went to get into the car and Karla reminded Sarah to take care of safety issues; you know, buckle your seat belt and sit up straight. "Oh, yes, thank you Karla," and smiled at her.

They had a good lunch at one of the small restaurants on the way to the hospital. Karla said, "Uncle Carl, I want one more good hamburger and fries before mommy tells me I must eat some fish and vegetables. I like those, but sometimes I really want a hamburger." Carl said, "Okay, I will too." Sarah spoke up and ordered the same; "Karla you know your mommy is right about a well-balanced diet." Karla replied, "Of course, but sometimes I just like a good ol' hamburger." Their food came and they began to eat and chat, well, Karla and Sarah chatted and Carl ate and listened.

Sarah said, "When I'm able to go to school to be a chef, I'll learn new ways to incorporate hamburgers within a balanced diet and when you all come to the restaurant, you will find it almost as good as a plain ol' hamburger. Karla, I'm really glad you showed me the schools rather near, in which I can become a real chef. That's been a goal of mine for a very long time. Karla, do you have your goals for life written down?" "Actually I do, but none are written "in stone" as mommy told me. Just write down your goals and when you are older, you can decide what you really want."

Carl spoke up and asked Karla what her goals were at this time. Karla replied, "Well, I'm really interested in becoming an electronic engineer, but I'm also interested in becoming a doctor who can specialize in helping our soldiers who have problems when they come home, often without limbs or eyes and the everyday stresses that causes them. However, I'm also interested in painting, like you, Uncle Carl, as well as writing. I seem to be interested in so much, it is hard to define at present; so that's why mommy said, 'write it all down' and you can decide when you're older. Uncle Carl, did you tell Sarah what a wonderful painter you are?" "No, Karla, I haven't told her much yet, but I will. We have all been concerned about each other, and the subject never came up."

Karla replied, "I understand that, but we are all better and mommy will be too. I say my prayers every night and ask God to be sure and watch over her while I'm asleep. I thanked Him for you, Sarah; you are a good friend and I think I've known you for 'just ages'." Sarah smiled at her and said, "Karla, that's one of the nicest things you could say to me. It really helps me, thank you."

They had finished their lunch and it was almost time to see Grace. Carl told the girls to go to the bathroom before we get to the hospital. "Okay," they both chimed together. While they were gone, Carl took care of the bill and tip and was waiting for them when they came out. "All ready?" "Yep!"

They got to the hospital and went upstairs to Grace's room. Karla said, "Hi mommy, we almost couldn't wait to see you, but Dr. Knowles said we must let you rest last night. Do you still have a bad headache? What is that thing on your head? It looks interesting, I'll get closer to see, but I won't touch it." Grace started smiling and said, "Karla, don't you think Uncle Carl could lift you up for a kiss on the cheek?" "Oh, I know he can, but I didn't know if that was allowed. The 'whatever' on your head is really interesting." Carl lifted Karla up and she kissed her mommy's cheek and said, "I love you, mommy and I've asked God every night to be with you, because I couldn't. God knows everything and He knows when I'm really worried about you or Uncle Carl or Sarah; when I ask Him to help all of you, well I just go to sleep."

Carl set her back on the floor and handed her the crutches. She walked around to the head of the bed and just looked. Meanwhile, Grace said, "Hello, Sarah, I knew I could rest so much better knowing that you would keep Carl and Karla in check. I really appreciate that." Carl had already kissed Grace's cheek. He told Grace what a good cook that Sarah was and they had her room ready when she could come home. "I hope you do so well that it won't be long." "I really think I am, Carl, my head hurts less and my vision is completely clear. Robert comes often and says, 'I really like your bonnet', but it won't be long before it can come off."

Karla said, "Hi, Dr. Knowles, did you see Sarah's face is better and I am as well, just sometimes mine hurts a little and Uncle Carl gives me that medicine you said I needed; but, you know what?" "What?" Robert asked her; "Well I just think you should hurry up and help mommy get well, I miss her and you fixed Sarah and me so well; I just wondered why you could not make mommy well sooner?" Robert was somewhat taken aback at this child's intelligence and reasoning ability. He said, "Well Karla, sometimes injuries may look similar, but they are very different inside the body." "Oh, I understand that," "Did you notice this contraption on mommy's head?" "Yes, I did;" but before Robert could go further, Karla said, "One of my goals is to be a doctor to help our wounded soldiers that come home. You realize that some of them hurt inside as well as outside."

Robert was still amazed at how God had gifted this little girl. He absolutely knew he loved her and her mother, but he didn't have a clue how to tell her. However, trying to remember and keep up with her questions, he finally answered, "Yes, Karla, I do know that, and you have a wonderful goal." Karla said, "Well that's only one of my goals; the others are to become an electronic engineer and possibly a physicist." "Whatever you decide on, you will succeed," he answered. "Well, that's not all, I also am very interested in painting like Uncle Carl, he paints so beautifully and I'm also interested in writing." "Well, Karla," Robert said, "You can do whatever you choose and even combine some of your goals." Karla answered, "You know, Dr. Knowles, I hadn't thought of that, thank you."

Carl said, "Karla, the rest of us haven't had much opportunity to talk with Robert; you know he fixed Sarah's head too. Let's let your mommy and Sarah talk a little while." "Okay," she replied and asked if she could sit in that chair over there? Robert said, "Certainly Karla, I'll help you in it and give your legs a rest." Robert looked at Grace, Carl, and Sarah and asked, "How do you manage?" Carl said, "It's easy, because of the love and wisdom some people have." Robert smiled at Grace and Carl and Sarah.

"Sarah is your face giving you any pain?" No, I just wish it wasn't quite so colorful," and they all got a chuckle. Robert said, "It will soon clear up."

Carl noticed how tired Karla was, as well as Sarah. He told Grace and Robert that he thought he might take the two of them home to rest a while. Grace said, "That's fine, Carl, but you and Sarah be sure that Karla doesn't hit you up for more hamburgers today. I could smell the one for lunch on her breath." Karla looked at Uncle Carl and mouthed, "Oh, my, I didn't brush after lunch." Grace said, "I know honey, but try to eat a few vegetables and salads." "I will, you know Sarah is a great cook and she believes in balanced diets as well." Carl gathered them up and kissed Grace and lifted Karla to kiss her mommy goodbye for now, and Sarah reached down and kissed Grace's cheek. "Thank you, Grace for the care you've shown me."

They got in the car and headed for home. Karla said, "Uncle Carl, I wanted to stay longer and look more at the 'bonnet' mommy calls that thing, but my head hurts a little bit and so does my leg." Carl said, "Karla, when we get home, I'll give you some medicine, and we will all three take a rest. I expect your mommy will too."

They got home and Carl carried Karla and asked Sarah if she could carry her crutches and of course she could. Carl gave Karla a drink of water and asked if she needed the bathroom, "Yes, I do," she replied. So Sarah handed the crutches to Karla and both 'girls' went to the bathroom. Then Karla was given the medicine and fairly soon went to sleep.

Carl said, "Sarah, would you be comfortable with me lying beside you; I've got something to talk with you about and I'm tired as well." "Of course, Carl, I feel safe when you are with me, wherever I am." They went into Sarah's room and lay on top of the covers and got comfortable. Carl said, "Sarah, I've told you before I love you, now, I'm asking you again to marry me. I'm not trying to pressure you, but please think about it. If you have feelings for me, I need to know, because I really want you for my wife." Sarah said, "Carl, I do love you, I wasn't sure before if it was love or gratitude; however, I dream about you, and my heart longs for you, but I too need to know if my past must all be revealed before we could get married? Some of it, I simply can't remember except it wasn't pleasant. Sometimes I go back to places I cannot remember and become very frightened and angry. When I awake, I realize it was only a dream."

"Sarah, our past is just that, 'the past'. I don't need to know anything that would make you uncomfortable in any way; I just want to know if you love me, warts and all, enough to marry me? I realize we are both wounded souls; I have seen your eyes, when your mask slipped, so I'm aware that past events still haunt us both; but do you love me?" "Yes, Carl, I do. Do we have to have a big wedding?" Carl kissed her deeply and she responded; then he said, "No, we don't; in fact, I wouldn't be comfortable with a large wedding unless you really wanted one." "Thank you, Carl, I love you dearly and I believe we can help one another and give each other space needed."

Sarah asked Carl if he knew a Pastor or Justice of the Peace who would marry them with only a few friends present. Carl said, "Grace, Karla and I go to the same Church and the Pastor there is a decent, caring man. I'll ask him if he could do a very simple ceremony with only family and a few friends around." This time Sarah reached over and kissed Carl. "That would be ideal. You know I haven't any close friends or family, but I would like Grace, Karla and perhaps your friends that are First Responders. They were so nice to me; after you left one evening; they both came to see me for themselves. Lucas did not talk much, but David did. He is a dedicated Christian, isn't he?" "Yes, I would trust him or Lucas with my life; they are good men who have been in difficult battles as well as you and I."

Carl and Sarah kissed and hugged a little while and Carl said, "Better stop a while." He kept his arm around Sarah and she fairly soon dozed off to sleep. Carl thanked God for Sarah and for the progress of Karla and Grace and asked Him to please put the right people in their lives. Carl was soon asleep. They all three rested about three hours and Carl and Sarah awoke almost at the same time. Sarah asked Carl if he had really asked her to marry him and he said, "Absolutely, and you said 'yes' and I hold you to that. I love you Sarah and I'd like to hear you say it once again." Sarah reached over and hugged and kissed Carl and said, "I love you!"

"Great!" They got up and started dinner and Carl said, "We'd better fix a more balanced meal than hamburger." Sarah said, "I can do that. Let me check the refrigerator and freezer and put a good dinner on the table." Carl hugged her and said, "I'll help."

Dinner was indeed good. Sarah found some fish fillets, broccoli, and salad makings. She also found some fruit and she would make a fruit salad as well. She broiled the fish fillets and made a lemon sauce, steamed the broccoli and made a green salad. She also made a fruit salad with small pieces of cheese to go with that for dessert. She had found a small angel food cake in the freezer and planned to put the fruit salad on top of a slice of cake. Carl set the table and by this time Karla was awake and in the kitchen with them. She said, "Wow, Sarah, you really are a good cook; everything is nice and balanced."

Later that evening, Carl took a walk out to his studio and simply looked at his canvasses. It had been a long while since he had a paintbrush in his hand, but a painting was in his head and had stayed a good while. He still had not prepared a canvas or really decided to paint, but he felt the urge to begin again when he had some weekends off.

He had his cell phone and called David. He told David that Sarah had agreed to marry him and that he was so glad. He asked David if Sheila was better and David said, "Yes, and she is a believer now. We talked to my Pastor the other evening and he has agreed to marry us. We both want it small and intimate in the little Church that I attend." "That's one reason I called you tonight, David. Sarah does not want a big wedding; only a small one with family and close friends. She has no family left and hasn't allowed herself to have close friends. David, you know as well as I, that some things a person is unable to recall or share. I simply know she loves me, for me and I definitely love her. Do you think it is possible for us to have a double wedding in your little Church, or is that asking too much David? I simply don't know; I know you and Lucas are closer to me than brothers, but I also like Molly's brother and his new wife. They are not back from their honeymoon."

"David said, Carl that is a wonderful idea, I want you to meet Sheila out of uniform – that's not what I meant – I mean in street clothes as a person instead of just a nurse. She is so dear to me and I can almost guarantee she would love a double wedding. She knows Grace and they have worked together and I think she would love to meet Sarah. I'll run the idea by her and see how she responds and get back with you. In the meantime, you need to check with Sarah to see if that might be agreeable with her."

"I will," Carl replied.

# David and Sheila Decide on a Double Ceremony with Carl and Sarah

Carl went back into the house and ensured Karla was down for the night and asked Sarah how she felt. "I'm fine, except a little tired." Carl asked if she minded if they slept on top of the covers in her room, he had something to talk with her about. "Of course, that would be great," Sarah replied. So Sarah got into sweat clothes without a bra and Carl put on a clean tee shirt and sweat pants. They lay down together and Carl reached over and kissed Sarah.

"You remember that you agreed to marry me?" "Yes, my dearest." "Well, I called David and asked him if it would be appropriate for us to have a double wedding in his small Church. He said he thought it was a great idea. Neither he nor Sheila want a big wedding. They already talked with his Pastor and he will marry them and have a small reception in the little reception room."

I asked him to run the idea by Sheila and he told me to find out what you thought. We all three (Lucas, David and me) will be tied up with training courses for the new recruits, so it will be about five weeks. "What do you think of the idea, Sarah?" "I think that would be wonderful if Sheila would not mind. In another five weeks, we will get to know one another better and I can meet Sheila. I'm a pretty good caterer as well as cook, but Sheila might want a large decorated cake and simple cake squares, nuts, mints and such. Please ask David when we could all meet and discuss this. Also ask him if Sheila wants a large buffet and florist designed wedding. It doesn't matter to me, but I don't want to feel like an intruder, either."

"You know that Grace will probably be out of the hospital by then. I expect Robert Knowles will keep close check on her and Karla. I know he wants to get to know Karla better. He looked somewhat bewildered at how bright Karla is and as though he didn't know if he could be a substitute daddy or not. Mind you, he didn't tell me that, but I read faces pretty well Carl, and the man was taken aback when he talked to Karla. I was at first until I learned what a kind heart she has and a loving spirit. You and Grace have done so well with her; I too, love her."

Carl said, "Thank you, Sarah. I didn't know you could read people so well, but I'm glad. I will call David back and let him know what we discussed so he can make Sheila aware. Maybe we could meet tomorrow for a little while." "That sounds wonderful," Sarah replied. "Sarah, I'd like to tell Lucas and Molly and when Michael and Lucy get home, I'd like them to come as well. Also, there is a young man that Michael is really close too; his name is Eli, (he's the one who accidentally kicked the lift that caused the car to fall on Michael). Michael said he had such a rough life at home; he never let the other guys know how bright he is. So I can tell Michael to invite Eli to our wedding, is that okay?" "Absolutely!"

As Carl was ready to pick up the phone and call David, but David called him. He said that Sheila said, "That would be a wonderful plan. She would like to invite two or three of the nurses with whom she works and she and Molly already are pretty close." Carl replied to David that he was really glad that Sheila thought it was a good idea. "Sheila wants to know what kind of reception Sarah would like?" "Almost anything will be fine with her." David said, "Carl, I think all four of us need to get together and discuss this. Doing a four-way conversation per phone is confusing me." Carl said, "Frankly I've been confused since Sarah definitely agreed to marry me. I am very thankful, though." David replied; "I'm pretty much the same; therefore, the girls need to talk and tell us what they want. That way, with a list of their desires we can pick up what they want." Carl said, "Fine, David, how would tomorrow at three p.m. sound to you and Sheila." David said, "We'll be there."

The next afternoon about three p.m. David and Sheila arrived. Carl had told Karla that the four of them had grown-up talk and he would tell her about it as soon as things were settled. Karla said, "That's fine, I'll go stay with Mrs. Strong. You know she sometimes needs my company, since she can't get out and walk so much. We sit and talk and sometimes I read to her, because her eyes are weak. Uncle Carl, you will have to drive me over there and I'd better call and ask her if she would like some company." Karla said, "I know you Sheila and of course, Sarah and Uncle Carl, but are you David, one of Uncle Carl's friends?" "That I am, Karla, we work closely together and I consider him like a brother." "Well, that is wonderful, welcome aboard."

Carl excused himself for a few minutes and ran Karla over to Mrs. Strong's. She was a close neighbor and dear friend and Karla seems to help with just her presence. Carl dropped Karla at the doorstep and waited for the bell ring and for Mrs. Strong to get to the door. She opened the door and opened her arms wide and Karla just stepped in and gave her a kiss on her cheek. Carl told them he would be back in a little while. "Make it a longer while, Karla and I haven't had much time to visit since the accident and I've been worried sick." "Well, as you can see, Mrs. Strong, I'm much better and soon the cast can come off, but I'll still need my crutches a while." They both went in the house and Carl was dismissed.

While Carl had been gone, David introduced Sheila to Sarah. "Oh Sarah, I was on duty when they brought you in. I'm so glad to see you looking so well. Do you still have bad headaches? I hope not, Dr. Knowles is one of the best 'face-men' around. He is also a really nice guy who wants to marry Grace. Grace accepted, but they want to wait a while until Karla can get to know him better."

"Is it true that you would like a double wedding with David and me?" Sarah noticed how friendly Sheila was and felt herself relax some. She could tell this young woman was very outgoing and loving. Sarah said, "Sheila, I would very much like that if I'm not intruding. You understand I have no family left and not many friends, I stay busy with my restaurant, well until the robbery." Sheila reminded her that she sure did want a double ceremony; you see David and Carl and Lucas are about as close as brothers. They all three have a three-week commitment to train the new recruits in areas of their expertise. "In about five weeks, we could have the ceremony. Grace will also be better at that time and I'm sure Robert will keep close watch over Grace and Karla."

Sarah had a notepad and asked Sheila if she would tell her what kind of reception and decoration she wanted. Sheila said; "I haven't had time to adjust to the fact that I'll be married in five weeks, certainly not enough time to plan for florist or flowers or reception foods. She also said that some of her nurse friends would know a good florist and cake maker, but she wasn't interested in a lot of flair. She liked simple things."

Sarah started laughing, "Believe it or not I told Carl about the same thing. I have a suggestion to ponder, if you'd like to hear." "What?" Sheila asked. "Well, I am a pretty good baker and I could make both of us a small wedding cake, one at one end of the table and the other at the other end. I could decorate with a few roses and write: 'Sheila and David', and then on the other write, 'Sarah and Carl'. We could have small cake squares, nuts, mints etc. on the table with the punch bowl in the center. I have a lovely tablecloth and punch bowl that we could use. We could have napkins embossed with Sheila and David and Sarah and Carl."

"That sounds wonderful Sarah; do you want me to take care of the florist? As I said, nothing to fancy, just pretty trees and flowers and candles." "That would be great," Sarah replied.

"I think the four of us should see your Pastor, David. I know he knows you two, but he doesn't know Carl and me, and certainly doesn't know of a double wedding ceremony."

"Do you and Carl like what Sheila and I have discussed?" David smiled his sweet smile and said, "Sarah, if you and Sheila like it, I know Carl and I will adore it." She looked quite a time at Carl and for the first time, he saw vulnerability in Sarah's face, David had noticed as well as Sheila. Carl said, "Sweetheart that sounds perfect to me. I know what a great cook you are, but was unaware until I just remembered you made beautiful desserts in your restaurant. That's a wonderful plan, since you and Sheila like it. I know David and I probably wouldn't notice if we were eating wood chips. We love you both and want you happy." Sarah smiled and looked at David and Sheila, "Well, done and done!"

They all relaxed and began talking like old friends. Sheila spoke up and said, "Sarah, I just remembered, we will need a few invitations." "Do you know about how many?" Sarah replied; "I don't need to mail any invitations because I know so few people that I'm close to." Sheila said, "Well, let's start counting: Molly and Lucas, Michael and Lucy, about three nurses besides Grace, and Robert (David help me remember), oh, a young man named Eli, but Michael will have to know his address, and how about that Mrs. Strong that Karla is visiting. Don't you think a dozen would be enough?" Sarah said, "It sounds about right to me, what do you think Carl?" Carl and David said, "We might need to add at least three; for our three Chiefs." "Oh, that's a great idea. Well let's just get twenty-four and that way we will have plenty in the event we remember someone else."

David said, let me call the Pastor and ask if he will see us all and what we've planned. He did and the Pastor told them to come on to his office. Carl asked how long have we been talking? "About forty-five minutes. Well I'll need to pick Karla up and have her sit in the Church while we are with the Pastor and then we can all go to dinner." "That's great," they all agreed.

David and Sheila and Carl and Sarah got into the car and went to pick Karla up and say goodbye to Mrs. Strong. Carl told her that David and Sheila and he and Sarah were going to see a Pastor about marrying them. Karla looked at Uncle Carl and Sarah and said; "I thought as much, but I didn't know about Sheila and David; that is wonderful. I guess I'll have to sit somewhere while you all talk to him, right?" "Right, Carl said. Karla said, "No problem, I have my reader with me in case Mrs. Strong needed me to read to her. Did you know that she used to teach school?" "No honey, I didn't, but you all have a lot to talk about when you do get together." "Yes, we enjoy one another's company."

They all got to the Church and went into the Pastor's office. Carl introduced Karla and Karla stuck out her hand to shake. "It is nice to meet you, sir; my Uncle Carl and Sarah want to ask if you will marry them too; oops!" "Please forgive me Uncle Carl, sometimes I forget things are between just you and me." "That's all right sweetheart, Sarah now knows how I feel." "Now, perhaps you need to go to the sanctuary and read." She turned to the Pastor and said; "I'm so glad to have met you." She then went to the sanctuary and began reading.

The Pastor looked at Carl and said, "That child is brilliant and so well-behaved and polite." Carl looked at the Pastor and David introduced both Carl and Sarah. Carl said; "Her dad was killed in the service when she was about two and a half years of age. She said she didn't remember too much, except he would toss her in the air and catch her. When I left the army, I came home to take care of my sister and Karla and we are all very close." Sarah and I took her up to see her mom yesterday (she had a skull fracture in an auto accident and Karla had a broken leg, as you saw, but when she saw her mommy, she said, "I've been praying every night for all of you and asked God to take care of you, because she couldn't." "I wish I could have that same innocent faith, but sadly, I'm not there yet."

David asked Pastor Jenkins if they could have a double ceremony and small reception in the reception hall. Both Sheila and Sarah are Christians, as well as Carl. Carl and I have about the same work schedule and we are committed to train new recruits for about three weeks. So they had intended to marry in about five weeks. Pastor said he thought he could do that and all four of them grinned at him and said, "Thank you."

Sheila asked if they could see the reception hall as well as the sanctuary. He of course took them around to see the Church Sanctuary and the reception hall. Both Sheila and Sarah loved the sanctuary and reception hall. They told him they thought it would be just right and thanked him for the use of the Church, Reception Hall and most of all agreeing to marry them.

Carl looked around for Karla and did not see her at first; then he spotted her crutches on the floor in the second pew. He went over to tell her they were ready to go and she was asleep with her electronic book open beside her. He spoke gently to her and Karla said, "Uncle Carl, I did not know I was tired. Thank you for awaking me." They all thanked the pastor and Carl said, "We are going to dinner, would you like to come?" Pastor Jenkins said, "Thank you, no, my wife will have dinner in a little while." Karla told him again how glad she was to meet him.

They all went to a small restaurant and ordered dinner. Karla said, "I know, Uncle Carl, no hamburger." Sarah and Sheila ordered grilled chicken breast and broccoli and Karla said, "That's balanced, I'll have the same." The men ordered a steak and baked potato and salads. They all talked until the dinner was served and then they ate with some gusto. Carl did not realize how late it was and he knew; Karla and Sarah were really tired. He told David and Sheila how much he appreciated their help and willingness to share their special day with them. David and Sheila said; "We are honored and thankful for you dear friends." They ate and Carl took care of the bill and then David and Sheila took them home.

Carl helped Karla in and handed Sarah her crutches and took Sarah's arm and said, "Welcome home." Sarah's fatigue was showing almost as much as Karla's. Carl helped Karla get her pajamas on and asked if she needed the bathroom. "I can do that on my own," Karla said. Carl said, "Okay," and went to get her some medicine to insure she rested well. She was out of the bathroom and leaning on the bed with her crutches. Carl put her into bed and gave her the medicine and kissed her goodnight.

He came out of Karla's room and told Sarah to please get undressed and lay down; if it's okay with you. "I will do the same. I enjoy lying side by side with you." Sarah smiled and said that she also enjoyed being with him. She put on sweats without a bra and Carl put on a clean tee shirt and some sweat pants. He insured the house was locked and knocked on Sarah's door and she said; "I'm in bed, Carl. Please come hold me a while and sleep beside me tonight. I don't know why I got a bit nervous a while ago." "My darling Sarah, I do. You had not met Sheila when you could recognize her, and you only met David and Lucas a short time; plus, you have been up all day with no rest period. I'm sorry about that, but we can now relax and sleep." He took her in his arms and held her and they kissed. He said; "I'd better just hold you." Sarah turned on her side and Carl put his arm around her and they both went to sleep.

# Michael and Lucy Return from Honeymoon

The week was almost over and Michael and Lucy had enjoyed most of the week; but they both thought it was time to go home. They had packed and the bellman had taken everything to the car, brought the car around to the front door and Michael went to pay the bill. Lucy asked quietly if Michael wanted her to drive. He said, "No, not at present." Lucy went to the front and waited for Michael to get there. The bellman opened Lucy's door and Michael got in on the driver's side. They started on the way home.

About an hour later, Michael pulled over to a small restaurant and they went in for a cup of coffee and light lunch. They had the lunch and Lucy looked at Michael and said; "Michael, you look tired and in pain. May I drive from here on to the house?" Michael said; "I hate to admit this, but my leg is throbbing and I am tired. Would you be up to driving on home? I know your entire bottom must still be sore, so we will get home and order dinner in when we want to eat." "That's fine," Lucy said. Michael reminded her how much he loved her and she returned the same.

They got in the car and continued home. When they got home, everything had been rearranged, was clean and fresh and looked like home to Lucy. She asked; "Michael do you think Molly and Lucas fixed our home so special?" "Yes, honey, I am not at all surprised and my guess is that the freezer and refrigerator are stocked. My sister and your brother are probably already settled in your old home place. Let's give them a call and let them know we are home. Also, tell Molly I miss my nephew and would like them to come visit a little while." Lucy told him that was a great idea. Lucy went to the bathroom and came out and said; "Michael, they cleaned everything, with fresh towels and linens already in place; I have to thank them."

Lucy got on the phone and called Lucas and Molly. She said; "First of all thank you both for fixing up the house and filling the refrigerator and freezer, secondly, Michael is quite anxious to see his nephew and so am I. Could you all come over for a little while before Luke's bedtime?" Lucas looked and Molly and repeated everything Lucy said and asked Molly how she felt. "I've love to see them, but, let's stay only a short time. They are both tired and we are too." "Okay, Lucy; we'll even let you hold Luke, if you are nice." Lucy started laughing and told Michael what Lucas said. "Michael promises to be real good; we'll see you all in a little while. Thanks, Lucas."

Lucas, Molly, and Luke got in the ATV, (Lucas had a pillow under Molly, and Luke in his car seat) and they headed over to see Michael and Lucy. Lucas was glad they were home, but he then realized, he must be back at work for three weeks extreme training of recruits; well, that would be good and some form of a normal life could begin for all of them.

Prior to Lucy's call, David had called Lucas, he and Carl would be having a double wedding in about five weeks. He told them to make sure Michael and Lucy knew and they also wanted to invite Eli and the three Chiefs. David said they had all four already talked with his pastor who agreed to marry them in the Church I attend, but they would have access to the Reception Hall, as well. "We all four want a small wedding that is blessed in the Church. I know now that Sheila really loves me and Carl had made Sarah aware of his feelings. Carl and Sarah are glad and so we set the wedding for five weeks. We have to do the three-week training sessions, and by that time Molly and Michael should be nearly well." Lucas told him congratulations and he meant that for all of them.

Lucas had told Molly about all this before Lucy called. Molly said, "Well, Lucas you have another reason for us to see them tonight, Michael will have to make Eli aware." "That's true, Molly, you and Luke are my heart!"

They soon arrived at Michael and Lucy's home and were welcomed like they hadn't seen one another in years, instead of a few days. Michael and

Lucy looked wonderful, except they both looked tired. "Did you have a good honeymoon?" "Oh yes! but, we are glad to be home."

They all went into the living room and Molly put Luke in his uncle's arms and Lucy was right beside them. Luke looked up and began his usual cooing. Michael said; "He knows us; he is really a smart little boy." Lucy said; "He is beautiful." They all played with Luke a while and Lucy put a pallet on the floor and some of the toys that they had gotten for Luke. Lucy lay down on the pallet with him and started playing.

Lucas spoke up and said; Michael and Lucy, "We have something to tell you, and it is good news." They looked at Lucas and said; "Well, tell us." So Lucas told them about David and Sheila having a double wedding with Carl and Sarah, in the small Church that David attends. "The weddings will be in about five weeks, so we can complete the recruits training. Sheila, Sarah, Molly and Lucy can get to know one another a bit more. Of course, Sheila and Molly work together, but they all need a closer relationship; that will give them time to know one another much better."

"Grace seems to be mending well," Molly said. "I'm so glad, Lucy and Michael; you both know some of what Carl has been through with the car accident and then the backset for Grace. Sarah must be a special young woman, because Carl actually smiles at times. Of course, David is very dear and is very founded in his belief in God and His leadership."

Lucy and Michael looked tired and he knew Molly and he were, so he told them, it's about time for us to go and put Master Luke to bed. "You all sleep well and we'll talk tomorrow." Michael and Lucy said, "That's a good idea and again, thank you for making the house so comfortable and welcoming for us."

Lucas picked Luke up and helped Molly up and they all said, "Good night, talk to you tomorrow."

# Lucas, David, and Carl Go Back to Work

All of them enjoyed the rest of the weekend and reminded the wife and brides that they had committed to train the recruits for a three-week period. "You girls need to get together and get to know each other well; plus, remember Karla. She will talk your ears off, but when you've had enough, tell her she needs to rest and read a while. She does need a nap in the afternoon."

Sarah, Sheila, and Molly reminded them they were adults and knew what needed to be done; well, Molly and Sheila said that. Sarah looked rather shocked that those two would speak up like that; but the guys started laughing, so she assumed this was a routine in this family and close friends.

Carl had gone back to the hospital to see Grace and find out if she knew when she might come home. "Not for a few more days, Carl, but since Sarah is with Karla, I won't worry about her."

Carl said; "Grace, I don't remember if I told you that Sarah has agreed to marry me and David and Sheila are getting married. We are planning a double wedding at David's Church in about five weeks. Grace, you know sometimes I forget the really important things because of intrusive thoughts; but if I haven't told you, I am now. I would like your approval. Sarah is so dear to me and loves me for myself."

Grace started laughing; "Carl you have only told me three times, when you came up here and saw how I was doing. Of course you have my approval and love. Sarah is very good for you and you are for her. She has had pain in her background; I don't know what, but occasionally one sees it in her face when she is unaware of another's presence. She is so good to Karla and Karla adores her, and I love her too for making you a happier man."

Molly and Lucas stayed together with Luke all weekend. They were bonding very quickly and enjoyed one another so much. Lucas hadn't needed to take a walk for quite some time lately. He knew it was because Molly loved him so much and he loved her and Luke.

David and Sheila spent as much time as possible together for the rest of the weekend. They would also see one another as often as Sheila had time off. They were also forming a bond of love and trust.

On Monday morning all three of the First-Responders showed up promptly on time, in uniform and ready to begin with the new recruits. All of the recruits came in together and went to each of their captains. The Captains came out to and reminded the recruits that this was a three week course in the various areas they had told them.

David said, "Men, we are going into a field and start a fire (of course with all safety equipment) and you all will take turns at being the leader of the group. You will be evaluated on timing, skill and ability to work together as a team or individually."

Carl told his men they would be learning shooting skills and rescue routines and the same time limit that was in place. "You too, will be evaluated on skills, ability to think 'on your feet' and the time it takes to become a team, working as one. You will learn various weapons in any situation; in a community with drug smuggling to taking of hostages."

Lucas said, "Gentlemen we will be special ops operations; with skills on spotting a real enemy, a fellow worker or innocent by stander. You will be able at the end of this course to take down a fortified village, smuggle people in or out of dangerous locations, find a specific target and take him or her out; as well as, (what I'll call now) a sniff test. I expect every man to work as a unit and separately to accomplish any mission you are called to do. Your evaluations will be judged on your ability to follow orders instantly, your reasoning ability, your ability to work together as a well-oiled machine. Now, let's go."

Each team went with their specific captain; David, Carl or Lucas. They were all young and Lucas could sense their fear, but they would learn to not allow fear to cause them to get off track.

All three teams began immediately to do what their captain told them to do. (The recruits called them chiefs), so eventually they referred to one another in the same way.

David's team went to an open field with a few trees scattered about, as well as some fodder. They had driven the safety trucks with them. David set the fire before the recruits were ready; however, when they saw it, they got ready quickly. They worked that field all day with different scenarios and about five o'clock, David said, "Well done, it's time to go. Please be sure every thing is safe before we leave. We use a different area every few days and each of you will learn all skills, from back fires to chemical sprays; whatever is needed to put a fire out and save lives."

Carl's team followed him to a mock-up town; this was to be a test of spotting and shooting without killing a fellow recruit or any by-stander. They would be timed and use paint bullets of different colors per team. The mock-up town was just that; cardboard store fronts, pull strings between buildings and some were not visible, the possibility of enemy attackers in the town or coming into the town, there were doors half open and windows in the store fronts. This would be no party. Carl divided his men into two groups with different colored paint cartridges, and shouted, "GO!" Very quickly the different people started coming into view and the recruits did not do well in identification or shooting. Carl said; "It's quitting time today; we meet back here in the morning promptly on time."

All of the teams worked vigorously in whatever their chief said to do. They all knew this was no picnic, but they had decided to become recruits to any unit in which they were needed. Today, they had learned to forget food, water only when necessary and to exercise their muscles well after the day's mission. Each chief worked their recruits hard. The same processes continued for three days; then another operation related to the area in which they were working began.

The Special Op team had the greatest difficulty in learning to spot and estimate the distance of the enemy and fire. Many times they missed and had to repeat the process. After three days, they were given different weapons to learn overnight and be able to use them the next day. They needed to look, listen, and smell any different smell whether fire, shooting, or holding hostages. The weapons were not only new to them; they had had no training in these skills. Lucas told them, "You will learn. You must think quickly and correctly and determine the course of action needed, dependent on the situation. The situations can and will change, from small villages, to larger towns, and to the city. Each situation calls for different strategy."

Each team worked extremely hard that first week. They were improving with fire extinguishing, but still not proficient in spotting potential fire sources, either weather related, or deliberately set fires, fuels used or any method to put the fire out.

The team that was supposed to learn shooting skills had progressed somewhat, but definitely not up to Carl's standards. Carl had found some literature on various weapons and the use of them; how to determine the distance of an enemy and determine the time a bullet would begin a downward move, as well as, learn they must all allow for wind changes. He gave each recruit the information and told them to study. They were to show up for work-outs promptly and to expect any change at any moment.

Lucas had also found literature on spotting an enemy, hostage taking procedure for rescue, how to recognize a sniper and use the right weapon to take him out. The literature was some that Lucas himself had to study when he was in the Marines. The team seemed grateful and assured him they would study. "Be prepared for any change at any time in your own location."

All the recruits were sent home for dinner and rest. David felt some pity for the guys, but nothing showed on any chief's face. David, Carl and Lucas knew they had pushed the recruits almost to the breaking point, but they knew the job had to be done. David asked Carl and Lucas where they got the literature they gave their recruits. Carl said, "Some of it is mine, from the army and part of it came from the office." Lucas said almost the same thing; some from his own literature in the Marines and the rest at the office. David decided he would look for some literature he could give his recruits. They all three went home to make today's notes for evaluation. Each day they would add to the folders.

When Carl got home, he looked pale and tired. Sarah had dinner waiting and Karla was waiting too. They all sat down to a wonderful dinner and Carl asked them about their day. They had a 'neat' time, according to Karla and she did take her rest and so did Sarah. "We looked up cooking schools and saw some classes on the reader you gave me, Uncle Carl." Sarah said, "Karla has been a big help and I have some new ideas for meals that I might test on you." "That's fine," Carl replied. Carl told her the dinner was great; he had been hungry. "We worked the recruits hard today and I never realized just how hard this work is on recruits."

David had gone home and showered and looked for some of his own literature. He found some good pamphlets and put them out to take to work. He then called Sheila and talked to her a while. She was still at work and wouldn't be off for a couple more days, but I love hearing your voice. David said, "I wish I could hold you now; it has been a difficult day for the recruits and me. I'm going to make a dinner and go to bed. I love you Sheila and good night."

Lucas got home and Molly had some dinner prepared and Luke was awake and playful. Lucas hugged Molly and kissed her and then took Luke to play with him a few minutes. Molly said, "Dinner is almost ready, just biscuits need to brown a bit more." "It smells wonderful," Lucas said. "David, Carl and I realize we aren't as young as these fellows, but we managed to stay ahead of them. They were wiped out, but not a one of them complained. I think we have some good guys in all three teams." Molly set up dinner and set the table and took Luke to put him on his pallet. He had begun to notice more toys and would play for a good while. "Lucas, darling, you must sit down and eat with me. You do look tired, but wonderful and you are not old. You are the dearest man I know. Now eat your dinner and I will too." Lucas smiled at his bossy little wife and said; "Yes dear." The dinner was delicious and Lucas told Molly how much he appreciated it. He said; "I'm going to hit the shower and hit the bed rather soon." Molly said, "Great, I'll finish tidying the kitchen and feed Luke and we will all go to bed." Lucas also made notes on today's events and put all in a folder. He could show and tell the recruits the progress they had made when the training was over.

The next two weeks were essentially the same; they did change locations, landscapes and enemy and standers-by, as well as hostage takers and learned different rescue efforts. They were all beginning to act as a team, wherever they were stationed. All three of their 'chiefs' were good trainers; but it was difficult to meet all the challenges they threw at them; however, they were beginning to understand and perform fairly well with any situation.

On the last day of training, Lucas, Carl and David told the recruits to come back to the base for their evaluations. They also asked all of the Captains to come to base for the recruit's evaluation. The Fire Chief told Lucas he had already heard how difficult the training was, but the recruit said he was glad they had their 'own chiefs', meaning all of the First Responders.

They all showed up at the base and all the Captains were there too. David presented his findings and evaluations first. He made everyone aware of the changes from the first day to now and how well they had performed. "I've kept daily performance records and a graph up here shows the progress and back-set each recruit has had. The entire graph showed ups and downs, the first week; however, the second week was more up grade and the third shows almost constant improvement." The basic training exercises had already been given to each Captain. David told the Captains that he was proud of every recruit and the hard work they had done.

Carl was next and he too had a graph. It was less steady in the upward climb, but toward the last week, it showed almost steady climb. He turned to his recruits and said; "Well done."

Lucas came last and to each of the Captains, Lucas' training exercises were the most difficult. However, Lucas had formed a graph with different colored lines to indicate each exercise they had performed and again, most of the lines showed an upward climb. They had all given their recruits individual tests and evaluations on Thursday; and the teams had finished. The recruits grinned and didn't say a word. Lucas turned to his recruits and said; "Men, you all did fine." No other compliments were given.

Each individual Captain congratulated the recruits and told them they were proud of them for 'sticking it out'; although every Captain knew they were made of 'good stuff'. To the 'chiefs', the Captains said, "Thank you, men. You too have done a remarkable job." The recruits started clapping and all three of the First Responders looked a bit shocked, except Lucas, who only smiled.

The three Captains had already agreed to give the First Responders two weeks off. They had heard about the up-coming weddings and knew the First Responders needed that time with pay. When they told the First Responders that, it really was a shock, even Lucas changed expression into one of gratitude and he smiled briefly, before his mask came back as well and the other First Responders. Again, the recruits started clapping. When the Captains told the recruits they would get one week off with pay; one could hear a pin drop. They were immensely grateful, but surprised. They all said almost in unison; "Thanks Captains." The Captains said; "Now off you all go and we'll see you at the appointed times."

They all left with 'thanks again' and the First Responders simply went home. Lucas went in and hugged Molly and kissed her rather deeply. Molly smiled and waited for the news. She knew something was up. Lucas said; "The Captains gave Carl, David and me two weeks off with pay." "Lucas, that's wonderful." Lucas said, "Somehow they had knowledge of the upcoming weddings and knew we all needed some time off. The evaluations went well and the Captains were very proud of the young men. I called them Men, in my exit as their chief." "Lucas Stone, you are a very special man, who understands what those boys, I mean men, went through and your comment reinforced their own choice to be in each department." Lucas hugged Molly again and said, "Thanks, my dearest Molly."

Carl went home and Sarah and Karla were in the kitchen, making dinner. Karla said, "Uncle Carl, have we got a surprise for you!" "What?" Carl asked. Karla said, "Can we tell him now or later?" Sarah said, "Why don't we show him, Karla?" They told Carl to close his eyes and each one took a hand and escorted him into Grace's bedroom. Grace nodded, and Karla said, "Open your eyes." Carl was absolutely shocked; there sat Grace up on pillows under her head and shoulders. Carl said, "When Grace, and how do you feel, and who brought you home, and fixed you up so well?" Grace smiled and pointed to the corner where Robert was seated. Carl was really smiling and went over and kissed his sister and turned to Robert and shook his hand and said, "How can I ever thank you, Robert?" Robert and Grace spoke up almost together to tell him some news, but Karla said, "Uncle Carl, guess what? Robert is going to marry mommy and he loves me too and will be a substitute for my daddy, if I'm agreeable. I told him if mommy was happy now, she was happy and she really liked him too. It will be a few weeks, so mommy and I can get used to it and see his house and I can pick my own room, and in one more week, I can walk without crutches if I continue with some rehab."

Carl was as near tears as Grace had ever seen. She said, "Carl the skull is healed and while I have to be quiet some of the time, I can get up and go to the bathroom and for short rides at times."

Carl said, "I am so glad, sis. You look great!" "Of course," Grace said and they all laughed and the tension was lifted. Grace went on and told Carl how much Sarah and Karla and Robert had helped her. She said, "Sarah is a good cook and makes well-balanced meals; Robert and I ate with Karla and Sarah last night; and it was wonderful to be out of bed for a short while. My bottom gets sore when I lay in bed too long."

Carl said; "Well, I knew Sarah and Karla could cook and they have been experimenting on me, but I'm sorry I wasn't here last night. I was so fatigued, I went to Sarah's place and finished my notes and evaluations and 'crashed' at Sarah's apartment. It is wonderful to see all of you looking so well. I also have some news." "What?" Karla and Grace and Sarah asked at the same time. "Well, the Captains gave all the First-Responders two weeks off with pay. Lucas nor David nor I asked for that, but they had heard that David and I were getting married and they figured Lucas needed the time to get to know his little boy. Has he grown much?" Sarah said, "Yes and he is so smart."

Robert said, "Excuse me Carl, but you look hungry and busted, so why don't the ladies put dinner out and I will help Grace to get out of bed and we can all have dinner together." "That sounds great," Carl responded.

They all went out of Grace's room and Carl went to take a shower while the 'ladies' were setting dinner out. The shower was very refreshing and he could hardly believe that he had been surprised. Karla usually let things 'slip' when they were on the phone together. He was smiling to himself and thanked God for His wonderful healing of them all.

David went home and picked up the phone to talk to Sheila, but she wasn't at the hospital tonight. She had gone home early, because she had an important task at home. David called her at home and she said, "David, my love, come over to my house and don't have dinner on the way; I've got you a good meal right here and I can't wait to see you." David said, "Sheila, you did not have to leave work, I would have come over and stayed with you until you could leave." Sheila said, "Yes, I did, I wanted to surprise you on the last day of exercise." "Thank you my darling. I'll be over as soon as I shower." "Okay," Sheila said.

David hit the shower and thanked God again for his dear Sheila. Lord, "You are God and nothing is impossible with You and I thank You for all the blessings You have sent us." His shower was too, refreshing. As soon as he showered and dressed casually, he left to see Sheila and be with her as long as possible. He got to her house and went in and everything smelled wonderful. Sheila came running and went into his arms and hugged and kissed him well. David hugged her and kissed her back. He still had his arms around her and said; "Whoa" and Sheila laughed and said, "Dinner is ready except for taking the rolls out." David sat down where she showed him and she served a delicious dinner. After dinner, Sheila told him all about meeting with Sarah, Molly and Lucy, who was back from her honeymoon. Grace also came home yesterday, but Sarah and Karla were going to surprise Carl.

"We have all decided on the florist, saw the florist and arranged to have the Church and Reception Hall decorated with beautiful pines and cream colored candles. There will also be some fill in the pines with other greenery. Sarah and I have already got our dresses and Sarah will make the cakes next week. I'll help with the cake squares, mints, nuts and rose petals to throw after we are married. The invitations have been sent and that's how the Captains knew you all needed some time off." David was again shocked at his wonderful Sheila. How did they keep that information to themselves and why? Sheila explained that they all agreed you all three had all on your plate you needed and we could do the other. "I hope you still want me as your wife." For the first time, David noticed a slight vulnerability in her face. He hugged and kissed her and said, "Absolutely, I want you for my wife forever, and I'm thankful you all could do that. It is wonderful news. I know you and I have talked to Pastor as well as Carl and Sarah, but have you contacted him again to insure everything is like you want it?" "Of course, darling, we are excited, but a bit nervous. Grace said, 'That is perfectly normal and stop worrying about such things'. So we've done a lot of 'girl talk', Karla included. Also, Grace told us she and Robert had talked to Karla and she was in agreement; she insisted on her own room and Robert said, 'You can pick any room in the house, except mine'. Karla started laughing and said, 'Of course, I knew that already'.

Wanda Hancock

The next two weeks seemed to fly by; everyone was preparing and talking and getting ready for their wedding. They had a wonderful response from Eli and he thinks it would be wonderful if Michael would let him be his assistant, until Michael was completely healed. Michael also told him what Lucas had said, "That perhaps he could go to community college and then join one of the departments who protect our community." Eli said, "He would do his best in college, but would need to work 'on the side' to pay for college." "Lucy, Sarah, and I decided between the three or (maybe the six of us) could help him through his first year of school. Molly is to ask Lucas if they could help too and I'm sure Lucas will agree."

The days were fast approaching when Sarah and Sheila and perhaps Molly if she is up to it, would begin on the wedding cakes and store them in the refrigerator. Sheila had already gotten the rose petals to throw after the wedding and Molly had arranged a photographer to take the wedding pictures. By Thursday the cakes were ready to be put in refrigerator, as well as the cake squares. Sheila was to pick up some good nuts, and nice mints for the table. The tablecloth was beautiful and rose petals had been placed around on the table cloth. Karla and Sarah had insured the Church and Reception Room was decorated as they wanted.

Carl had been in his studio and no one was allowed in that room unless invited. Carl kept it locked and Karla told us that was 'off limits', even to her. Lucas and Molly had mostly played with Luke and Lucas took him into the woods with him one day. Molly told them that Luke really seemed to enjoy being out of doors.

Well the wedding day was upon them. Both brides got dressed at Sheila's house and had their bags packed, but David would have to drive them to the Church. Everyone was dressed and ready to go to the Church. Robert and Karla were sitting with Grace, who seemed much improved. Robert told Carl that he would see that she rested in bed when the wedding was over and Karla would help him. He would stay in Carl's room with Grace and Karla to insure they were both all right. Carl agreed.

There were a number of cars at the Church, some were not recognized. They got out and Carl met Sarah at the car. He looked so nice in his dark suit and Sarah had a beautiful off white dress, almost egg shell color. Carl and Sarah were to walk down the aisle first and David and Sheila would follow.

The music was playing and the photographer was snapping pictures. He had already done pictures of the Church and Reception Hall.

Carl and Sarah started down the aisle and reached the Pastor and stayed turned toward him. David and Sheila came down the aisle (Sheila's dress was a beautiful cream color that looked great with her red hair). They reached the Pastor and he motioned them all to turn to the audience for a minute and then turn back to him. He married Carl and Sarah first and the David and Sheila. They did exchange rings and each pair was pronounced husband and wife. "You gentlemen may kiss your brides." They all four turned toward the audience and saw Eli, Lucas, Molly and Luke; as well as Michael and Lucy and Mrs. Strong, beside Grace, Robert and Karla. They also noticed the various Captains and the most surprising was all the recruits they had trained were there as well.

The bride and groom (Carl and Sarah) went ahead, followed by David and Sheila. When they got to the vestibule, there were ladies there to escort them to the Reception. David knew the ladies and smiled at them. They got into the Reception Room and the table was beautiful. Carl and Sarah stood beside their cake and David and Sheila stood beside theirs.

Lucas stood up and faced the reception group and said, "Ladies and Gentlemen, these men are like my brothers and their beautiful brides are very dear to Molly and me. Would you all come by and greet them and have some refreshments?" (The recruits looked at one another and realized that was the most sentences they had ever heard Lucas say at one time). Robert, Grace, Karla and Mrs. Strong began the line. They kissed the brides and hugged the grooms. The Captains came next and congratulated the men on beautiful brides and then the recruits all came by. They smiled at all the brides and Lucas and had refreshments and left. Lucas and Molly and Luke came next and Molly hugged them all and Lucas shook hands with his buddies and smiled at their brides.

Everything was accomplished and there were bowls of rose petals at each door. Everyone grabbed a handful of petals and threw them onto the brides and grooms, calling out to both pairs, "The best to all of you."

David and Sheila got into David's car and headed one way and Carl and Sarah headed the other way. Lucas had previously put every bag in the car that belonged to each couple. They were on their way for a brief honeymoon.

David and Sheila got back late Sunday afternoon and went to David's house. Sheila had had the map that she had obtained for David, matted and hung in the appropriate place. The house was spotless and when David saw the map; his shock was so obvious, that Sheila thought for a moment he might cry. He did and asked "Where in the world did you get that and how did you get in here to hang it?" She said, "I stole your key and had a duplicate made and came and hung it. You aren't angry are you?" David took her in his arms and almost kissed her breath away. "No my darling, I just never expected this; you are so wonderful to be my wife and just your wonderful self. Thank you with all my heart." They began to put their bags away and had already decided to live at David's so Sheila had moved a number of her clothes and cookware to David's.

Carl and Sarah got back late Sunday afternoon as well. Karla had given Sarah a key to Carl's house and she, mommy, and Robert were staying in his house. The house was nicely clean and welcoming to them. Carl hugged Sarah and told her again how much he loved her and how glad he was that she married him. He then took her by the hand and they went outside. Carl said, "Now, you must close your eyes until I tell you to open them." Sarah did as she was told and Carl directed her into his studio, and said, "Open your eyes." Sarah almost fainted, "Carl, How? When? Why?" Carl hugged and kissed her almost senseless and he almost lost control of himself. He said, "I did this for us, for you especially, on my time off, and because I love you." There on the easel perched an absolutely gorgeous picture of the little Church in which they married. Sarah said, "That is the most beautiful wonderful thing you could do, Carl. I love you with all my heart and thank you for the wonderful wedding present."

They all spent the night in their new homes and the next day was Monday and the First Responders had to report to duty. Lucas, David, and Carl were back at the base headquarter and went to their offices to see what needed to be done. Soon after, all three Captains came in and asked how everything went? Carl and David said great and Lucas said, "My son and I took our first walk in the forest; he seemed to like it."

Carl and David said, "What is the assignment now, sirs? Well gentlemen we have a new set of recruits for you to meet and you have done a tremendous job with the information you shared with us. We want you all to continue in this training role, except when you are needed. Take your phones and be ready with the recruits to respond to any situation that arises." "We can do that, sirs. Where are the recruits?" "Right this way. They met the recruits and each group was assigned a "chief" (seems the other recruits had named them 'chief' and it stuck). They gathered each group into a section and spoke briefly to them. Meanwhile, the Captains left and returned with the literature that Lucas, David, and Carl had used. They had made pamphlets with the material and it was ready to be distributed to the recruits. All three 'chiefs' gave the literature and told the recruits to study the rest of the day and tonight and be back here at eight o'clock in the morning.

Carl, Lucas and David thanked the Captains for having the literature duplicated. Then each of them went into their office to see what had been done on their leave. Nothing of great need, except, there was a strong rumor that the men who had been robbing and beating women, had now advanced to actually killing one woman. They didn't have many clues, but thought they hung out sometimes in an area in the city that most drugs were run.

# Conclusion

Lucas went to the Captains and said he could train his men, but didn't know if they would be ready when more leads came in regarding these men. I could use some of the first recruits I had and mix them with this group in week number two. That will give all of them some live practice. He also asked if Carl could be excused from this particular man hunt. They all said, we know and that's already handled. "When more is known we will have some members of the swat team with you all. We ask that you try to take them alive, but don't put our men in danger." "Understood," Lucas said.

The First Responders met with their recruits the next morning and started their training exercises. As usual at night they kept a record of progress. This process continued until about middle of the second week. The Police Captain called Lucas into his office and told him about some new, most probably accurate leads on those men. They told Lucas he could take two of his old recruits and two of the swat team with his new recruits and find these men. "Remember, we want them alive to gather more information, but don't risk our men's lives. We will start that exercise in the morning and I'll make my men aware this is not the usual exercise. They will probably know that when they see the swat team and old recruits."

The next morning Lucas told the recruits that today they would be going on a live exercise. "There are several men who are responsible for several robberies and beatings, mostly of women, but they have now killed a woman. This exercise will be difficult and not always safe; therefore, we have two members of the swat team with us, as well as, two of the recruits that were in my unit before. The place is an area in town that is known for drug dealing and a good place for these men to hide out. We will all quietly arrive from various areas around the potential hideout. One member of the swat team will go with one group and one recruit that graduated. The next team will go with another member of the swat team and another member of the recruit that graduated. The last team will go with me. We may need some face paint for one area, but I don't think so. We have strong leads on the potential hideout, so quietness and team work is essential. Once the first team gets in place (remember the roof), the second team will get in place on the other side and front, again remember you can use windows in the opposite site and the roof. My team will bring up the rear with some on the roof, some of the best shooters farther away, and the area will be swarmed quietly and quickly. Do you understand?" "Yes, sir." "Now all three teams will go in about two minutes apart, you will not have a vehicle because they will be left a distance away. You all have real bullets and are protected with chest vests. We'll try to bring them in without killing one, but do not risk your own life for these men. They will have no qualms about killing you or hiding behind an innocent civilian. Each team captain will have a headphone which will keep us all aware of the situation. They probably won't expect an attack in the early hours and that is to our advantage, as well as staying quiet and focused. Now let's go."

They got about a mile outside the target area and left the vehicles and took the equipment they needed on their backs and walked to the target area. When they were all in place they rushed the building. There were three men who had been asleep, but awoke quickly and grabbed their weapons. They saw not a soul and went out the back way. Two of them had guns firing at anything they saw; the third man was dragging a child with him in front of him. Lucas knew he was the best shot and so he took that man with the child down. The other two stopped firing and held their hands up. Lucas motioned for one of the other teams to keep them covered and told one of his team members to go get the child. Lucas then called headquarters and told the Police Captain that the men were caught, but he would need some help from probably the fire team. He thought he had seen smoke coming from one window. He also needed a few officers to aid in taking two men to jail. He said; "I killed the man who was dragging a child as a safety shield. I'll make a full report."

It was less than ten minutes until the others, he asked for, were on the premises. He glanced at some of his team and knew they had never seen an actual person shot down. Well, he did what he had to do to protect his men and that child.

When the police and fire department showed up, he sent his team to the vehicles they had driven. "Guard yourself and the vehicles in case there are others who intended to get away." There did not seem to be any more, but one never knew.

When the Police Chief and other crews were present and doing their job; Lucas said to the Captain, "I know you said bring them in alive; however the man I shot was dragging a child and firing at my men, so to save the others, I shot him." The Police Captain said, "I know, Lucas, you did what was right." When the mess was cleaned up, they all went back to base. Lucas instructed every member that had been with him to tell the Captain exactly what happened. He also asked the other team leaders to give him a full report of the recruits they had and they said, they would.

When everything was cleared out, Lucas went to his office and David was still there. Lucas told David that he had killed a man today. David said, "Lucas, one of the recruits told me what happened." He said, "You know, I think he is a good and decent man, but he will not see his men or a child mistreated." The recruit told him that he had never seen a man shot and that your face didn't show any emotion. The recruit said, "I felt like crying for the 'chief', but not for that man. He intended to use a child to protect himself. I still don't understand how 'chief' killed him and the child was uninjured; but I literally felt the heat from a bullet aimed at me. I was afraid to shoot back because of that little child." Lucas said, "I knew the recruits were not ready to shoot a real person, but I did not intend anyone of them to be injured. I saw how close that bullet got to a recruit (It could have been the one who talked to you), but I simply killed him. David, I'm not sorry; I feel like I'm going backward toward AFGANISTAN. I need to go home to my Molly. Thanks David for writing the report. I did talk to the Police Captain and told him what I had done; he said I did the right thing; but inside I don't know if I feel anything. I'll ask for your prayers."

Carl came in and asked David where Lucas was. David said, "Carl, sit down a minute. You were not supposed to know about this attack today.

The Police Captain told Lucas that he had kept you out of the loop on this particular project, however they had good clues on where the men were who hurt Sarah were and they had advanced to murdering one woman. Lucas took a team hand-picked of previous recruits and two members of the swat-team and they swarmed the place and caught all three of them. Lucas had to kill one of them, because the coward was dragging a little child with him as a shield. Lucas knew his recruits couldn't do it; so he killed the man. A recruit told me about it (this recruit was with Lucas) and he said, 'You know chief, that man never changed expression, but told me to get the child'. He didn't realize I couldn't really shoot someone who had a child in front of him." "I told him that Lucas could sense another person's feelings and he knew he was the only one who could kill that rascal."

Carl asked if Lucas was all right. David said, "He said he needed to see Molly and asked me to pray for him; he did not want to go back to AFGANISTAN. Those surviving men will be put away a long time and you can rest assured of that." Carl said, "I'm glad Lucas protected me, because, I would have killed them all. I'm sorry David, I hate so much, especially when someone I love is injured." David said, "Lucas understands that and so did the Police Captain; I don't know how he knew, but the Captain did not want you involved. Now Carl, please go home and hug your wife and thank God for her. You can relieve her mind, because I believe that the man Lucas killed was the ring leader. Anyway, let your precious wife know she is safe, and you are so thankful for her." Carl said, "Thanks, David, I will. It's about time for you to go see your wife as well."

When Lucas got in, he hugged Molly tightly and she could feel his muscles almost in knots. She simply held him and kissed him and began to rub his back. He began to relax and asked how Luke was doing. "He is fine, he's resting a while. We have played a good bit this afternoon." Lucas asked her if she could lie beside him and let him just hold her; "I'm about on the edge again, sweetheart." Molly said, "I know, I could sense something today about noon and had no idea what, but I knew it concerned you. Let's lie down a while and just hold one another." Lucas slipped his outer shirt off and his shoes and they lay down and held each other. Lucas began to feel himself relax some and Molly was so warm and loving, he told her that her senses were 'on the money'. "I had to kill a man today about that time and it has been so difficult to finish my reports. I talked briefly to David who was still at work and told him what happened and he said he already knew. One of the recruits said that the man dragging a child as a shield shot at the recruit and had no intention of surrendering, so 'chief' brought him down." "The recruits have never seen a man killed and I knew that, but if they are going to be any good at their job, they have to understand that sometimes there are no happy endings." David said, "Go home and hold your wife and just love her; she is a good woman Lucas." "I told him thanks and I came home. He is doing a report, because some of his team and the swat team had to insure there were no other creeps there and they had set a small fire in one of the rooms. I smelled it and called the Captain and told him what had happened." He said, "Lucas, you did what you had to do to save lives and you did the right thing."

Molly continued to rub Lucas' back and arms and he finally did relax. Molly also told him that he did the right thing. "Now, please just let me hold you and try to take a nap. I have dinner almost complete and you can rest with me until Luke wakes up, I don't think he will for a while." Lucas put his arms around Molly and she continued to rub his back and arms and he dozed off. Molly stayed where she was and continued to comfort him with her massage and warm body.

Carl also went home and hugged Sarah tightly and told her he really loved her. "You don't have to be afraid any longer Sarah, the men who hurt you are in custody and one is dead. Lucas and his team raided the place that the Captain said was the best lead they had. As it happened, Lucas killed the ring leader and the other two were arrested. The robbing hadn't been enough for them; the last straw was when they killed a woman they were robbing. I'm glad he is dead and I'm equally glad Lucas took care of it; I would have killed them all."

The next morning they all met at the base and the exercises began again in full swing. No one congratulated one another or any chief; they simply did their exercises the best they could. They all had studied the material their 'chief' gave them and were working hard to learn and put into practice what they were learning. They had one more week before evaluations and they were all determined to do well.

When the week was almost complete the 'chiefs' did the personal evaluation of each recruit and then they went for the various Captains to be evaluated. The 'chiefs' had again made a graph that showed steady progress, but Lucas' team had a sharp upward climb after the real job had been completed. The Captains told each one "Congratulations"; and asked each recruit if they need some time off? They all said, "No Sir, we want to continue to learn." The Captains did not even ask the First Responders, they just said, "We'll see all the First Responders next Thursday." Lucas, Carl and David knew they needed the time and apparently so did the Captains. They all went home to their wives.

The next morning, Michael called Lucas and told him about Eli. He said, "Lucy, Sarah, and Sheila volunteered to help with his first year of school. Molly said she would discuss it with you, but she was pretty sure you could help too." "Absolutely! Tell that young man to get on the stick and put in his application; that his first year is already taken care of." Michael said, "He is going to be my assistant for the rest of the year, until I can stand up longer." All the students seemed to agree and were really happy that Michael was back. Michael told him, "Thanks, Lucas. Lucy has been somewhat worried about you, Lucas, since yesterday. She knows something isn't right and so do I. If you need help with something, you know we are here and will help any way we can." "Thanks, Michael, but tell that little bossy sister that I am fine now. My Molly has already helped me, thank you both. Both of you have good instincts, but I am fine now."

It seems, "After the 'Blackness of Midnight'; a Glimmer of Sunrise, is really present!"